The Women of Robertson Place

A Family Saga

The Women of Robertson Place

A Family Saga

Lynn H. Carden

ORANGE *frazer* PRESS
Wilmington, Ohio

Published for the author by:
Orange Frazer Press
37½ West Main St.
P.O. Box 214
Wilmington, OH 45177

For price and shipping information, call: 937.382.3196
Or visit: www.orangefrazer.com

Book and cover design by: Kelly Schutte and Orange Frazer Press

Note to the Reader: Book illustrations were created by the author
and depict items she discovered at Robertson Place.

Library of Congress Control Number: 2019916223

First Printing

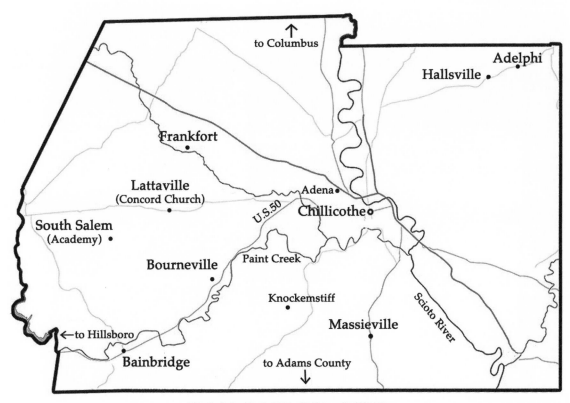

ROSS COUNTY, OHIO

Family Tree
Maternal Line

Mary (Williams) Vinsonhaller 1767–1859
m. George Vinsonhaller

|

Mary "Little Mary" (Vinsonhaller) Poole 1804–1872
m. Henry Poole

|

Martha (Poole) Robertson 1830–1911
m. Robert I. Robertson

|

Margarite (Robertson) Anderson 1847–1922
m. Erskine Anderson

|

Sadie (Anderson) Butler 1874–1945
m. Delano Butler

|

Marian (Butler) Hammond 1908–1982
m. George Hammond

|

Lynn (Hammond) Carden b.1941
m. Douglas Carden

Amy (Carden) Suardi b.1969   Jenny Carden b.1972
m. Enrico Suardi   m. Lucas Caro

Table of Contents

Introduction

"Mom, I want to do a documentary!" These were the first words out of my daughter's mouth as she burst into the farmhouse. It was the summer of 1996, and I was hovering over the kitchen table trying to arrange things for a still life painting.

Jenny, a film major in college, was referring to our family history and to the tales she'd heard me tell—stories about a prison escape and slaves hidden away, stories about someone eloping and a little boy drowning.

But I was here at the family homestead to do my own work, to churn out paintings for an upcoming show. This was where I came when I needed to sequester myself. And yet, ever since I had left the city to spend summers alone in the country, I'd been wondering about the ancestors who looked down at me from their portraits on the wall. What were they really like? I was curious about their stories and how to pass them down.

Robertson Place, as it was known over the past century, had become a repository for several generations. None had ever moved out. But why? And why had it been passed down through the women? I knew so little about them. My mother had not been the type to talk of olden days, and my grandmother had been gone for a half century. Throughout the house were letters and diaries, books and photographs; portraits, poems, ledgers and lists: a tantalizing cache of mementos awaiting someone's curiosity.

"I'll help, Mom," Jenny insisted. Here was the much needed energy and urgency of youth. Dropping everything, I surrendered myself. We started by opening the family Bible, then pulled open drawers and closets. Out came letters and long dresses, photographs and newspaper clippings. Tables soon groaned under stacks of artifacts from the past. And then I remembered the trunk. Up in the attic of the old wash house was a carved and domed trunk. Although I had long been aware of its existence, I had never wanted to lift its lid. Opening that old trunk was something to be avoided. What would I find? How would I catalog its contents? Regardless. Now was that time.

The air was stifling hot in the cramped attic. Struggling under the weight of the trunk, we dragged it down the rickety stairs into the light of day. The latch was rusted shut. Prying it open, we gasped.

Inside, wrapped in ribbons and string, crumbling with age, were the contents of a life. Gingerly, we peeked at the tintypes in their velvet and gold cases. Jenny shook out the horsehair lap robe. Most of the mementos, especially the gossamer wedding dress, were ravaged by silverfish, a wingless insect that feeds on fabric, paper, hair, and even leather. Here came a pair of men's boots, along with a tiny diary from the Civil War. I picked up the phone to call my contacts at the Ross County Historical Society; Jenny ran for her camera. We hung a clothesline to air out the dresses and quilts. "What else is up there, Mom?" called Jenny up the dark staircase. I saw a wooden baby buggy from the mid 1800s, then a rusty bicycle, several bed pans and chamber pots, and finally, a wreath made of hair.

As night fell, Jenny started to photograph the history we had dismantled. Our daughter was enrolled in Northwestern University; her major was Radio, Television, and Film. Tonight, she would have to improvise. In the living room, intense at her work, she set up a tripod, and against the hall door Jenny began to prop the artifacts, one by one. Sitting cross-legged on the floor, she aimed her lens at the tintypes of the men and women of Robertson Place; focus and click, focus and click. Flashes went off as I retold the stories.

This is how it all began. This is how I was inspired to set aside my paint brushes in order to continue my daughter's work. Because when summer was over, her 250 minutes of film would be edited down to thirty-six. The finished documentary was a watershed, but there was much left to tell. And so, I went back to the letters and the diaries. Timelines went up on the wall; chronologies spun out of my typewriter. The deeper I went, the more clearly I heard the voices of my forebears. The more time I spent living in the old house, the stronger was its pull.

In fact, the house itself had stories to tell. In my self-imposed solitude I began to appreciate its own history. The character of the house became almost as important as the people who had loved it so much that they returned again and again. I must tell you about this house because its time may be running out. My own time, too.

The Women *of* Robertson Place

A Family Saga

Part 1
1793–1899

What Holds the Heart

Deep in the heart of America, nestled among the foothills of the Appalachian Mountains, a house is perched atop a small hill. Lush pastures spill away from it like cascading skirts into the fertile valley below. Towering stalks of corn and fields of golden soybeans rise from the rich soil.

A lazy stream meanders along its eastern border to join a deeper, swifter body of water called Paint Creek. It is said that the reddish-brown clay of its banks made good war paint for the Shawnees. Even before, the land was the site of sacred mounds and earthworks built by an ancient people.

Each fall, a giant harvest moon of orange rises above the distant Spruce Hill; in spring an iridescent fog of blue spreads over the valley. But what holds the heart is not the setting, but the house itself. Locals call it the old Robertson Place. Architects call it Greek Revival. Two Doric columns frame the recessed doorway, ironwork trims its balcony, and the facade is made of red brick, which today is showing itself once again after shedding so many coats of paint. Historians declare that the house played a part in the Underground Railroad, and this is one of its mysteries. But there is an unexplainable charm about the place. Perhaps it is due to its provenance; because Robertson Place was passed down—not by design, but by coincidence—solely through its daughters.

Although a single family has owned Robertson Place for over 150 years, during the late 1800s it was only the female members of three generations who inhabited it. But its crops were no longer able to support both the house and its inhabitants. Still, my ancestors could not leave it. And neither can I. Though it strains me, I hang on, because I love it too much. Again and again I return to the house in Paint Valley, allowing it to cast its spell upon my daughters and their daughters. And now, I, too, call it home.

And yet, when I came to adulthood, I knew little about the house that loomed so large in my life. I might have learned about it at my mother's knee, but by the time I was curious enough to ask questions, she was gone. Instead, my father filled in some of its history. Even so, it took years of digging and sorting through the detritus of the house and its outbuildings, more than a decade to reconstruct its poignant history.

Martha Robertson (1830–1911) was the first of my grandmothers to inhabit the house we still call Robertson Place. She was born in a cabin just one mile up the road. At seventeen, Martha married her teacher, but it would take ambition and luck and twenty years of hard work before the couple would make the fine house on the hill their own.

Earlier still, when Martha was but a toddler, her own mother witnessed the house rising from a pile of bricks. And even before that, Martha's pioneering grandmother wrenched herself from a comfortable life back East and struck out for a place that was not yet on any map. Her destination was located just two miles from Robertson Place. So I begin the saga of the women of Robertson Place by first telling her story, the story of my own great-great-great-great-grandmother, Mary Williams Vinsonhaller (1767–1859), the pioneer.

Mary Risks Her Future

*M*ary Williams was born in Richmond, Virginia, when it was still a colony. Americans owed allegiance to the King of England. But there was revolution in the air, and by the time Mary was nine, her country had declared its independence.

Women in Mary's world had limited status and rights. To vote or hold office was prohibited by law: to become educated or join the professions was discouraged by custom. If Mary remained single, she could buy and sell property, make a will. But once married, she would have to give up those rights. Essentially, her husband would own whatever belonged to her, including any children she might bear.

Little is known about Mary's childhood, but when she reached adulthood, she married a man of adventure. Casting aside all that was familiar, she left her hometown of Richmond (which had by then become a bustling state capital) and set out across the great barrier mountains to become part of history. It was on the other side of those mountains, in a great unknown wilderness, that Mary Williams Vinsonhaller became one of the Northwest Territory's earliest settlers.

Mary's future, however, might have taken a different turn. George Vinsonhaller was the son of a prosperous German farmer, and if he were in line to inherit land, Mary might have spent a secure, conventional life right there in Shenandoah Valley. As a young man, George would have known something of soil management, carpentry, blacksmithing, coopering, timbering and animal husbandry. But the Virginian was also book-educated. So, the young couple might have chosen to live in town amongst merchants and bankers. Though there were no public schools in Mary's time, Virginians of wealth and standing typically educated their sons, and Mary's new husband had a classical education. He was versed in Greek and Latin and could have gone on to study medicine or the law—in which case Mary might have become a socialite.

In any case, as landed gentry along the south branch of the Potomac, the Vinsonhaller family would have possessed many of the trappings of country life in England such as servants and silver tea services. On special occasions, Mary might have worn high-busted dresses in the fashionable Empire style and toted a parasol to protect her fair skin. Indeed, before they gave up everything to become pioneers, life for this couple would have been one of relative ease and sophistication.

Bursting upon this genteel scene in Virginia, there sounded a siren call that would prove irresistible. FREE LAND! read the broadsides and newspapers. The word was out. Men were needed in the Northwest Territory to survey and settle it. Land would be the payment.

War was over and the country was busy building a nation. Congress looked west to expand its borders, in part because there wasn't enough money in the treasury to pay the soldiers who had fought and won the revolution; land was to be used as a substitute for cash. President George Washington was about to send out surveyors to draw maps of the uncharted territory beyond the Allegheny Mountains—land still occupied by the Ottawa, Iroquois, Delaware, Miami, Wyandot and Shawnee tribes. His generals would be close behind, securing or forcing treaties with those tribes. The newly married Vinsonhallers would have known little about what lay beyond the Alleghenies, but everyone understood that if Washington's men were to get a truce, settlers would soon follow.

A once-in-a-lifetime opportunity, thought Mary and George—the chance to get there first! She was twenty-six, and he twenty-three; beating the others would have had its appeal. Striking out on their own was another heady thought. Homesteading would have its challenges, but owning property meant everything to early Americans. Hearsay from trappers and scouts began to fill the Vinsonhallers' minds with images of virgin forests festooned with vines and berries, streams flush with trout, and soil fertile with the rot of millennia. An endeavor such as this would take years if not decades and would be pitted with unknowable dangers. Yet its lure was great enough to pry an ambitious couple such as Mary and George Vinsonhaller from the security of the only world they had ever known. Setting their sights on an amorphous region on the map, the couple began to prepare for the journey to a tree-filled expanse in which there were no trading posts, no churches—no neighbors!—and where they would have to learn how to survive alone.

To live without the benefit of doctors, post offices, and roads might have been frightening. Perhaps Mary and George would never return home, never again see their parents. But it turned out that Jacob Vinsonhaller, George's older brother, was also enthusiastic about the idea of pioneering. So there would be two Vinsonhaller boys leaving home at the same time. And with Jacob's wife Margaret, the four were now a team.[1]

In a wagon pulled by oxen there would be room for only necessities; so the four young people began to cast off their luxuries and make the hard decisions of what to take. Firearms were essential, along with logging tools and basic farm implements. Mary and Margaret would need pots and pans, some bedding, clothing, and a spinning wheel. In the spring of 1793, the four Vinsonhallers left their families behind and set out on horseback on their one-way journey.[2] In less than a week, the Vinsonhaller party arrived at the base of their first great adversary, the Appalachian Mountains, or what they would have called the Alleghenies.[3]

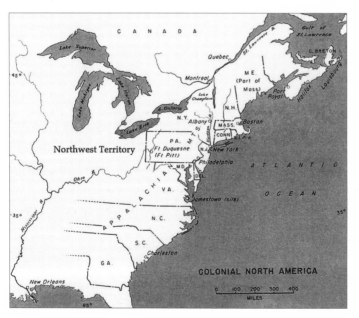

Towering and steep, the rocky eastern face of the range would challenge both man and beast. George and Jacob urged their oxen up the escarpment and down its gorges and valleys, following the Wilderness Road which Daniel Boone had blazed with his team of thirty-five men bearing axes. Yet to navigate was the Cumberland Gap, but after nearly two months of arduous travel, the jubilant foursome finally left the mountains behind and joined other pioneers and recruits in Kentucky to form a caravan of covered wagons and pack horses headed north for the Ohio River. Once there, after selling their oxen, for the final leg of the trip, the exhausted party boarded flatboats and surrendered themselves to the gentle current of the wide Ohio.

A Trustworthy Leader—Happy as Kittens

Waiting to meet the recruits on the northern banks of the Ohio River was Nathaniel Massie. He was the man who would lead the Vinsonhaller brothers on the surveys which would earn them free land. When he was only seventeen, Massie had served for his father in the Revolutionary War; he had become an expert woodsman and surveyor. Along the way he dabbled in land speculation. And now at age twenty-seven, he was hired by the government to survey Virginia military land located in both Kentucky and the Ohio Country. But before any surveying could take place, Massie would have to build a stockade. Would the native people who inhabited this land tolerate an intrusion into their territory? This he would have to find out.

George and Mary Vinsonhaller may have wondered whether their young leader was capable of such a weighty assignment. But Nathaniel Massie was a born leader. According to historian Henry Howe, Massie "could steer his course truly in clear or cloudy weather, and compute distances more correctly than most of the old hunters. He could endure fatigue and hunger with more composure than most of those persons who were inured to want on the frontier. He could live upon meat without bread, and bread without meat, and was perfectly cheerful and contented with his fare. In all the perilous situations in which he was placed, he was always conspicuous for his good feeling and the happy temperament of his mind. His courage was of a cool and dispassionate character, which, added to great circumspection in times of danger, gave him a complete ascendancy over his companions, who were always willing to follow when Massie led the way."[4]

Indeed, Massie was a man who could lead the Vinsonhaller brothers beyond the known world and into their futures. Already this likable man and his volunteers had

GENERAL NATHANIEL MASSIE.
FOUNDER OF CHILLICOTHE.

built a fort called Massie's Station. It stood along the Ohio River near present-day Manchester, Ohio, and with its tall, pointed timbers for walls and lookout towers on four corners, the fortress appeared ready for warfare. Yet Massie's first exploratory hike into the new territory had penetrated some seventy miles without sighting any natives. On his second foray, however, only four miles from the fortress gates one of his party was kidnapped. Surveying the Military District would not be so easy; it would take years and enough men to make an imposing show of force.

The Vinsonhaller brothers would now become part of this team of forty, and in the cover of night, clothed in buckskin, George and Jacob Vinsonhaller would carry Massie's rod and chains.[5]

During the survey years, while the brothers measured the new territory in increments of sixty-six feet, it is not known whether Mary and Margaret Vinsonhaller stayed on the southern side of the river in Kentucky or whether they lived and worked within Massie's settlement and its protective stockade. Although these were located in what was called hostile territory, most of the married women did live with their husbands and were key to the survey teams' survival. In relative safety these wives planted gardens and set up a bakery; they established a nursery, a chapel, and an infirmary. Women like Mary and Margaret Vinsonhaller practiced a host of pioneer skills in this government outpost, including skinning wild game, making medicine from herbs, and delivering babies. In chronicles of the Massie years, we learn that when day was done, the volunteers often gathered around campfires to sing and tell stories. In his *Biographical Sketches*, John McDonald describes Massie's recruits and their families as being "happy as kittens."

But battles still raged throughout the territory between land-hungry white men and the Shawnees. So despite the happy times in their commune, Mary would have worried about her husband's safety whenever he left the fort. However, Massie was an adept strategist and he laid out a strict formula for his men's safety. Half the team was to go north by water, half by land. To avoid detection, those who paddled upstream on the Ohio and Scioto Rivers were to sink their wide-bodied canoes at night. The others, traveling by foot, were to proceed stealthily along the river banks in tandem with the canoes.[6]

Silence was strictly enforced. Hunters took the lead, serving as scouts; surveyors and their assistants, known as chain-carriers, followed close behind. Next came a marksman, then packhorses laden with cooking and survey equipment. Finally, the cook, who carried only flour and salt, brought up the rear and kept lookout. When darkness fell, the men extinguished the fire, and without so much as a whisper or a tent, divided themselves into four squadrons and fanned out some five-hundred paces from the center to bed down for the night.

In this fashion, much survey work was accomplished without incident. However, there were two exceptions. One become known as the "starving tour." To explore the north fork of Paint Creek, Massie planned a late February foray, when the cold had lost its grip and the Shawnee were still away at their winter quarters. But a sudden snow storm arose and caught the men by surprise. Marooned by waist-high drifts, they began to run out of food. To make things worse, the snow crusted over, making it impossible to walk. On day three, a dazed turkey wandered within their reach and provided a meager meal, but the situation was still dire. Finally the men decided to force their way single file through the drifts, using a lone set of footprints. At the same time, warm droplets of rain began to fall, melting their impasse and, no doubt, restoring their hopes.

The "starving tour" would later be recalled in jest, but the very last of the Massie tours held no such humor. Only weeks before the United States would sign its final treaty with the Native Americans, it was at Reeves Crossing—a place quite near the future site of Robertson Place—that Massie unwittingly made camp near a group of Shawnees. Realizing that his men would be discovered and raided, the Revolutionary War veteran felt he had no choice but to order his men to preempt an attack, and in this resulting fray one of George Vinsonhaller's companions was killed.

Luck, however, was with the Vinsonhaller brothers; they both survived the survey years. In 1795, Chief Little Turtle, on behalf of a confederation of tribes—and in exchange for gifts such as blankets, utensils and horses—signed his X on the Greenville Treaty, thus ceding all rights to the land that George and Jacob had been measuring in the Ohio Country.

At last the surveyors and settlers were officially allowed into this part of the Virginia Military District. The Vinsonhaller men had by now spent two years with Massie, surveying and locating land that matched the soldiers' grants in nearly 6,570 square miles of wooded terrain; they had helped map the Paint Valley region. Soon they would get their payoff.

But first, there was the task of laying out a town. Massie instructed his men to plot a European-style town near the banks of a big bend in the Scioto River. It was the perfect site for such a town. Back from the shores of the Scioto, in a grove of trees near the mouth of Paint Creek, George Vinsonhaller and his comrades began to swing their axes. Although most of the native inhabitants had already left the region, when it came time for naming, Massie chose for his town the Shawnee word for "gathering place"—Chillicothe.

Massie offered each member of the survey team a free lot in the newly plotted town. Unlike these plots, land suitable for farming would not be free, but that did not deter George and Jacob. They wanted to farm. And since it could take a man an entire season to clear a mere ten to fifteen acres of wooded land—only the rare plain or prairie would suit these ambitious men. With this in mind, the Vinsonhaller brothers put in their canoes at the mouth of Paint Creek and paddled westward, against the current. What they remembered seeing on an earlier survey was a broad, flat expanse of promising bottom land. Sure enough, several miles from the town site, a vast plain spread out from the banks of the creek. It was bordered by sheltering hills and dense forests, and it was a settler's dream. Creek beds were teaming with beaver, otter, bass, pike, and catfish: forests were thick with oak and ash, sugar-maple and walnut trees. Birds populated the skies in such number that they sometimes blotted out the sun. Grazing the hills were deer, flocks of turkeys, and the occasional elk and bison. And in the distance, gentle hills of pine folded into one another in soft shades of blue, perhaps reminding the Vinsonhallers of their home in the Shenandoah Valley.[7]

It was here that the German descendants put down their stakes. About seventy miles into the new territory, this long, skinny flood plain would be known for the next two centuries as Haller's Bottom. And it was about to become Mary Vinsonhaller's first real home.[8]

Camping in the Wilderness—A Pack of Wolves

Paying with silver and gold, George and Jacob Vinsonhaller purchased their first of many parcels of Paint Valley bottom land from Nathaniel Massie.[9] But before heading back downstream to fetch their wives, the brothers may have lingered, as others often did, long enough to go hunting and to fill a hollow tree with smoked venison and elk meat.

But it was not just the women that the brothers would be fetching from the stockade; it was their families. For by now the young men were fathers. In 1793, during the first year of migration, the year the Vinsonhallers had crossed the mountains, Mary had given birth to twin boys. And now John and William circled her skirts as their father bent down to kiss the new babe in her arms. Little Ada was delivered on a cold January night in 1795, presumably by a midwife in the security of the fort's makeshift infirmary. But if Mary were to have another baby, how and where would she deliver her fourth? In early spring of 1796, (dates vary), Mary and Margaret Vinsonhaller bundled up their children and once again prepared to leave behind their friends and safety.

In the bottoms of Paint Creek Valley where the two Vinsonhaller families had bought their land, they set up camp in the wilderness. Few explorers, if any, had set foot on this forest floor where trees of three- and four-hundred years towered above, where wigwams dotted the dark landscape and where deer, buffalo, wolves and bears outnumbered their hunters. Faced with the urgency of protecting their families, George and his brother must have first cleared just enough of the old-growth forest to build shelters. Real cabins would have to wait. Working together, the brothers hoisted heavy slabs of timber into upright positions to make walls for a shelter. For a roof they spanned the puncheons with yet more hewn slabs and covered them with layers of wild grasses. During the spring, the new shanties protected the frontier families from the rains, but what followed were months of stifling humidity and swarms of mosquitoes.

Decades later, when a reporter tramped through the region gathering tales from settlers for a book about the region's history, Mary Vinsonhaller's daughter explained how her family survived that first winter in the bottoms. Her mother had lined their walls with the skins of bears and bison. One entire side of their enclosure was left open to accommodate a huge log campfire, and by continually feeding its flames her parents had hoped to keep the warmth in and the wild animals out. One night her parents awakened to see a circle of glowing eyes beyond the flames. That pack of wolves, according to their daughter, was the only thing that ever caused her mother to question their judgment about coming to the new territory.[10]

When summer arrived, a proper cabin was finally built. Life gradually improved for the frontier families, and their numbers were increasing. Mary and Margaret continued to bear children. On the first day of March 1798, another son, Jacob, was born to George and Mary Vinsonhaller. Other settlers slowly trickled into the area.

But even so, Mary's existence in Haller's Bottom was essentially one of relative isolation and self-sufficiency, surviving much as people had done for centuries. Mary and George hunted for their food and lit the night with fire.

During these early years Mary must have had to shoulder many unfamiliar chores, things she would not have thought about—let alone mastered—back in Richmond, such as butchering small game and tanning hides. If she had been a farm girl back in Virginia she would have left home knowing how to cook and sew, weave and spin, grow vegetables and preserve them. Back at the fort Mary probably picked up some additional skills necessary for surviving on the frontier, and it is possible that she learned some things from the dwindling population of friendly Native Americans whose wigwams lay sprinkled along the banks of the creek. Now she would pass those life skills down to her daughters, for all hands were needed to keep the family alive. Cloth was scarce: all the females were required to take turns at the spinning wheel. And when her husband brought sheep into the territory, it is likely that Mary learned to card and spin the wool to make night caps and booties, and to weave it with flax for linsey-woolsey tunics. By necessity she might even have learned how to fashion animal skin into coats, and fur into blankets.

Typical of frontier life, as soon as the Vinsonhaller children were big enough, they were given chores. They planted seeds and pulled weeds. They fetched water from the creek for cooking and drinking, bathing and washing. Mary instructed the girls to find berries and nuts; their father showed the boys how to fish and hunt. Lacking toys or entertainment, jobs filled their days.

One of the stories that survives Mary's early years in Haller's bottom comes from *The History of Ross and Highland County*, and it illustrates the settlers' fear of bears. Her husband was known for his accurate aim, and one Sunday morning while walking with his brother the men spotted bear tracks. Word spread from cabin to cabin and soon a small crowd gathered below the trunk of a hollow tree which appeared to be the bear's home. Daring one another to peer into the hole, Jacob finally climbed a ladder, and with a long lighted branch, he shone light into the bear's hiding place. A shaggy brown face suddenly appeared and George fired his rifle. When Jacob turned to face the onlookers his face was spattered with bear blood. Screams of horror echoed through the woods because everyone thought that George Vinsonhaller had killed his brother.[11]

Tales such as this became the folklore of early life in Paint Valley. Regrettably, not much is known about the state of affairs between the invading white settlers and the native Shawnees in the early days of their cohabitation. Several Paint Valley families told historians a story which stemmed from the scarcity of salt, and it always involved a surly brave who frightened a pioneer woman by demanding salt at the door of her isolated cabin. In one such case, the revered local Chief Waw-wil-a-way made the brave return to apologize to the woman. Chief Waw-wil-a-way was a hunting companion of Massie, and during the early 1800s the two were instrumental in the task of maintaining peace between the two races.

Shawnee Man, 1796

Adventures such as these would have filled Mary Vinsonhaller's days. However, her life was probably shaped even more by her pregnancies and child-birth. She and her sister-in-law, Margaret Vinsonhaller, would have helped one another during deliveries, but each and every time Mary began labor, her life was on the line. Over her twenty-three years of childbearing Mary was to bear twelve babies. Where there were no nearby doctors to treat a host of life-threatening illnesses, it is remarkable that every one of Mary's children survived to adulthood.

As other settlers arrived, bringing with them needed skills and friendship, Mary Vinsonhaller's life may have became a little easier. By 1800, in the fledgling town of Chillicothe, there were now 150 houses, a tavern and a church. Soon there would be a market, a mill and a newspaper. From all directions settlers began to flood into the new territory, especially into the northern portions, but Paint Valley, with its rich potential for large scale farming, remained sparsely populated. Only eight or ten families were pioneering in the vicinity. Still, there were jobs to do and the neighbors asked Mary's husband to take on a few civic responsibilities. Would he be their fence viewer, the person to settle boundary disputes? Would he check on all their neighbors, be an Overseer of the Poor? George Vinsonhaller became these and more. Between the Vinsonhaller brothers, they would hold the jobs of house appraiser, trustee, clerk, lister, supervisor and constable. Later Mary's husband served as justice of the peace, and during a period when prudery and morality swept the young nation, he took on the role of preacher.

Religion was integral to the lives of most of the early settlers, but formal education was not. Schooling was uneven. No such thing as public education existed in the young nation, and in 1810 only one in ten children attended any classes at all. Yet as early as 1802 Chillicothe established an academy for female students and was soon to be dubbed the "Athens of the West." In Haller's Bottom, as soon as George Vinsonhaller was able to convince his neighbors to hire a teacher, he stepped up to offer a piece of his land for a schoolhouse.[12]

Little Mary is Born

It was into this world that Little Mary Vinsonhaller was born. Seventh amongst the children, she was but the second girl, and since she was given her mother's name, she soon acquired the diminutive "Little Mary." Thomas Jefferson was in the White House—a sprawling new edifice on the Potomac—when Little Mary was born on October 24, 1804. Explorers Lewis and Clark were in the Northwest, about to befriend the Mandans who would shelter them in earth lodges over the coming winter. Ohio had just become the seventeenth state in the Union, making Little Mary the first of the Vinsonhaller children to be born in the new state. The portion of the Northwest Territory in which her parents were settling had reached a population of 60,000, thus allowing it to apply to Congress for statehood. And when statehood was won in 1803, Chillicothe became its first capital.

Every day now, life was catching up with what Little Mary's parents had left behind in Virginia. Ever since they'd left the East Coast, mail to and from their loved ones had been unreliable and agonizingly slow. But now, if George and Mary Vinsonhaller had wanted to send word of their newborn's arrival, they could expect that letter to arrive in Richmond a mere two weeks later. Taken to the post office in Chillicothe, the precious news would be carried in saddle bags by a series of postal riders to the baby's grandparents. Livestock, too, was making its way back across the mountains. 1805 saw the first cattle drive. From Paint Valley drovers herded their animals to the markets back East.

Not all of the changes in the Vinsonhaller family's drama-filled lives would prove helpful. The very year Little Mary was born, her family was uprooted by flooding. Access to the water of Paint Creek had attracted the pioneers, but its annual flooding caused enormous problems. Tales of uprooted cabins and boat rescues fill the valley's history books. So it is not surprising that after a major flood in 1804 the Vinsonhallers decided to abandon their homestead and move to higher ground. From their new perch on Kilbourne Hill, the settlers still had a view of the flood plain and much of their property, but looking west, the family began to observe something else rising in the distance. Just two miles further down the trail they could see curls of smoke rising from the first log cabins of what would soon become another settlement.

This new settlement, equidistant between two tributaries that lead to Paint Creek, would be called Twintown, and Twintown would be the future site of Robertson Place. In the years to come, George Vinsonhaller would take on leadership roles in the vibrant young community. He would help build its first log church and later become justice of the peace. Little Mary would meet her new neighbors at log rollings and barn raisings.

All for Nothing

Meanwhile, a drama was enfolding in the larger world. The country had fallen into war. The War of 1812 would become the last battle with England over territory in the New World, and thousands of men from the region volunteered to serve in the Army of the Northwest. At one point Chillicothe had to throw up tents to hold an overflow of British prisoners until the army could build more stockades.

The Vinsonhaller twins, William and John, were of fighting age. Perhaps they wanted to sign up to fight. But as unsettling as wartime would have been, in 1815 another series of events began to unravel the very foundation upon which the Vinsonhallers had built their lives. Ever since coming to the Northwest Territory, the German-speaking farmer from Virginia had been buying up land. In Ross County, of which Chillicothe was the county seat, George Vinsonhaller owned nearly three-thousand acres. Only a small portion of his investment was productive, because the cost of transforming some of that dense virgin forest into farm land came at enormous expense and years of backbreaking labor. However, with statehood established in 1803, even without developing his acreage, the monetary value of his holdings had increased fourfold. On paper George Vinsonhaller was wealthy. But over the next fifteen years, due to what surviving letters refer to as "bad writings," these holdings would come into question.

Little Mary's father was not the only landowner caught in what became a serious financial crisis. By the end of the War of 1812, the federal government was deeply in debt, its currency was depreciated and foreign goods were flooding the market. At the same time there were local reasons for worry. Ross County historian, Pat Medert, explains that unease spread through the valley when it was discovered that some of the land granted by George Washington to Virginia's veterans had been sold twice. These duplications were presumed to have been accidental, but they caused several Ohio landowners to lose their homesteads. Perhaps if George Vinsonhaller had been able to sell some of his property before the financial crisis was widespread, he might have fared better, but now he was left with worthless promissory notes.

Complicating matters further, the methods of Nathaniel Massie's own survey work came under attack. He and the other land locators had employed the old English tradition of siting rocks, trees and streams to define borders. But over the course of time, rocks had been moved; trees had fallen, streams had changed courses. Border disputes clogged the Ross County courts early in the nineteenth century and caused banks to call in their loans. It would take nearly fifteen years, but in the end, according to his daughter Asenath, every last acre of the vast Vinsonhaller holdings would be lost.[13]

Little Mary was an adolescent when the family's hard-earned prosperity was threatened. Her twin brothers were twenty-two and her mother, Mary Vinsonhaller, was still bearing children. At age forty-eight, she now had eleven. As early as 1811, George Vinsonhaller may have foreseen the coming collapse, because at that time he began to purchase raw land in an adjacent county. Adams County lay southwest of Ross, and its more rugged terrain remained undeveloped and unpopulated. Land there was still cheap. With its rolling hills, it was picturesque like his birthplace in Shenandoah, but therefore harder to farm than Paint Valley. Month after month, year after year, George went to the dimly-lit log courthouse in Adams County to record the purchase of another parcel of wooded property. His holdings there would eventually amount to 2,500 acres.[14]

Because of his losses, in 1817 the Vinsonhaller family moved to the village of West Union, the seat of Adams County. Little Mary's mother had just given birth to her twelfth, whom she named Flavius, and he would be her last. Settling themselves into a small clapboard house across from the courthouse, (a house which, at this printing, still stands at 205 West Walnut Street), the family would stay there only a year before moving to a permanent site on higher ground in what is now Bratton Township.

To get to West Union, the family would have transported their chattels and children in wagons. Southward over Zane's Trace they traveled, over the route which before 1796 had been a mere buffalo trail when Ebenezer Zane slashed the underbrush and formed a green tunnel. Now it was wider and considered a road, but nevertheless, the forty-five-mile distance that would separate them from family and friends and their former homestead would have seemed a great distance to Little Mary. And one can imagine that the loss of status would have been quite painful for Mary Vinsonhaller, the wife of such a prominent citizen. But would the move have depressed her? Or would the change have merely re-energized a restless adventurer? Other families bearing her maiden name Williams had already put down roots in the region, so perhaps there were happy reunions. It is impossible to know how Little Mary's mother felt about the move, but we do know that she stayed put in Adams County and lived to be ninety-two years of age.

Back in Ross County, the Vinsonhaller presence was dwindling. In 1823 an epidemic broke out, and it may have been what took the life of George's brother Jacob, who died that same year. But it could have been the family's reversal of fortune that caused the older Vinsonhaller children to leave the area. One of the children would later return to Paint Valley, brought by a suitor. But the twins John and William, left—perhaps to find other land to farm. Lorenzo Dow Vinsonhaller joined Colonel John Fremont's Mountain Men to explore the West. Jacob went to Kentucky to study the law, his father having arranged to "trade" sons with an old friend who ran a college in Louisville. Eventually this son would work for Ohio Governor McArthur. Miriam married and followed her husband to yet another early Ohio town, Hillsboro. And while Ada, the first born daughter, would eventually settle back in Twintown, it was Flavius, the last born, who would stay close to his parents and call Bratton Township his home.[15]

By 1829 there were no more Vinsonhallers living in Haller's Bottom. But this was about to change.

The Poole Family Arrives

Sixteen years before the Vinsonhallers were entirely gone from the region, this next story began. One day, in the little schoolhouse in Haller's Bottom where nine-year-old Little Mary was doing her lessons, there arrived at the doorway a father and his three sons. They were newcomers. The teacher, knowing of Little Mary's gentle nature, may have asked her pupil to move over to make room on the bench for Henry. Henry Poole was the middle son, the one with tousled blond curls and gray-green eyes.

No doubt Little Mary already knew Henry, because in the fall of 1813, soon after his family had arrived from Baltimore, Maryland, they had purchased land just up the road, making them close neighbors to the large Vinsonhaller family. Since the Poole boys were motherless, one can imagine that they began to spend time at the Vinsonhaller homestead. Amidst this backdrop, Little Mary and Henry Poole grew up together. But when the Vinsonhaller family lost its holdings and moved to Adams County, Little Mary, then thirteen, went away with her family. It was Henry Poole who, some twelve years later, would bring her back to Paint Valley as his wife, Mary Poole.

But while Mary was away in Adams County, the scene of her childhood had changed dramatically. Paint Valley had gone from "wilderness territory" to "settlement territory." In her youth, the towering trees had been so thick that the settlers had complained of suffering from "green gloom." In his book about the early settlers, Conrad Richter writes that "women settlers hated the trees like poison. They were your mortal enemy. All your life you had to fight them, chop, split, [niggle] them off till nothing was left. And then their wild sprouts kept coming up to plague you." He describes the trees as "standing thick as thieves with their heads together plotting against humans."[16]

When in 1829 Mary and Henry Poole returned to Ross County as husband and wife, they were met by a landscape so denuded it was nearly unrecognizable. Over the years, most of the centuries-old trees had been cut down or killed by girdling; their branches were burned, and if the clearing was to be farmed, their stumps were yanked or dug out. Any second growth appeared weak and spindly next to the severed butts. These giant reminders of the old virgin forest now littered the horizon as far as one could see, and from their smoldering branches rose a smoke which shrouded the valley with an acrid odor.

Decapitated trees, their stumps leaning this way or that, populated Mary and Henry Poole's world. To their generation, the constant thunder of timber crashing to the earth signaled progress. It meant the wilderness was shrinking, civilization gaining the upper hand. It meant opportunity.[17]

A Rough Start

Opportunity was the magnet that attracted most of the settlers to the new territory. However, it was not what had motivated Henry Poole's father to leave Baltimore sixteen years ago. Instead, it was tragedy.

In Maryland the Poole family had been living in a large stone house inherited from their English grandparents. Henry's father John was a businessman; his mother, Anna Pierce Poole, was said to be "talented." And with help from thirteen slaves the young family hosted parties for dignitaries and authors. Present at some of those gatherings may have been two of Anna's young cousins who would later become famous: the author, Nathaniel Hawthorne, and the nation's fourteenth president, Franklin Pierce. One can only imagine the active life lived in that large stone mansion.

But in 1813, Henry's mother Anna died. Their gay life came to a sudden end. His father quit working and, according to a surviving letter, "...let all the black folks go, except for the black mammy who wanted to stay with the family, wanted to go with them to the new country." However, just before their departure on September 10, 1813, "Mammy took sick and died."[18]

In the new land of Ohio, Henry Poole's father bought 150 acres of land between Haller's Bottom and Twintown. It was on higher ground (on the current Lower Twin Road) that John and his sons built a cabin. Back in Maryland, father Poole had learned to work with iron; now, at the age of 40, he transformed himself into a blacksmith. And then, he took a new wife.

Rebecca was a young widow at age twenty-six. She came to the marriage with three daughters. It looked for a while as though the Poole family might once again have a happy family life. Two more daughters were born. But in a few short years, not only had the youngest of the Poole boys died, but death had claimed all four of the little girls. And now Rebecca was dead. Buried in a row, among the maple and ash trees on nearby Teter Hill, their hand-carved head stones signaled the end of hope for Henry's father. When a virulent epidemic swept through the valley in 1823, the widower, still in mourning, prepared his will. Ten days later Henry's father, age fifty, was dead.

With Confidence and Ambition

At the time of their father's death, two of the Poole brothers were courting Vinsonhaller girls. Six years later, when Little Mary and Henry were both twenty-five, they married, and as newlyweds, they moved into the old Poole cabin. As a boy, Henry had helped to clear the land which lay between Haller's Bottom and the fledgling Twintown settlement. He'd helped plant the farm's crops, and build this very cabin. It had been home to Henry for eleven years. But now the place looked neglected, heavy and dark from leftover sorrow.

Young and full of energy, it is likely that Mary and Henry Poole embarked on their new life together with confidence and ambition. If so, they would have been typical of their times, for in the 1820s a sense of optimism prevailed across America. It was a time of discovery and great feats. John Audubon was trekking through swamps to record the nation's birds, trappers were harvesting boatloads of beaver pelts, and the famed Mountain Men were about to discover the great Salt Lake. Back East, men were using pick and shovel to gouge out a canal which would become the engineering marvel of the nineteenth century. The 363-mile waterway, known as the Erie Canal, would connect Lake Erie with the eastern seaboard, and its construction would spur the building of another water-route, the Ohio and Erie Canal. Spanning Ohio from north to south, the Ohio and Erie Canal would pass through Chillicothe and provide a way for the settlers of Ross County to get their products to market.

Yet to come were railroads. Even in the 1820s and 1830s, ambitious men were laying down tracks and experimenting with steam-powered engines. Out West it would be decades before the first transcontinental railroad tracks would meet at a point in the newly created Utah Territory. Meanwhile, many Americans thought the steam-powered engines were monsters from the pits of hell. Filling the quiet landscape with unearthly thunder and fire, the trains were called "iron horses who breathe smoke" by the indigenous people. When their whistles screamed, dogs cowered and ran away.

In time, these fierce conveyances would carry settlers and goods to the rapidly expanding western territories, and in distant prairie towns, the locomotive would be taken apart and shipped back by water to the East Coast for yet another load. The nation was feeling strong, and when President Andrew Jackson took his oath of office in 1828, Congress warned Europe to keep its hands off this bountiful country.

Back in Paint Valley, inside the sturdy confines of the Poole cabin, things may have started out with high hopes and confidence, but their outlook would soon be tempered. Within a year, Mary Poole's first pregnancy ended in grief. Child mortality was a curse in the Old World as well as the New, and their baby boy died before his name could be recorded. Unlike her mother, Mary Poole would experience the overwhelming sorrow that envelopes a woman after losing a child. And although Mary's second child would survive, she would lose her third. Even so, it is unlikely that it ever crossed Mary Poole's mind to abandon what she probably considered to be her duty and destiny—to have a large family. For as long as anyone could remember, babies had come in rapid succession until a woman died or reached menopause. What's more, Mary's generation of women were under increasing pressure to have lots of babies because the birthrate in Protestant Anglo-Saxon families was actually declining. During a time of massive immigration from Roman Catholic countries, some social critics worried. Who would rule, if not those of their own "good native stock?" From bully pulpits and state-house steps, preachers and statesmen pronounced it a woman's job to have babies.[19]

But had Mary been able to resist social pressure, had she wanted to limit her family or her risk, she might well have failed, because as yet, women did not have the means or knowledge to control their fertility. Because the rhythm method was misunderstood, total abstinence was the only sure contraceptive.[20]

Nevertheless, for Mary Poole and all the other women of the region, conditions were about to get better. Relief was close at hand in the form of a midwife who would win many a heart. Enter Captain Molly.

Captain Molly

Captain Molly was an eccentric widow from Kentucky, who in 1831 came galloping into the new settlement of Twintown. Dressed in jodhpurs and a peculiar homemade straw hat that covered her short-cropped hair, she often arrived in the nick of time at the township's doorsteps. Straddling her horse with both legs was a sight that raised eyebrows. Dressing like a man provoked ridicule and gained Mary Edmiston a nickname.

Despite her idiosyncrasies, to the residents of Paint Valley, Captain Molly became a sort of heroine. Early historians said this about her: "She was unusually intelligent and quick-witted, and whoever attempted to have a little sport at her expense, as was often the case, generally got more than he wanted." If a family could not pay for her services as midwife, the colorful widow accepted as her payment a side of beef, a cord of firewood or perhaps some mutton to feed Molly's several children back home.[21]

As a result of Captain Molly's good work, perhaps Mary Poole's own life or that of an offspring was spared. After a rocky start, Mary went on to deliver seven more babies, and all of these children lived to adulthood. But in 1830, just one year before Captain Molly arrived on the scene, the first of Mary's babies to survive was born. This child was Martha. And Martha would live to become the first of the women to occupy the house that would carry the name Robertson Place.

Although she might never be described as a beauty, Martha would prove to be quite capable: as the eldest of eight children, she would be given many responsibilities. But more important than beauty or even her capabilities, was her strong constitution. Martha was born sturdy. And while still a toddler, her stamina was put to a formidable test.

Little is Known

Cholera cut its first swath through Paint Valley in 1832. For two years the pandemic had been laying waste in Europe, killing thousands across the continent and the British Isles. Now the disease was hitching a ride with emigrants to the New World, and as the canal diggers approached Chillicothe, along came cholera. Citizens of Ross County braced for the worst, for they had neither resistance nor effective treatments against what would become the most feared disease of the nineteenth century.

Cholera may well have struck the Poole cabin, may well have taken the most vulnerable, for in 1832 Mary Poole buried another infant. Humphrey was not yet one-year old when he died. And although his sister Martha, now two years old, would have been too young to have fully appreciated the finality of death, its power to snuff out her tiny brother's breath and to silence his cries would be forever etched upon her brain.

In all, Mary and Henry Poole suffered the loss of three children. Their first and third died in infancy and daughter Eleanor would die of diphtheria at the age of twenty-five. But beyond the list of children Mary Poole delivered and lost, little else is known about her adult life. At the time, women did not often write about their lives, nor were they written about. That she was the daughter of a pioneer and among the first children born in the new state of Ohio were both her pride and identity. The *Chillicothe Advertiser*'s obituary of her death on April 15, 1872, spent six paragraphs regaling the life of George Vinsonhaller and one sentence about its subject, Mary Poole. "As wife and mother sister Pool had few superiors." Only by inference could I track the life she must have lived as the wife of Henry Poole. Repeated entries in the ledgers of the township's general store reveal that her husband continued to farm and to purchase only basic supplies in trade for wood, corn, sausage and wool.

From Mary Poole's elusive record we should not surmise, however, that her life was dull; instead her life was one of rapid change, and indeed, drama. During her lifetime her father's fortune was won and lost. Forests gave way to farms and farms gave way to towns. Busy roads replaced what had been mere trails blazed by moccasin-footed Shawnees. In fact, Mary Poole's generation may have been the last to have come in daily contact with the Native Americans of the Northwest Territory, some of whom continued to hunt and fish on the land her family had bought with gold and silver. For the most part these early encounters would have been peaceful, and one of her peers left a memoir in which she describes having played with "young squaws."[22]

Tecumseh

But as a child, Little Mary may also have been present when her father mediated the occasional conflicts that arose between the native population and the settlers who were displacing them. Not all peace agreements held. In 1803, her father's chain-carrying friend, Captain Tom Herrod, was thought to have been shot and scalped by a Shawnee in nearby Frankfort.[23] Tecumseh, the great Shawnee leader, undoubtedly loomed large in Little Mary's lifetime. She was a child of nine when, late in the War of 1812, this charismatic figure met his death in a one-sided battle in Upper Canada. This battle turned out to be the last stand for his confederacy of Native American tribes.

Bourneville—A Village is Born

When Mary Poole was twenty-four years old, something would occur just down the road from the Poole cabin which would shape the remainder of her life. It was 1832, and just three miles away in the sparse settlement of Twintown two men were plotting out a village. At this time the Pooles were mourning the loss of their baby boy, Humphrey, and would likely have carried the two-year-old Martha papoose-style wherever they went. Eager to see what was happening down the road, they may have taken Martha to Twintown to watch a surveyor work with his brass surveyor's transit and compass, a rod, and his sixty-six-foot chain. A man named E. P. Kendrick was measuring a strip of land through the middle of the settlement, and under the supervision of the cartographer from Pennsylvania, Alexander Bourne, they were dividing that strip into forty lots.

Mr. Bourne received such high praise for his work that his bosses decided to rename the settlement. And so, Bourneville it became. Founders, John Boswell and Isaac McCracken, held high hopes for their project. They wanted Bourneville to thrive not only as a stage-coach stop and a place to post mail, but as a center of commerce. Indeed Bourneville did thrive. Soon it would have an inn and a general store and would go on to serve as the heart of Twin Township for the next century. Most importantly for this history, it would become Martha's home.[24]

Aboard horse and buggy, or wagons and stage coaches, new settlers began to arrive. A broad mixture of adventurous people soon called Bourneville home: war veterans who had won land grants in the territory, professionals looking for a place to practice their trades, and newlyweds wanting to start from scratch. There were young widows, retirees and former slaves. Altogether they comprised the first wave of the great migration west.

When Mary Poole's children were old enough to start school they would mix with and learn from the offspring of these colorful newcomers. When their Vinsonhaller grandparents came to visit, the children probably heard about the local lore of Paint Valley. Martha may have discovered where to search for ginseng and watercress, blackberries and the prized morel mushrooms. From her father, she had already learned the names of the different trees in the valley: the tupelos and tulip trees, the ash and black walnut. Martha would have delighted in collecting the mitten-shaped leaves of the sassafras tree and the shiny brown seeds of the giant buckeyes. "He was almost a 'tree worshiper,'" Martha's Aunt Asenath wrote about her father Henry Poole. "I used to know [the] different varieties of nearly all the trees that grew in the woods."[25]

Under the tutelage of Grandmother Vinsonhaller, young Martha discovered that she had a knack for working with textiles, a facility which would spark a lifelong affinity for sewing and quilting. Surely George Vinsonhaller showed this grandchild his favorite fishing spots along Paint Creek where, as a young frontiersman, he had caught bass, pike, catfish and sturgeon. And the beaver lodges? Where were they? Martha might have wondered.

Even more memorable to Martha might have been treks into Haller's Bottom to look for the remains of her grandparents' first shanty and to find the cabin they were forced to abandon during that great flood back in 1804, the year Martha's mother was born. Perhaps they explored the vine-covered, empty school house in Haller's Bottom while the pioneers reminisced about how it had taken in water like the rest of the homesteads lying in the flood plain. And the great flood of 1817? Martha had heard the story of how her mother had gone by boat with her grandfather into their submerged cornfield to warn their tenants, and how, when the water had receded, he and Grandmother had discovered a calf stranded high in a tree.[26] Now over there, Grandfather might have gestured, was how high the water had come when it spilled over its banks, and over there was the tree where he and Uncle Jacob had shot the bear.

Grandfather Vinsonhaller had touched many lives in the valley and was credited for first bringing sheep into the territory. But in 1839, when Martha was nine years old, her grandfather died. Obituaries were rarely published in those days because word of mouth spread the news much quicker than a weekly newspaper, but The *Scioto Gazette* made an exception when this pioneer died.

> *The deceased was one of the first settlers in Ohio, and assisted laying out the town of Chillicothe. He was in several engagements with the Indians, and was one of the pioneers whose passing from amongst us deserves especial note.*[27]

Undoubtedly Martha's childhood was layered with rich stories from her elders. Tidbits of news from the outside world would have trickled down to her by word of mouth or the region's newspapers. Beyond this, however, Martha would learn little about the history of her young nation, because America's history was not yet in her school books. Writers and artists of the day complained that the country had no history yet—or certainly none worth romanticizing. But in fact Americans were making their own swashbuckling history every day. Even in the few years since Martha's own birth in 1830, several noteworthy events had occurred, events which would one day fill entire shelves in school libraries. Nat Turner instigated a slave revolt in Virginia and was hanged for his rebellion. Out West a territorial war had erupted with Mexico. And on their long exodus to the reservations of Oklahoma, Native Americans were walking what would later be referred to as the Trail of Tears.

As dramatic and tragic as these events were, Martha would learn other things in school. She would learn to read from McGuffey's readers and to write—although from her letters, it appears that penmanship was not her strong suit. Arithmetic, spelling and oration were subjects taught to all, and the advanced students of her rural school even learned a bit of ancient history.

But what Martha learned at the clapboard school on Black Run, she learned in spite of its bullies. For always present were a group of older boys who made it their business to frighten the weaker children and to pester their teacher. At the end of nearly every year, it seemed, another beleaguered teacher would give up, another have to be found. When Martha was near graduation, the brave soul who took the job of schoolmaster was the clerk of Bourneville's village store. Though not a large man, he was thought to be well-educated and up to the challenge. It was none other than Robert Robertson.

Master Robertson

Robert Robertson would have been among the area's most eligible of bachelors. His current standing was hard-earned. Back in 1833, when Martha was a toddling three-year-old, the boy Robert had arrived in Bourneville from Rockingham County, Virginia, aboard a covered wagon. At that time, Robert was fifteen. And he was fatherless.

Premature death of one's father would have cast a deep shadow across many a boy, but instead, or perhaps because of this, one can imagine the strong-willed Robert pleading with his widowed mother to begin the adventure. Across the Appalachian Mountains was a new land where newcomers could get a footing, could make a contribution, perhaps a fortune.

Alongside his mother and sister on the seat of their covered wagon, Robert coaxed and prodded their beasts of burden up the steep mountains, down the muddy ravines, around giant fallen trees and across raging streams. Earlier travelers had cobbled together logs to ford the muddy stretches, giving the Allegheny trails the appearance of corduroy, but over such terrain the Robertsons could have covered no more than a few miles each day.

Weeks later, the family emerged from the ridges and passes, but they still had a long way to go. Instead of heading west on the Ohio River, as did many pioneers here in Wheeling, Virginia, (now West Virginia) the Robertsons crossed the river and picked up Zane's Trace. Young Robert drove his team over what had been the native footpaths just a few decades ago, until at long last the Virginia Military District came into his view. In Chillicothe his pace would have slowed, and after passing Slate Mills and fording Lower Twin Creek, he pulled on the reins. It was to be here in a fledgling settlement called Bourneville that Robert Robertson would come of age. It was to be here that he would gain his manhood, become a teacher, buy his first property. Here that he would be elected justice of the peace and leave behind a library of records charting the daily trials and tribulations, purchases and sales, marriages and deaths of a village of early American settlers. And here that he would meet his future wife.

In the center of the freshly laid out village of Bourneville, Robert's mother purchased a small lot. To one side was a lot owned by her brother-in-law, Joseph Robertson. Nothing is known about this relative or whether he ever lived there. On the other side, however, was the settlement's store, and it was in this store that Robert, at the age of seventeen, would gain a job and a foothold.

In the Robertson family there were land holders and a future governor back in Virginia, and Robert may have been mentored by such capable people back home. Perhaps even more important for his advancement and for the position of leadership he was to take later in life was the strategic timing of his arrival. Bourneville and Robert Robertson would grow up together. They would form and influence one another, and soon marriage into the prominent Vinsonhaller/Poole family would help to cement the position of the newcomer. Likewise, Martha's marriage to the ambitious outsider would assure her future. Together they would give their descendants a reason to stay here for generations to come.

A Dashing Presence

Maybe the child Martha met the new boy in town when she played with his younger sister, Emily. But sooner or later Martha would have encountered Robert when he clerked at the general store. Martha was twelve years younger than Robert: he was seventeen and she was five. Martha could have met Robert when she came to purchase her first spelling book. Once inside the bustling store, a mere smile from the mahogany-haired clerk might have sent the five-year-old for refuge into the folds of her mother's long skirts.

A busy young man might have quickly forgotten this casual introduction to a customer's child, but a small impressionable girl could have remembered every detail about her first encounter with Robert Robertson. His confident stature, the intelligent eyes, the dark and thick wavy hair would have given the young man a dashing presence in the sparsely-settled valley. It is probable that when Robert later took a job as the local school teacher, his students would have already known quite a bit about him. Undoubtedly, some of the girls in his classroom had a crush on him. When Martha graduated at age sixteen, was she surprised when Master Robertson came to call?

An offer of marriage likely pleased Martha's parents, and the discrepancy between the couple's ages probably left the Pooles unfazed. It was on January 7, 1847, a day when the valley lay shivering under ice, when hoarfrost sparkled like diamonds and etched the outline of every tiny twig, that Martha Poole and her school teacher began their new lives as Mr. and Mrs. Robertson.

Martha Starts a Family

A small clapboard cottage in the heart of Bourneville was to be the first home of the newlyweds. It was also the home of Robert's mother Sarah and sister

Emily. As a guest, the young bride Martha made herself useful. Newly reconfigured, the Robertson family regained its equilibrium with Sarah Robertson retaining her role as matron of the household, and the new arrangement must have worked surprisingly well because it was to last many, many years.

Barely had the females perfected their choreography in the cottage's tiny kitchen, when Martha suspected pregnancy. News traveled quickly back to the Poole cabin where Martha's mother, Mary Poole, was also pregnant. After eighteen years of childbearing, at forty-three she would for the tenth time be carrying a child. But since two of Mary Poole's early deliveries had ended in disaster, she and Martha's father would no doubt worry about the simultaneous pregnancies. Captain Molly could be summoned, but even so, the excitement in the air would have been tinged with apprehension.

Despite their worries, Martha Robertson's first baby, Margarite, was a lusty newborn. Some called her Maggie, but almost no one used the name Mary Margaret—the formal one her parents had chosen at her birth. It didn't matter. The infant would soon establish her own personality.

After Martha's confinement, it must have been pleasant to have callers. A favorite was her Aunt Ada Vinsonhaller McMillan who now lived in Bourneville, just a few steps away from the Robertson abode. This pioneer woman liked to reminisce about her own babyhood in Haller's Bottom where she spent that first winter in the now legendary three-sided shanty. Other relatives came and went. Martha's own siblings, though technically the baby's aunts and uncles, were but toddlers themselves and they all wanted to see the new baby.

The coming and going of curious well-wishers, the new noises, the clatter of crockery, the sudden outbursts—all must have charged the atmosphere in the Robertson household and made it hard for Robert to concentrate. As a new father, he may have enjoyed the attention toward his firstborn, but he had other things to think about. He was about to take on new responsibilities.

Justice of the Peace

Nearly everyone in the region knew of the handsome southerner, Robert Robertson, and in 1848 Twin Township would be choosing a new justice of the peace. Despite his youth—Robert was just thirty at the time—the townspeople cast their votes for the former school teacher. Soon he began to travel the countryside by day and study the law by candlelight. Aside from taking care of small matters, such as witnessing legal documents and deeds as the township's magistrate, Robert would be expected to officiate at marriages, collect taxes, settle minor disputes and oversee the town's jail. Occasionally his services would require that he referee a paternity suit as he would do in the Case of Bastardy commenced on August 17, 1854 when he filed in his leather-bound legal journal a lawsuit on behalf of Eliza Looss against the accused father of her child, Washington Gregg.[28] Robert sent out a warrant for the man's arrest, and the very next day ruled that the defendant, who acknowledged his paternity, pay Eliza a sum of $213. The errant father was to pay $20 down and $20 annually for the "first" years. On another occasion the new JP was called upon to settle a domestic violence case when a resident of Twin Township accused her husband of threatening her with a broom. These may have been cases that broke the boredom for Robert, but for the most part, his work, recorded in ink on the light-blue pages of his journal, dealt with money and property. Occasionally, if a man defaulted or could not pay his penalty, Robert might assign him work, as he did on November 2, 1854, when he fined a man "1 day of work feeding cattle."[29]

Clerking at the town's general store had given Robert Robertson a glimpse into the community's business, but this new work opened other vistas. He was privy to matters both personal and financial, and soon the Virginian began to purchase land. Robert would never become a land speculator on the scale of Martha's grandfather, George Vinsonhaller, but, parcel by parcel, the squire (as some of the town's residents began to refer to him) began to buy and trade property in and around Bourneville. He taught himself to use a compass and to survey. At first his purchases were small—ten acres here, thirty there—but the pace quickened and the scale increased.

While the Robertsons were buying up land and putting down roots in Paint Valley, it seemed that many Ohioans were pulling up stakes to move on to bigger opportunities. In 1848 John Sutter discovered a vein of gold in California, and many Americans bet their last penny on what would become for most a mere siren's song. Not twenty feet from their cottage door, the Robertson family could hear the rumble of wagon wheels heading west in what eventually felt like a stampede. It was the Gold Rush.

A new and unprecedented period of optimism took hold in America as a result of its rush for gold. It seemed to the settlers of European ancestry that their good luck was about to reach historic proportions. All around them was evidence of their progress and success. Following the pioneers into the new territory had come cabinet makers, tin smiths, and shop keepers; their stores now lined the streets of Chillicothe and provided families like the Robertsons with luxuries that were unobtainable during both Martha's mother's and grandmother's generations. The most primitive of log tables and three-legged stools were replaced by European-style furniture crafted of walnut and cherry; queen's ware took the place of wooden chargers, and instead of coarse linen, shawls of silk wrapped the shoulders of some of the women of Bourneville. Where once shanties and log cabins had dotted the countryside, clapboard houses now lined the pike, and, as bookends to the village, on the east and west ends of the town of Bourneville, were now rising two grand brick houses—the very essence of stability and wealth.

Martha and Robert Robertson were active participants in this rapid and uplifting change: their own lives were proof of the extraordinary opportunities inherent in mid-century America. To anyone looking, their futures could not have seemed brighter. Nothing, it seemed, could go wrong.

But there had been and would continue to be challenges. In 1847, the very year Martha had moved into the Robertson cottage, a week of rains sent Paint Creek gushing over its banks. Flood waters swept into the bottomland behind Bourneville and burst over the Robertson threshold, depositing an ugly layer of mud on the kitchen floor. As housekeepers, Martha and her mother-in-law would have been dismayed by the slime that clung to their bare feet, and by the sight of their children holding their noses at the stench of rotting debris floating by the back door.

What's more, ever since the arrival of the Ohio and Erie Canal in 1831, Martha and all the residents of Ross County were menaced by periodic outbreaks of cholera. In 1849, when she was pregnant with her second child, the killer disease hovered over the valley and put the Robertson family on high alert. But once again this family survived unscathed.

It was not, however, the case for poor Nelson Prather and his family. The Prathers were friends who lived on the eastern edge of Bourneville in one of the town's two fine new brick houses. And this house would eventually become Robertson

Place. At the time, however, no one could have fathomed such a future because the Prathers and their children seemed permanently ensconced in their stately home. No floods could reach them: they lived on high ground. No flames could destroy the fireproof bricks of their sturdy house. But now Robert and Martha might have winced every time they glanced up at the house on the hill. It was frightening to see how fast a family's luck could go bad.

The Prather Story

In 1841, when Martha was eleven years old and Robert was her teacher, three young Prather men had sauntered into town: Enos, Nelson, and Erasmus. The brothers were farmers. They knew good land when they saw it, and they had money in their pockets. By 1845, the brothers had found just what they had been looking for.

It was on a cold and bleak January day when news broke that the Prather brothers had made purchases in the vicinity. Enos, the eldest, chose land about a mile west from the center of the village; Nelson and Erasmus Prather bought 333 acres bordering the east end of Bourneville. Pooling their money, these two men paid $17,000 for the eastern tracts (in 1845 a pair of men's shoes cost $1.75), making the land worth fifty-five dollars per acre—a far cry from the price Massie had commanded back before statehood in 1802. For the two-thousand acres in the original survey, Massie had been paid five-hundred English pounds. Had Virginia's veterans seen the territory's potential—land rich in wildlife, fertile from glacier debris and watered by rivers and streams—they might not have sold their land grants so readily. It had taken settlers and the hand of man to shape its beauty, to realize its potential.[30]

Since Massie's early sale in 1802, a string of land speculators had continued to buy and sell the tracts that the Prather brothers were now buying in 1845. Each new sale had brought whistles to the lips. So when word of their purchase reached the ears of Robert Robertson, it might have served to put a fire under him. Within a year the ambitious former schoolteacher bought his very first piece of property. It was a small tract of land, only fourteen acres, and he bought it from his exuberant new neighbor, Nelson Prather.

It turned out that Nelson's big brother, Enos, may have become the wealthiest man in Twin Township because by 1857 his real estate holdings were valued at $120,000.

"Oakland Farm."
Residence of Mr. Wm. A. JONES, Twin Township. Oct. 13. 1874

With his wife Zero, he began to build their dream home. What began as an explosion of activity ended some twenty years later in a house with eighteen rooms (and as many fireplaces), a semi-circular self supporting staircase, an exterior stairway to a drovers room, and a name. Oakland Farm it would be called for several generations.[31]

Here on the east end of Bourneville, alongside the log Methodist church and its cemetery, the middle Prather brother, Nelson, sited a more modest house. It would face west and would replace an earlier timber structure which had been built on the property in the 1820s by settlers. Just as did Oakland Farm, this Prather house would sit high on a hill.

When Nelson Prather started to build the foundation for his brick house, Martha was just fifteen. The Poole family lived on the other side of a stream which ran through this Prather property, and from her family's cabin Martha and her younger brothers and sisters could walk over the hill to see all the activity. No doubt they loved the excitement, the grand gesture of it all. They would have thrilled to the sound of the sledge hammers hewing the stones for the foundation, marveled at a brick house taking shape in a world of log and clapboard.

During the summers of 1845 and 1846 the sounds of carpenters' hammers echoed throughout the valley. Old men and small children gathered at the base of Prather's hill to watch the workers create their rectangular bricks of clay from the banks of Paint Creek.[32]

Nelson Prather was on the site every day. He guided the builders, often pitching in to help in the construction of his house. And when his wife Mahala—herself not much older than Martha—asked for cupboards, the carpenters fashioned them from the property's hickory and ash, and built them into a wall beside the main hearth. On the other side of the fireplace the workmen created a curved and winding staircase leading to two bedrooms for the Prathers and their five children. It seemed everyone was happy in those days.

But in 1849, another virulent epidemic of cholera swept through the valley, and it took few prisoners. One by one, the Prather family dwindled. After a fourth child succumbed, Mahala fought on, but at last she too was taken by the dreaded disease.

And so it was that a microscopic organism, a bacillus not even visualized by the world's doctors and scientists, would in two weeks time nearly decimate this healthy young family. Also taken by cholera in 1849 was Nelson's younger brother, Erasmus. So by the spring of 1850, Mahala Prather and her four children lay in the cemetery next door, and Nelson Prather was a thirty-five-year-old widower.

Martha and Robert mourned alongside the others, but by comparison, they were blessed. Not only had they escaped the dreaded epidemic, they now had another healthy child. Just as Margarite had begun to wobble around on her two chubby legs, along came another baby girl. Virginia was the chosen name for the Robertsons' second daughter, but her perky, delicate nature led many to call her Ginnie. Virginia's looks set her apart, even as a child. She had a long oval face. And, squinting out at the world from atop tall ivory cheekbones were a pair of intense, hazel-colored eyes.

Martha, now nineteen, was forced to spend more time at home these days, especially during the winter months. And yet, or possibly because of being housebound, it was at this time that Martha took on a new enterprise. She began to earn money by sewing.

Sewing

Sewing was huge in the lives of American women during the nineteenth century. Aside from child rearing and food preparation, it was a woman's biggest job. Thanks to the Industrial Revolution, ready-made fabric allowed Martha's generation the luxury of setting aside the spinning wheel and loom. However, the creation of a family's wardrobe still consumed much of a their time and energy. As a matter of necessity or thrift, many women like Martha learned to cut and stitch the household's curtains and table linens, not to mention the bed sheets and pillow cases. She also knitted and thus supplied the family with mittens and mufflers, sweaters and socks. Waistcoats and mattress covers, knapsacks and nightshirts—all were produced at home by women like Martha. Sometimes they got together with friends to quilt or cut out patterns.

Martha Robertson had always sewed for her family, but now she began to put her skills to work for profit. In the midst of the Robertson cottage—probably in the kitchen—sat a new device which was to make this possible. It was a sewing machine—the family's pride, and probably the first machine ever to be brought into the Robertson home. A precursor to the Singer, this heavy black symbol of the new machine age had a long and graceful arm and side wheel. Under its table was a treadle which Martha could pump to make a needle and thread hum in miraculous precision and dizzying speed atop the seams of shirts, vests, and collars. Whereas it used to take her more than fourteen hours of hand labor to make a man's shirt, the salesmen claimed she could now do the job in one hour and sixteen minutes.[33]

In 1854, Martha Robertson began to make shirts and collars to sell next door at Bourneville's general store. Its new clerk, hoisting a heavy, hand-bound, leather ledger from under the counter, would then open the marbleized cover and turn to a page which bore the account of Robert I. Robertson. On October 14, 1854, he dipped his pen into a pot of ink, and, in graceful script wrote, "one fine muslin shirt….$.50."[34]

In her day, it was highly unusual for a woman to earn anything but "pin money." When a man could earn a dollar for a day's work, no doubt the tangible result of Martha's labor was quite satisfying to the young wife and mother. Although she would have to subtract her costs, a half dollar could buy four pounds of butter, a new dish pan or five yards of calico. If she were to make three more shirts before the holidays, Martha could buy something special at the store such as the beautiful pair of Moroccan slippers. On that same day in October her efforts paid only for necessities: butter, eggs, candles, molasses and, of course, more fabric. Robert often brought firewood to the store in trade, but unlike most of his neighbors who frequented the establishment, the squire did not purchase tobacco—at least not from this store. Once he purchased a whalebone umbrella, but on most occasions his firewood bought more sheets of fine writing paper for his legal work.

In November Martha stocked up on muslin, flannel and velvet. In December of 1854, she earned credit for another nine shirts and ten collars. After placing her perfunctory order of butter and eggs, she selected six yards of calico and a large woolen shawl. In addition she paid for the rental of a buggy. Perhaps it was for visiting her ailing grandmother Vinsonhaller in Adams County.[35]

Robertson General Store Ledger, 1854

After asking the clerk to tally the rest for credit, when she turned to go, Martha might have encountered the store's new owner, their friend, Nelson Prather. In 1853 the widower rebounded from his melancholy to remarry. His new wife was Sara Robinson (similar in name, but not to be confused with Robert's mother, Sarah Robertson). The couple would have two more children, and by 1857 Nelson was off and running again. Together with older brother Enos and a brother-in-law Jeremiah Shelton, Nelson Prather purchased the town's general store. They asked Robert Robertson to be a trustee.

A New Facade

Nelson Prather's newfound enthusiasm did not end with this large purchase. Buying and building seemed to be in his blood. With the second Mrs. Prather along came two more children and big ideas for expanding their house on the hill. Once again the brick makers assembled at the foot of the Prather property to begin their work. At right angles to the original house, in limestone blocks, workmen laid out the foundation for what would become four large rooms. Two front parlors with large bedrooms above them would comprise the new facade for the brick house, giving it an appearance far grander. And for its residents, along with the new reorientation came a commanding view; in the foreground, reaching all the way to Paint Creek, was their lush cropland. Beyond, in the distance, they could see Spruce Hill, where, it was rumored, rose a stone fortress built by a vanished race.

For a decade Martha Robertson and her husband had been observing the evolution of the house on the hill. No doubt curiosity first attracted them, but when cholera and death visited its door, perhaps their feelings toward the fine house became ambivalent. Now, despite its history, when the place again became a beehive of activity, they may have found themselves curious, if not covetous.

Care and precision guided the builders as they stitched together the two structures. Thousands of bricks would be needed to build the addition that lay in the mind's eye of Nelson Prather. Its Greek Revival style, so clean and dignified, might have given the new facade a look of severity, had it not been for the introduction of the Italianate cornices. A note of domesticity and decoration was achieved when the front door was recessed behind a pair of fluted columns and the motif repeated in a recessed balcony.

For the hip roof, wood was split into shakes, and for ventilation and light, glass windows were fitted into its many openings. Large windows were a marvel in the settlement and it might have occurred to Martha and Robert that the valley's heat and humidity would be more tolerable if one could throw open one of those windows at night. As it was, during a heat wave, their damp bedding clung to their bodies as they lay in their little clapboard cottage in the low-lying village. Martha and Robert could only imagine sleeping on a four-poster bed in one of the high-ceilinged bedrooms of the Prather house whose thick brick walls would be cool to the touch and whose many doors and windows could be opened to the breezes.

Careful Living

In contrast to the house on the hill, by the mid 1850s the Robertson residence might have suffered by comparison. Back in 1830 it was built on a shoe-string. Improvements were needed. Now there were five sharing the space and once again, Martha was pregnant.

Dare they wish for a boy? Alas, it was another girl. But Robert may have soon forgotten that he ever wished for a boy, because this newborn had an especially sweet disposition. Sally was her name. Her sisters soon took to calling her Sadie Lady, and over the years she also went by Sarah and eventually, Aunt Sadie. But here, we will use her given name, Sally.

Margarite and Virginia, now eight and six, were away at school all day, but when they came home each evening they certainly would have vied for the baby's attention. Baby bottles with rubber nipples were an invention of their era, so in addition to rocking or changing her diapers, the girls could have fed little Sally.

Martha and Robert Robertson were very busy these days. In addition to his family and civic work, the squire had been accumulating even more responsibilities. He was about to take on the job of superintendent of the Methodist Church, a job he would keep for the rest of his life. All along, the squire continued to haul wagon-loads of firewood to trade at the store next door, and Martha continued to sew up dozens of shirts and waistcoats to sell. Everyone could see that the Robertsons were careful with their money.

Regular purchases of milk and eggs indicate that the family kept no cow or chickens, but like all the villagers, the Robertson family kept a garden. Plenty of clear water lies under Bourneville; the Robertsons needed only to dig down twelve feet to reach it, and except for the well, an outhouse, and perhaps a small play area, the rest of their deep back yard was plowed under each spring to make way for row upon row of vegetables. Martha's generation benefited from the invention of glass canning jars with their lids of porcelain and lead. Each summer Bourneville's housewives sealed into those jars the vitamins and minerals of their tomatoes, beans, and berries.

Perhaps Martha's children gathered apples from one of Johnny Appleseed's trees. He'd passed through the valley in the early 1800s, planting seeds wherever he found a likely spot. Later, when the barefooted nurseryman returned to harvest the saplings, he sold those little trees to the settlers. Now his ruddy apples would be stowed away in a cold cellar alongside the Robertsons' supply of potatoes and carrots, beets and cabbage.

Bankruptcy Notice

*I*ndeed, the Robertsons worked hard and spent their money with care. Perhaps it alarmed the staid couple when news surfaced that the Prather brothers were in financial straits. And yet, some may have seen it coming because a monetary crisis was beginning to engulf the region.

Bad weather had ruined the crops in the summer of 1857. Poor crops meant two things for the ambitious brothers. Not only would their farm income decrease, so would that of their customers. Enos and Nelson owned not one, but two businesses now: in addition to the general store, they owned a mill. More than anything, the Prathers' lavish life-style was costing a king's ransom.

Robert, the store's trustee, extended his friends a loan, but it was not nearly enough. Soon after this infusion of cash, the Prather brothers had to mortgage 564 acres of land to provide more cash. But after they mortgaged it a second and yet a third time, Enos and Nelson were still short of money.[36]

By August 18, 1857, the brothers were in desperate straits. Both were forced to sell their homes and their land. Yet even in this dark hour, hope remained. Members of their extended families stepped forward to buy the properties, although at a fraction of its value. It was Nelson's sister and her husband John Barger, who, along with two others, were the buyers of Nelson's house, and no doubt it was Robert Robertson, as justice of the peace and notary, who engineered the transfer.

Mercifully, the new buyers allowed Nelson's family to remain in the fine brick house. However, the downward slide of their luck continued. On August 21, 1857, Amasa Sproat of Chillicothe filed a lien against Nelson's brother Enos for failing to pay his bill. It was for fifty-one pounds of putty, fifteen kegs of white lead, plus linseed oil, turpentine, sand paper and colorants (including the hues of yellow ochre, rose pink, terra sienna) "furnished for his dwelling house in Twin Township, Ross County." One day later, the brothers declared bankruptcy.[37]

Such an abrupt reversal put Robert back into the sudden position of being a merchant. As the Prather store's trustee, he was at the very eye of the storm. Robert I. Robertson and Nathaniel Core, the store's other trustee, were named by the bankruptcy court to take over all the credits and debits left behind by the Prathers—all "goods, chattels, merchandise and sums of money due or coming to them."[38]

Within hours of the court order, the center of power shifted from the small frame house in which Robert carried out his duties as justice of the peace over to lot #8 where stood the Shelton, Prather & Company store. Behind closed doors and shuttered windows, where so recently the townspeople had come to trade and meet their neighbors, the accountants now tallied each can of sardines, pound of nails, and yard of dimity. In order to match their tabulations against those of the store's ledgers, the men worked their way silently up and down the wooden aisles of the general store, counting every bag of feathers, yard of bed cording and sheet of window paper.

Even for Robert, such a sudden plunge into the mercantile business took its toll. In 1858 he resigned his post as justice of the peace. One year later, however, the townspeople persuaded him to return to the job, and they would keep him as their law enforcer for the rest of his life.

During this chaotic juncture, Martha was pregnant with her fourth child. At the same time, her mother-in-law was failing. Up until now, Robert's mother had been a steadying force in Martha's household; she'd been a help rather than a burden. But now she herself needed care. Martha was the only one to take up the slack because there were no reinforcements coming from the Poole cabin. Martha's mother, Mary Poole, was in Adams County tending her own mother, Grandmother Vinsonhaller, who was dying. During times of stress in the Robertson household when bursts of wails and whining may have spilled over its threshold into the stifling air of the bankrupt store, it was not Martha's voice that Robert heard through the walls. According to Martha's Aunt Asenath, a frequent visitor, never did Martha Robertson raise her voice to shout.[39]

Meanwhile, up on the hill, Nelson Prather lay dying. After losing his first family and then his house, the forty-two-year-old father was now losing his health. Nelson's and Sara's little boy John had just died on July 22. Looking back, I think that what took their provider just two weeks later, on August 4, 1858, was not cholera, but a broken heart. A lover and dreamer can only bear so much.

Shutters pulled, the darkened house announced the end of a family tragedy which had been breathtaking in both speed and breadth.

On the Brink of War, A House Stands Empty

The house is for sale. But times are not right for selling real estate. In fact they are terrible. The Panic of 1857 has given the nation's investors and businessmen a severe case of the jitters. Local farmers are unnerved by freak weather. A cyclone ripped through the valley last year, and in 1858, crops stood frozen in the fields. Beneath the economic unease lies a still greater concern; in Washington, Congress seems to be locked in controversy, North against South. Will the nation itself even survive?

It was during this uneasy time that the sale of the former Prather property proceeded. John Barger, Nelson Prather's brother-in-law, sold it quickly for nearly twice what he had paid. And in such a climate Robert Robertson was also to take a bold move. With Nathanial Core as partner, he would buy the village's bankrupt store.

Bourneville's general store not only sold goods, it acted as a bank. Folks paid bills there, borrowed money and withdrew cash. Robert may have wondered if owning such an establishment could be considered a conflict of interest, but buying it seemed to be a risk worth taking. For the rest of his life, however, it seems as though the squire played down his part-ownership of the town's general store. Never would he list himself as a merchant to the census takers. Instead, to the county's documentarians, he continued to be "Robert I. Robertson, Justice of the Peace."

To enter the general store with its wooden floors and potbellied stove was to enter a different world. Aromas of coffee and nutmeg filled the air; ribbons and laces lined the shelves. Peddlers from Chillicothe arrived to replenish the store's stock, and one of them brought a box of spectacles for the trying. Fresh-smelling soap and balls of candlewick awaited a customer's inspection, and on a long counter in the back of the store were dress patterns and colorful fabric.

Girls were tempted to run their fingertips along the bolts of gay calicos, striped ticking, and red flannel. Of course the village boys would be interested in other things. Gun powder or tobacco, plow points or a pair of calf-skin boots would have lured them into the store. Occasionally, if a wedding or a funeral were in the offing, a man of style might ask for a satin vest and suspenders, or perhaps a top hat of beaver fur.[40]

The three Robertson girls may have whooped with glee when they learned of their father's decision to buy the store in 1858, but everything stood still in the Robertson cottage when it came time for the drama of childbirth. When Martha gave the signal, the girls ran for their father who summoned help. Martha was both strong and lucky; she survived yet one more delivery. It was another baby girl!

Martha and Robert named their fourth daughter Jane. Her grandmother Sarah had regained enough strength to be of some help, and the Robertson nursery once again brimmed with domestic activity. Robert returned to work and eventually Martha took up her sewing again, turning out shirts to sell next door. But Martha had been confined to her home for a long time now because to appear in public while pregnant or nursing was considered unseemly. So to keep Martha apprised of the world, Robert would have gathered local news from the store, the village, and the township. He brought her the daily newspaper and perhaps a copy of *Harper's Weekly*.

Chit Chat

Anesthesia was one of the hot topics during Martha Robertson's confinement. In England Queen Victoria had shocked her subjects by breathing an experimental gas which would render childbirth nearly painless. Out in Utah a group of Mormons and Native Americans had attacked 120 settlers in the Mountain Meadows Massacre. The cause of cholera had been discovered, but a new lethal disease called diphtheria was making its way across the continent. And in that same year of 1857, the Supreme Court, in its infamous Dred Scott decision, concluded that people of African descent could never be citizens of this country.

Folks traded news among themselves while rocking and knitting, chewing and whittling. When finally the young matron was able to venture out of their house, the fact that she came armed with enlightened conversation would have made her a welcome visitor on any of the village's porches. Tales of the terrible fire that destroyed half the town of Chillicothe had alarmed the villagers back in 1852. More recently, their imaginations were riveted by a local murderer and his disappearance. Refrigerators and elevators were newsworthy in the late 1850s, but if laughter were wanted, one subject which would have been certain to bring guffaws was Charles Darwin's outlandish new theory that we all came from apes.

Chillicothe built its first library in 1859, and if the conversation turned to the arts, perhaps they would critique a performance at one of the town's entertainment houses. In February of 1854, at the Atheneum on Second and Walnut Streets in Chillicothe, folks witnessed a performance of *Uncle Tom's Cabin*. Harriet Beecher Stowe's sympathetic book and subsequent play about slaves was still being fussed about in Washington as well as in every little village in the nation. Its writer had become nearly as famous as the Queen of England. During that same year of 1854, a war nearly broke out in Kansas over whether to allow slavery. For years, Chillicothe's two newspapers, *The Scioto Gazette* and *The Chillicothe Advertiser*, carried on a battle of words over the issue. Finally, in 1860, each took an opposing stance.

In the small town of Bourneville feelings were mixed about the issues of states' rights and slavery. 1860 was a presidential election year, and the men in the town would soon have to take a stand if they intended to vote in the back of the general store for their next president. According to Beverly Gray, the region's authority on local African-American history, Bainbridge likely sided with their southern kin, Bourneville with the North.

On November 6, 1860, the headlines declared the victor to be the lawyer from Illinois, Abraham Lincoln. Within hours, aided by the speed of the telegraph, South Carolina notified the nation of its intention to secede from the Union. Nerves grew taut between free and slave states, between neighbors and co-workers, between fathers and sons.

Impending war was one thing, but the abandoned Prather house was another. It had been purchased, but not inhabited, and now it was for sale again. Attempts to find a suitable buyer for the big house were proving to be difficult because the region's potential buyers were mired in fear, afraid to take on new risk. In the year of Prather's death there had been a run on the banks. Lots of folks were still out of jobs. To make matters worse, the government in Washington had decided to lay a tax on earnings. With the possibility of war breaking out, who could predict the future of the house on the hill?

Ridicule and Neglect

Throughout these unsettling times the Robertsons watched the shuttered house on the hill suffer the ignominy of ridicule and neglect. Like a hot potato, it seemed to bounce among half-hearted investors. And now yet another buyer stood in line. The townspeople could barely keep up with the turnovers, and nature was beginning to have its way with the grounds.

Over the winter, Alexander McMillan had teamed up with an eager young physician and farmer named John Poage, and on January 8, 1859, the two men bought the stately brick house, along with 341 frozen acres for $22,881.75.[41] Alex McMillan was Martha's uncle, and he and his wife Ada lived in Bourneville, just a few steps away from the Robertsons. Aunt Ada was Martha's favorite aunt, the one born in Massie's fort in 1795.

The elder McMillans didn't move into their purchase and probably never intended to. Instead, the young Dr. Poage brought his family to live in the house on the hill. Soon his wife and daughter Alice, along with maid Mary Bowen, arrived to cut back the ivy, open the shutters and hang lace curtains in its front windows.

Margarite Robertson was thirteen when she befriended Alice Poage, but it seemed that the grand, columned house was plagued with bad luck. Margarite's friend soon moved out of the brick house and once again it stood vacant. It seemed that nobody could make of the place a home.

Martha's Aunt Ada and Uncle Alex would have been in a quandary. What could they do with the ill-fated property? At their advanced age, would they be up to its challenge? And yet to leave it empty very long would invite trouble. The house was set apart from the village just enough for vandals to enter and depart unseen, and mischievous humans weren't the only worry. Vacancy would invite varmints, too. When Ada lived in her family's log cabin in the bottoms, she'd witnessed the mess made by rodents and chimney swallows, not to mention those pesky wood squirrels. Already vines were beginning to attack the brick house on the hill; trees had since toppled and weeds were taking over.

Diversion

One cannot help wondering whether, on a muggy summer night in Bourneville back around 1862 or 1863—on a night when the cicadas were tuning up and the neighbors spilling out of their houses to catch a little breeze—Ada McMillan may have asked her niece Martha to stop by for a chat. Sitting side by side on the porch swing, Aunt Ada would have pointed up the hill, and in a calm but pleading tone she might even have declared that she really thought a family like the Robertsons should live up there. If Ada McMillan had made such a comment it would have caught Martha by surprise, and that may have been exactly what her aunt had intended. Because on that humid evening back in 1862, her niece was wearing a dress of black. Martha Robertson was in mourning.

Life for the Robertson family was on hold now. Not long ago, the fourth and last child, their baby, had died. Little Jane Robertson was never to know her nickname, was never to learn to walk. She would never live in the house on the hill. It was only recently that her name was discovered on a Ross County census of 1860. For the infants of Bourneville during the mid-nineteenth century, after Captain Molly brought then into the world, they were on their own. If Jane's desperate parents had summoned a doctor to their cottage, he would have had in his black leather bag only useless elixirs, poultices, and bloodletting devices; there would have been no vials of antibiotics to save the life of tiny Jane Robertson.

After months and even years, the Robertson family would bear the scar of the baby's death, but here, on Aunt Ada's front porch, I imagine that the women were looking for a chance to set aside grief. Had it not been for the tragedy, Ada McMillan might not have thought up her scheme, the dual purpose of which was to return the light to her niece's sad eyes and to rescue the house on the hill.

What the neglected house on the hill clearly needed was the energy and enthusiasm of younger people such as Martha and Robert. For an instant, in the dim light of that summer evening, when Ada MacMillan and Martha sat fanning themselves in their rockers, a tiny spark may have appeared in the dull eyes of a mourning mother. For years Aunt Ada had observed her niece gazing up at the mansion, and by now everybody in town would have been aware of her husband's ambition. All but the blind could have guessed that he too admired the big house. As the rockers creaked and swayed on the McMillan front porch, Ada, the first Vinson-

haller daughter born in the Northwest Territory, might have elaborated on her proposal. Could Robert and Martha rescue the Prather place, clean it up, make it habitable? Would they agree to become its caretakers?

Ada's offer may well have stunned the Robertsons. Wide-eyed and slack-jawed, they might have let go of their grieving for a moment. Soon a list of projects would have spun from their brains. Fences to be built, gravel spread and brush cleared. Perhaps from his cane-seated chair, Uncle Alex offered to help scythe the yard's prairie grass. All the floors needed to be scrubbed, the windows washed and shutters opened. Inevitably, to this list the ladies would have added their own ambitious landscaping plans. Should they plant snowball or beauty bushes by the long side porch? Where could they start a hedge of lilacs? Planning new gardens would have been strong medicine for Martha's melancholy.

No gardeners tended the grounds back in the 1860s. Random trees hung their shaggy branches this way and that, giving the place a look of abandonment. After so many deaths under its roof, the house itself looked forlorn, and the village youth would have thought it haunted.

When Martha and Robert announced their plans to move into the house, perhaps their daughters were willing to put aside their fear of bats and spiders and ghosts because what really would have captured their imagination was the house's potential for romance. Margarite, then in her early teens, was the family's budding poet. How grand that house must have seemed to her. She had listened to her mother tell about exploring its construction site back in 1845 when she herself was a girl of fifteen: of watching as great stones were laid in place to form the very first outlines of the house; of seeing bricks, three deep, stacked higher and higher atop the stone foundation to define the original four rooms, and of questioning why the carpenters were sawing boards into triangles. And Margarite herself could remember witnessing the rise of the large two-story addition in 1857. She could remember it distinctly because she was ten at the time. It had more than doubled the original brick house in size and made it more impressive. It must have seemed that any one of those new square rooms could have swallowed up her own little house.

The Big Move

When it finally came to time move, the Robertson family was in for some surprises. Long-ignored, the house on the hill was not inclined to welcome the newcomers. Martha may not have bargained for the mice droppings and bat guano, nor the sight of snake skins. The dark and cavernous rooms reeked of mold. Bird nests were lodged in the chimneys, and the nests of wasps and hornets clung to the pillars. The high plastered ceilings sent echoes of shrieks up and down the staircases, putting everyone's nerves on edge.

Martha and her husband were not deterred. They got busy ridding the house of its pests and superstition. Martha mixed up buckets of whitewash to freshen the walls; she gathered bars of lye soap to scrub the floors. Robert rounded up some carpenters to make repairs and the sound of hammer against nail rang out beyond the cavernous space, announcing to the village that the Robertson family was taking charge.

A single open wagon might have transferred all the earthly belongings of the Robertson family up the dirt lane to their new residence. All in the squire's household were busy that historic moving day; all that is, except for Robert's mother. On New Year's Eve in 1862, Sarah Robertson had passed away. Her death came shortly after baby Jane's, and some said it was a mercy. Had she lived to make the move with her family, would Sarah Robertson have been worrying herself about the risk or foolishness of moving into a house they did not own? Perhaps. But more than likely, she would have been proud for her son to be living in the fine brick house they had admired over the years, might even have predicted that he would figure out a way to make it his own.

At the funeral of this seventy-four-year-old Virginian some of the old-timers remembered the vigorous young woman who had ridden into the settlement some forty-odd years ago atop the seat of a covered wagon. Some may have remembered the powerful look of determination they saw in her eyes when they looked through the long tunnel of her sunbonnet. Way before the time came for Robert to lay his mother to rest in the cemetery next to the house on the hill, he must have realized that he owed nearly everything to his mother's vision and courage. She had abandoned her kin and all that was dear to bring her children to a new world. No parent could have done more. To him, then an ambitious adolescent, she had given a remarkable opportunity to make something of himself—perhaps to make his fortune—in this fertile new Ohio territory.

As he unloaded his mother's enormous walnut blanket chest from the moving wagon, Robert's thoughts may have returned to the eve of his departure from Virginia when his mother had packed that trunk with all the family linens and clothing. This walnut trunk, a replica of a giant tool chest, is lined with cedar and fitted with small wheels and a handsome brass closure. We still use it today, and I can see in my mind's eye the men struggling back then to lug this heavy piece of furniture up and around the winding front stair steps. Filled once again with linens and quilts, the Robertson's chest was placed between the two front bedrooms in a broad hallway which, if one swung open the balcony door, commanded a panoramic view of the valley.

Looking around the upstairs, Martha may have started wondering. Should she close off a room or two? Keeping six fireplaces and three stoves fueled all winter long would require too much effort for a family without servants. The Prathers had kept servants. At least during the cold months Martha could close off the east bedroom and the parlor below. She and Robert claimed for their bedroom the large sleeping chamber on the west side of the house; its window faced southward and flooded the room with sunlight during the winter. A smaller window looked west and gave Martha a view of the village.

Margarite, who had just turned fourteen, was given a room all to herself—the one in the original house near the back stairs. Between these two bedrooms was one in which Virginia and Sally would sleep. And though at first the two younger girls may have put up a fuss, later, when the wind howled through the crevices of the strange and darkened house, they may have rediscovered the merits of sharing a bedroom.[42]

Life in the Big House

As the Robertson girls would soon discover, just as did I as a child, the house had many quirks. Sunspots were to be claimed on the west side of the house, drafty corners avoided on the north. Small closets tucked under the staircases made good places to hide. But to clamor up the spiral back staircase became a favorite exercise for the younger generation. When the parents were nowhere to be seen, the furtive pleasure of grabbing onto the floor above and swinging out over the stairs, feet arching over the dining table below, was beyond resisting.

Margarite, Virginia and Sally would have adored the front balcony. From it they could view much of the village, and when not spying on a neighbor doing this or that, they could have turned the tiny space into their stage. For their more ambitious dramas, the girls could run downstairs to pull back the heavy pocket doors which separated the old parlor from the big new one.

Pocket doors may have served as stage curtains for the girls, but the paneled dividers with their ornate brass pulls would have fascinated their parents as well. One can picture Martha standing with her hands on her hips wondering why on earth Nelson Prather's wife had put a black stripe around the upper portion of the parlor walls. The remainder of the room was painted an apple green. Wallpaper would be a nice improvement, Martha must have mused, as she assessed the place where the Robertson family would receive callers.

And callers there were. In the front hall Martha put a silver-plated dish into which visitors might place their calling cards. Friends and relatives were eager to see inside the big house and the girls never tired of showing it. But did Martha detect a bit of envy in her curious visitors? Maybe it is not surprising that the Robertson family began to draw inward a bit, for like it or not, they were learning that living in the house on the hill tended to set them apart from everyday life in the village.

Tintypes

Still, moving into the town's fine brick home would have been cause for celebration. It is around this time that the Robertsons recorded their family's prosperity. A new invention called photography was all the rage. Before their move to the hill Martha may have intended to shepherd her family into town to get their portraits made, but something must have come up to postpone their trip. The window of opportunity slipped by, and for baby Jane's memory it was now too late. The family would have no permanent record of her cherubic face.

Two decades earlier, the first photographic portraits had seemed astonishing. Were men meant to stop time? Some witnesses claimed the process involved magic; others deemed it heretical. But by the 1860s the images had become popular, and when a horse-pulled wagon full of chemicals and metal plates stopped in a town such as Bourneville, it commanded a great deal of attention and business. With a war going on, photographs as keepsakes took on even more importance, and a line would form alongside the wagon if the photographer brought with him military props such as a sash, a sword or a drum.

In the echo-filled house on the hill, the very idea of having their appearances recorded for posterity would have set the three Robertson girls atwitter. What should they wear? Chafing against convention, the elder sisters might have fallen into argu-

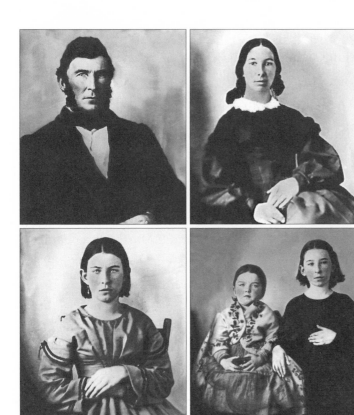

ments with their mother over what was and was not appropriate for a formal portrait. Martha herself may have yearned for a new outfit to mark the historic occasion, while Sally, the family's four-year-old, would have flitted from room to room begging to try on this or that from among her sisters' castoffs until she too caught the enthusiasm and joined the chorus of pleas for a fancier outfit.

Once at the photographer's studio, the dynamics changed. Sally, in her embroidered vest, would have been forced to place her head against an iron neck rest to prevent her from fidgeting and thus becoming a smear on the photographer's precious plate. Virginia, still angular and gawky at the age of eleven, assumed an expression of resignation in this, her first portrait. In contrast, Margarite gathered her composure and looked mature and self-assured in a dress of satin.

But wait! Margarite's confident appearance in this 1860s tintype is deceiving. More than a century later, amongst the letters and diaries in the moldy confines

of a dust-laden trunk, I found another tintype of a slightly younger Margarite. Defaced with scratches, here is the likeness which had to be replaced in the handsome, gilded frame on the wall.

Did a younger sibling, in a fit of revenge, scratch Margarite's image? If not, what was it that made the adolescent Margarite want to destroy the image of her younger self? In the earlier take she appears to be sulking. Perhaps she was self conscious about her changing body and thought none of her dresses was

The Women of Robertson Place

flattering. I can imagine her sticking out her tongue when her mother put her foot down, insisting that the polka-dot dress was perfectly fine. Martha, in her well-modulated voice, may have reminded her pouting child that she herself had selected the fabric. A year later, Margarite may have thought it looked so babyish. At fourteen, Margarite was teetering between childhood and adulthood.

Boarding School

*I*t was not until Margarite left home and attended boarding school that she would become the Margarite Robertson known to her heirs. Early in Ohio's history, colleges and universities began to spring up around the state, and in 1842 a group of Presbyterians in nearby South Salem established The South Salem Academy, a co-ed school for the purpose of preparing the region's youth for entry into those institutions of higher learning.

Margarite must have pleaded with all her heart when she heard that there was to be a music teacher at the Salem Academy because she had always wanted to study music. For quite a while Margarite had been trying to persuade her father to buy a piano. She well understood that the idea of education was different, however, and maybe her father could be persuaded to spend money on quality schooling.

Perhaps it was the right time to send their first-born off to boarding school. The academy was only an hour away by horse and carriage, and for an enrollment fee of fifty cents, Margarite could attend classes at a cost of twelve cents per term. English literature and composition were mandatory, as was Bible study. In Robert's mind it was important that his daughter be versed in the ancient history of Rome and Greece. On the other hand, French, German and Greek demanded a hefty surcharge. He would have to pay an additional $1.50 for his daughter to learn a foreign language.[43]

Whether or not Margarite's parents realized it, when their dreamy and

Salem Academy, South Salem, Ohio

artistic daughter left their nest, it would be her new friends, not the academic courses, which would influence her most. Salem Academy was known for its staunch support of abolition. Back when the Robertson family was consumed with the death of their fourth daughter and the failing health of Grandmother Sarah, the nation had fallen into war. The family may have been caught off guard in 1861 when the war between the North and the South began, but now they joined their neighbors in constant discourse about the war. The townspeople could talk of almost nothing else. Many had kin on the other side of the Mason-Dixon line and the idea of shooting at one's cousin was a horrifying one.

Despite the mounting unease, the Robertsons enrolled Margarite in the Salem Academy. At about that same time, this devout family began to attend the Concord Church in nearby Lattaville. The old Concord Church had been drawing Presbyterians to its services since 1803, but recently it was gaining a reputation for being a bastion of anti-slavery sentiment. Although Robert Robertson was to keep his post as superintendent of the Methodist Church in Bourneville until his death, during the war years he traveled the seven miles to join fellow abolitionists in the pews of Concord Church.

In the church's youth group were many of Margarite's friends from the school in South Salem. Soon after she arrived at the academy, Margarite began to hear rumors about enlistment, even though everyone expected the nation's conflagration to last only a few months. But the war did not peter out. Instead, it began to escalate. Week after week, some of Margarite's classmates left to join the war effort. Referred to as "boy soldiers," they had been Margarite's playmates just yesterday. And when Margarite returned to Bourneville, her biased talk no doubt raised concern. Even though Martha and Robert shared Margarite's sympathies, as parents they would have been wise to warn their daughter against repeating the school's fiery rhetoric around Bourneville because in their hometown lived several Confederate sympathizers.

War altered everyone's mood and behavior. As it grew worse and its boundaries less certain, the Robertson family may have wanted all their children living at home under their roof. Withdrawal from the academy would have been for Margarite a terrible disappointment. Margarite stood up for her beliefs: she loved her school without reservation. She seemed made for it and it for her. Nevertheless, three years into the battle between the states, Margarite left the academy.

Perhaps it was to balance this setback that her father reconsidered the purchase of a piano. No doubt the Robertson family needed a diversion, and it would have been the perfect time for such a luxury to enter the Robertson household.[44]

The Piano

How and when did the upright piano make its grand entrance? I wonder if it was on a soft summer afternoon, when Robert may have been napping as Sally lay on the carpet playing with the family dog, that a team of horses was spotted by the eight-year-old?

Bounding up the staircase, one can imagine little Sally barging into Margarite's bedroom. "Come quick!" Margarite, always off writing somewhere, was probably sprawled on her four-poster bed and poised in mid-sentence when she was so rudely interrupted. Before the two of them could dash back to the balcony, the team of horses was cresting the hill. From the balcony the girls could see the horses enter the drive's turnaround. What was the mysterious cargo behind the sweating chestnut-colored horses?

For the adults in the house, the afternoon's siesta ended in ear-shattering squeals. Dashing down the front staircase, the girls called out to their parents. And by the time Robert glanced through the parlor's wavy window panes on his way to the front door, his fingers were stuck in his ears in mock pain. On the balcony above, one can imagine Margarite standing in disbelief with her hands cradling her tear-streaked face.

When at last the precious piano was pushed against a wall in the back parlor, Margarite pulled shut the heavy pocket-doors and spun the seat of the three-legged piano stool round and round until it was just the right height. Her bare feet searching for the pedals, her petite hands spread across the shiny keys, eyes closed, brows arched in anticipation, the eldest Robertson daughter gingerly placed her finger tips on the ivories. When the sound of that first tentative set of scales seeped under the doors and reached the ears of eager family members, it could have—ever so briefly—replaced the nation's doom and gloom with a little hope and gaiety.

The Secret at Concord Church

The war was now in its third year, and while chaos reigned in other parts of the nation, the Robertsons remained as bystanders. But this was about to end; they were about to take a small part in history. In her research, Beverly

Gray discovered that Robert Robertson acted as a "superintendent" for the Underground Railroad. [45]

On a summer afternoon in 1863, when Margarite was picking out the chords for *When Johnny Comes Marching Home*, her concentration was interrupted by an explosion of barking dogs. Up the gravel driveway on a coal-black steed came her father's friend, James Steel.

Mr. Steel would no doubt be calling upon Margarite's father to discuss church matters. It was common knowledge that the two saw eye-to-eye on the controversial issues facing both the nation and the parishioners at Concord Church. President Lincoln, in his Emancipation Proclamation of January, 1, 1863, had freed all slaves living in the ten states that were in rebellion. However, under the old Fugitive Slave Act of 1850, support for those who ran away was still punishable by law. Confusion reigned. Several brave families in southern Ohio had opened their homes to the escapees, explained Mr. Steel, but more hideouts were needed.

While Margarite listened on one side of the pocket doors, on the other, sitting in the comfort and apparent privacy of the squire's parlor, the two men pondered the dilemma. Margarite had heard rumors at the academy. Mr. Steel and his five sons were ardent abolitionists and all were conductors on the Underground Railroad. Their self-appointed task was to organize way stations and to escort the runaways in the cover of night. Thousands of runaways had made their way across the Ohio River and many were fanning out through the valley. Few slave masters had the resources to stop the escapees once they left the plantations, but the more vindictive and tenacious owners were known to hire hunters to take chase, to cross the Mason-Dixon Line in hot pursuit of their bounty. Some of the runaways, especially those traveling with their families, would be desperate for protection. When Mr. Steel informed her father that a new location must be found in this vicinity, Margarite clutched her hands to her heart and held her breath.

Create no records, leave no evidence; this would be the oath her father would have to take. Did she hear the words "resting place?" Mr. Steel's voice was now muffled. Superintendent? What did that mean? And Lattaville? That was where the Robertsons went to church! It was well known that somewhere in the vicinity of Bainbridge was a hideout for runaway slaves. To get from Bainbridge to Lattaville was a long way, fifteen miles. Escapees would need a stop in between. And in between was Bourneville.

Perhaps on that spring afternoon Margarite did not overhear the next question on Mr. Steel's tongue, but if she had, she would have dropped to the floor and

Concord Presbyterian Church   125 Anniversary   Sept 21 1930

buried her face into the warm belly of the family cat. With the shuffling of men's boots and the high-pitched whinny of Mr. Steel's rearing horse, the house grew quiet.

Although Margarite may have intuited the meaning of the meeting in the Robertson parlor, she was not privy to the secret at Concord Church. Only a tiny few knew of the church's defiance of the Fugitive Slave Act. Robert Robertson was one of them who knew that its elders had cut a large hole in the sanctuary's ceiling (one that could later be concealed), and that they had carried cots into the newly opened attic. Now, in two long rows, behind the deception of wood molding and fresh paint, lay twenty-six beds hidden and ready for the weary runaways.

As for Margarite's mother, the thought of aiding the escapees might very well have been appealing. After reading Harriet Stowe's anti-slavery novel, (several copies of *Uncle Tom's Cabin* were found in the house), little persuasion would have been needed. Right on their own property, just across the creek, was a perfect hideout. It was an old log cabin. Abandoned some years ago, the dark low-slung building now stood surrounded by crops. And by mid-summer and into fall the corn rose high around it, obscuring its location. From the balcony of their house the Robertsons could see not only the cabin, but also the pike in both directions. A perfect position from which to signal a warning! Margarite, the eldest and most likely to be able to keep a secret, would be entrusted to act as lookout when escapees were hiding in the cabin.

Without doubt, all this clandestine activity would have made Robert Robertson, the law-abiding, law-enforcing justice of the peace, exceedingly nervous. However, one can imagine that a romantic Margarite and her tenderhearted mother were exhilarated by the risk of this challenge, by the thought that while others might provide food or nursing skills to help the war cause, perhaps they could provide a safe haven for the runaways, perhaps they could make the desperate flight a little less wretched.

Robert's old brass hand bell was put to a new use. It was the one whose clapper had caused Martha's young heart to flutter when her husband had called his pupils

to class. To test the bell's reach, one of them had to cross over the old foot bridge to the pasture and then wade through its high fescue to the crest of the bank above the ancient creek bed. Beyond the towering cottonwoods and over the golden cornstalks a person could barely make out the cabin's chimney on the other side. According to plan, the other accomplice was to crouch beside its log walls to listen for the bell's distant clanging.

With all her vigor, Martha swung the bell. Could it be heard at that distance? Together, the family decided that a short repeated ringing would act as a summons—"Come to the big house for food or news." A prolonged clanging would signal alarm—"Bounty hunters sighted! Hide in the creek or head for the hills!"

Morgan's Raiders

Paint Valley was now in a high level of alert. Ever since the North had declared war, its citizenry had been on edge, but as of July 1863, they were nearly in a frenzy.

Rumors that Morgan and his raiders were racing toward Ross County were rampant. If not for his terrifying tactics, Confederate General John Hunt Morgan would have been the epitome of a southern gentleman. With a carefully trimmed goatee and a long swooping mustache, the blue-eyed Confederate carried his six-foot frame with pride and swagger. Women reported that if he happened to pick your farm as a resting spot for his men, he would dismount, dust off his hat, light up a cigar and ask you kindly, ma'am, to cook up some rations for two-hundred or so of his band.

For two weeks the general and his brigand of fifteen-hundred or more men bivouacked and wreaked mayhem across the southern part of Ohio. According to Robert Harper's *Ohio Handbook of the Civil War*, approximately 2,500 horses were

General John Morgan

stolen and nearly 4,375 homes and businesses were raided. In a line that passed through Ross County, he ordered his men to rip up railroad tracks and cut telegraph lines in order to retain the advantage of surprise. Rumors of his sightings were transmitted with such speed that warnings of his progress far outpaced the general's advances.

Would the outlaws pass through Bourneville? Would they steal horses? Maybe they would pillage their way through the Robertson-Core general store! What should the town's JP do if the village came under attack?

If the raiders chose to plunder, casualties might ensue, and there could be panic. Furthermore, General Morgan might look to the spacious Robertson property as a good place to quarter his cavalry. What if his Union counterpart got there first and commandeered the house as a hospital?

Margarite's heart, true to its dramatic nature, must have beat a little faster, and I can picture the women of the house taking inventory of the bedding and making a separate pile of old sheets for tearing into bandages. Even though her younger sisters might not have fully understood the concept of commandeering, they would have wanted to be part of the whirlwind, planning how they would help their father hide the animals and wondering what they would do if the wild-eyed raiders came galloping up their gravel lane.

Looking back, the Robertson household may have gone a little overboard in their fear of a raid by the infamous southerner. But they were not alone. Once General James Worthington of the Ohio Militia arrived in Chillicothe, he ordered his aides to post hand bills emblazoned with the cry "CITIZENS TO ARMS!" Volunteers were asked to come to the court house with a rifle, shotgun, or pistol; a sword or dagger; a blanket; some rations; and a tin cup.

Nearly two-thousand citizens of Ross Country rushed to the court house steps and vowed to "fight to the last—to surrender never." General Worthington declared martial law. Businesses shut down and by the next day the town was overrun with volunteers and onlookers. But confusion reigned because it became apparent that the township had only one cannon at its disposal. There was no ammunition in the armory—"not a bullet, a grain of powder, or a pound of shot."

Relief soon arrived in the person of Colonel Runkle of the United States Army, who came to take command. He quickly collected all the weapons, marked them with identification, and stored them for reissue if needed. He also thought to tie up the volunteers' horses so that no one could go AWOL.

But did General Morgan and his raiders thunder up the Chillicothe-Cincinnati Pike in a shooting and whooping stampede? Did they ransack and loot the Robertson and Core Mercantile, or charge up the gravel lane to the Robertson front door in a flourish of gun-waving?

Historians say the hell-raisers dipped south before passing through Bourneville on their way east. Sally Robertson, Margarite's younger sister, later told a *Gazette* reporter that she saw one of Morgan's horses fall off the little bridge at the east end of her village. Although this would have been the bridge over the creek that ran through the Robertson property, Sally's "citing" was likely due to mistaken identity during a time of hysteria. In any case, Chillicothe itself was spared, and only later did Runkle's volunteers admit with chagrin that they had needlessly burned up Chillicothe's southern bridge when, in a state of panic, they thought they had spotted the raiders.[46]

On July 19 most of Morgan's raiders were captured as they attempted to cross the Ohio River into West Virginia, and a week later the remaining two-hundred were forced to surrender. However, behind bars, a captive Morgan once again thrilled his followers by managing to pull off the century's only successful escape from the ominous Ohio State Penitentiary. The flamboyant general made it back to the South, but a year later he came to a rather sudden end when he was shot by Union troops in Greenville, Tennessee.

Boy Soldiers

When the heart-stopping Confederate raids of the summer of 1863 were but colorful and disputed history, the mood within the Robertson household returned to the sick acknowledgment of the cost of this war. On the kitchen table lay the daily local newspaper with death lists of local husbands, brothers, and fathers. Letters bearing reports from the battlefront circulated within the community, and the popular periodical, *Harper's Weekly*, displayed large-format, double-page renderings of scenes from the battlefields. In graphic detail its quick-sketch artists conveyed the thunder of a cavalry attack, the night-time drama of a battle at sea and the horror of post-battle carnage. The famous society photographer, Mathew Brady, made history by driving his wagon of photographic equipment into the midst of the fray in order to record the aftermath of the great conflict which would define the century.

Yet after three years of this war, its end was nowhere in sight. Northern generals had come and gone; things seemed to be at a stalemate. Invitations to wartime fundraising galas in Chillicothe's great halls gave way to rations and calls for food. Women in the farming community pickled extra cucumbers and onions. Others knitted warm socks, made soap, collected straight pins and wool blankets to fill the wagons heading south.

Measles and dysentery broke out in Union camps and many young women signed up to be nurses' aids. A few of the braver ones got permission to follow the troops in order to help cook and care for their brothers or husbands.

Then along came the rains of April and a flurry of tiny letters addressed to Margarite from South Salem. Had she heard? Several of her classmates were signing up for the war cause. They were heading for Camp Dennison, near Cincinnati, where they would start training. Jeb, Will, Erskine—all of them close friends.

The news might have taken away Margarite's breath. It would have both exhilarated and frightened her to realize that the consequences for her friends could be life or death. Although she had not yet admitted to having a sweetheart among her classmates, from then on Margarite Robertson would follow every detail about the 149th Regiment in the daily *Gazette*. It was *her* regiment.

Yet to those who knew the young men of the regiment, the thought of sending them to war—if even for three months—would have been shocking. But on May 2, 1864, these sons of local families—these seventeen, eighteen, and nineteen-year-olds who had just days before been playing practical jokes on one another, frolicking together in a swimming hole—joined the Ohio National Guard and committed themselves to fight for one-hundred days.

Two days later, on May 4, the newly organized 149th Regiment began maneuvers at Camp Dennison. Soon another Ross County regiment was formed; the 188th. In it was a young man by the name of Thomas Steadman from Bainbridge, a town just seven miles west of Bourneville. Tom had recently begun paying attention to Margarite's younger sister, Virginia. Perhaps Virginia had met the Steadman boy when the young people of Bourneville and Bainbridge had met in the snowy foothills between the two villages with lanterns and horse-drawn sleds for an evening sleigh ride. Soon after that he had come to call at the Robertson home. But even if Virginia had not been smitten by Tom, her girlfriends would have nudged the two into a flirtatious relationship because in her circle nearly everyone wanted to have a boyfriend. However, Tom was eighteen, and Virginia, at fifteen, was considered by

Erskine Anderson

her father to be too young for courting. Still, it would be fun to write to a boyfriend in uniform because the fighting boys got all the attention.

Soon reports about the local regiments filtered back to Ross County, and hence to Margarite and Virginia. Local names such as Cutwright and Caldwell, Florah and Steel, Purdum and Poole cropped up in the news. Shoemaker, McGinnis and Darbyshire were named as officers. Among the seventeen officers and sixty-nine enlisted men who formed Company C of the Ohio National Guard's 149th Regiment were Wisehart, Latta, and one of the four Jones boys whose family lived just beyond Bourneville in Oakland, the eighteen-room house formerly belonging to Enos and Zero Prather. From Frankfort, Ohio, came a boy whose framed portrait still hangs on a wall inside the brick house on the hill: Erskine Anderson.[47]

On May 11, when training was complete, the volunteers of the 149th climbed aboard boxcars on a train headed for Baltimore, Maryland. Northern spies reported that Confederate soldiers were amassing across the Potomac and Union generals now feared an attack on the nation's capital. They had asked the president for fresh troops to hold off the enemy until their own armies could reach the capital. Erskine's would be the regiment called upon for this task.

Back home, Margarite and Virginia scoured each issue of the *Gazette* for news of her friends. Finally they were rewarded with a report. On July 4, 1864, General Tyler ordered the 149th to advance to a bridge at Monocacy Junction, just east of Frederick, Maryland. They were to protect the railroads and bridges leading to the nation's capital.

Five days later the boy-soldiers engaged in battle. Theirs was a small but vital attempt to halt a Confederate invasion of Washington. However, the Battle of Monocacy was severely lopsided. The young men of the 149th were inexperienced and outnumbered, and try as they might, they were unable to hold the bridge as ordered, "to the last extremity." Their commanding officer was forced to retreat, but the young soldiers did buy valuable time for the Union veterans to arrive to defend the capital.

Of his erstwhile young soldiers, General Tyler later reported that, "No troops could have done more than did the men under Colonel Brown's command in that unequal combat. It seldom falls to the lot of veterans to be more severely tried than were the Ohio National Guard at the stone bridge, and none ever carried out trying and hazardous orders better or with a more determined spirit than did the 149th."[48]

This battle would later be called "The Battle that Saved Washington." But for the Ohio regiment it was costly; on the battlefield lay 130 soldiers, wounded or dead.

Back home the wires began to pulse with a staccato beat, listing the names of the dead and wounded. Rumors about prisoner-taking ricocheted through the valley. Over 100 of the young men were reported to have been taken into captivity and herded across the bridge to Richmond, Virginia, the capital of the Confederacy. Richmond was home to Libby Prison, whose mere mention could send shudders down one's spine.

Fear gripped the parents of the young prisoners. The entire region kept vigil for weeks on end while tales of heroic escape gave them hope. On August 20, exactly one-hundred days and two battles later, the much reduced regiment returned to Ohio and fell into the waiting embraces of their loved ones, where the truth spilled over in a fall of tears.

Some of the soldiers were wrapped in bandages, some were on crutches. In Maryland's cemeteries, some of Margarite Robertson's friends were left behind. But all three of the Anderson boys, sons of the well known missionary family in Frankfort, made it home. Margarite was sickened yet relieved to find that Erskine Anderson, the youngest, had been one of the thirty soldiers who managed to escape from the horrors of Libby Prison. Sandy soil under the brick walls of the waterfront prison had made tunneling possible, although the soft walls of those tunnels had sometimes caved in, trapping many who attempted to flee.

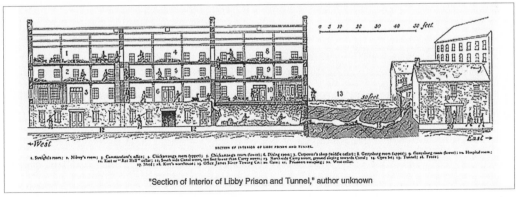

"Section of Interior of Libby Prison and Tunnel," author unknown

Finally, the long wait was over. A special camp meeting was called by the church elders to welcome home the young heroes. But the carefree and sunny boys Margarite remembered did not show up, for those one-hundred days had seemed a decade to the tenderfoots—many of whom had never before slept a night away from their mothers' care. Barely recognizable in their faded blue, Margarite's friends were changed by their brush with war. Thin and slump-shouldered, they walked as if still carrying packs. Their skin was sunburned or sallow, and while to their families they appeared as heroes, to a stranger they might have been mistaken for the vanquished. It would take time to heal Hiram and Levi, Jeb and Will, Charles, Edwin, and Erskine.

While the crippled 149th regiment had been hopping westbound trains to get back to Camp Dennison, elsewhere in the nation General William Tecumseh Sherman was leading his Union army in the opposite direction toward the sea. He was burning a swath across Georgia. Atlanta lay in ashes, and the war was nearing its end.

On the afternoon of April 9, in the spring of 1865, General Robert E. Lee, sword by his side and dressed in his immaculate uniform, surrendered his men to a mud-spattered, sloping-shouldered, casually dressed General Ulysses S. Grant. The formality took place in the front parlor of a private home in Appomattox Court House, Virginia. The American Civil War was finally over.

Shock

It was just five days after the war's end, as the Robertsons and their country-men were heaving a collective sigh of relief and when the nations' beleaguered and exhausted president was enjoying a rare evening of entertainment at Ford's Theatre, that a terrible shock ripped through the land.

LINCOLN ASSASSINATED!!! tapped the wires. People ran into the streets with the news. The nation staggered and came to a halt.

Right on cue, the actor John Wilkes Booth had fulfilled his goal by shooting the unsuspecting president in the back of his head with a derringer pistol. He was part of a group of conspirators who meant to disrupt the Union cause. Six days later, a coal-burning funeral train, swaged in red, white, and blue and belching smoke as it blew its mournful whistle, pulled away from the nation's capital. On front of the engine was strapped a large photograph of the man whose flag-draped coffin lay behind in a railroad funeral car. On its way to Illinois for burial, at every town stop along the way, a sea of mourners clad in black gathered alongside the tracks to view the likeness of Abraham Lincoln's craggy face and to stand in mute tribute.

Scramble

*L*incoln's cortège stopped in Columbus, Ohio's capital, where great crowds flocked to the statehouse hoping to view the president's casket as it lay in state. But in Bourneville life stood still. People walked around in a trance. Small talk dried up. Scant business took place. In all likelihood, Robert Robertson took to his library where he could brood in private and warm himself by the heating stove.

Only grudgingly would he have looked up from his newspaper to catch the sound of hoof-beats and of gravel crunching under the wheels of a carriage. It was James Steel and his son. What could they want? Slavery was over; the Underground shut down, and bounty hunters a thing of the past. Were the Steels here on business? If Margarite had been anywhere in the house, she would have taken up her listening post.

Later that evening Martha was to learn the news. The Steels were buying the house her family was living in! For $15,000, the brick house and 164 acres would go from the Poages and McMillans to the Steels.

Had the squire seen this coming? Maybe the men had conspired. Maybe it was a plan concocted by the Steel men to secure the property until their friend Robertson could come up with the funds to buy it, because the Steels had no intention of living in the house on the hill. They had their own farm up the road, north of Bourneville.[49]

Perhaps this is why Ada McMillan had not worried her niece with her husband's plans. She would not have wanted Martha's children to be alarmed. Ada's nieces loved the house; they thought they belonged to the house and it to them.

Regardless. The sale put the squire on notice. His work was cut out for him. For the next three years Robert Robertson's single-minded goal was to gain title to the property his family called home.

Getting it Together

*A*ll along, the alert Virginian had been buying up small parcels of land. But at this time, the entire country was experiencing paralysis. A man didn't know what the future held. The South's economy was in shambles, and great swaths of land lay decimated by the war. Carpetbaggers roamed the red soil, extracting profits. Perhaps Robert Robertson foresaw that when the nation came out of its shock people would migrate north and the price of land would rise.

On the heels of the war and the Steel purchase, in 1865, Robert sold all his small parcels of land in order to buy the much larger tract of 315 acres which lay directly across the little creek from the house he inhabited. This newly purchased tract of land (on which the old log cabin was its only improvement) ran along side the Steel tract where it crossed the pike and followed the stream all the way to the swift-flowing, annual-flooding, Paint Creek.

A good head for trade seemed to be his strong trait. Since their marriage nearly twenty years before, the Robertsons had increased their holdings fivefold. Martha's management of the family's resources most certainly played a role in the family's prosperity. Ownership of the village's general store had required the resources of the entire family, but it was proving to be a good investment. Robert must have reasoned that as long as the corn crops kept growing and Bourneville kept expanding, he could justify a feeling of optimism.

Bourneville was indeed growing. By 1865 its trustees figured that over 130 people lived in cabins and frame houses along the pike. Many others came to the town to do their trading. They could go to the Robertson-Core general store for groceries and other necessities or to several other establishments such as the one for stoves and tinwork or a small drug store which supplied cigars and tobacco, trusses and porcelain teeth along with cough candy and stomach bitters.

Machine shops had sprung up to fix farm implements and other machine-age contraptions. Two doctors, a couple of teachers and a lawyer had also made Bourneville their home. In addition to a schoolhouse and post office, to serve the community were now two churches with their manses and cemeteries. And, as of late, a new hotel sign swung above the old tavern.

Just as predicted, when the Union states began to rebound from the great conflict, folks migrated north. The price for Midwestern farmland escalated, but the price for residential real estate did not rise. Instead, it fell. When it seemed that prices could fall no further, Robert and Martha Robertson summoned all their resources and made an offer. It was 1868. For $8,000, they were able to buy forty-seven of the 164 acres of the Steel tract, those forty-seven holding what was most important to the Robertson family and their heirs for generations to come—the big brick house on the hill. Together with his 1865 purchase of 315 acres across the creek, Robert

Robertson figured he now had more than enough tillable acreage to support his family. It would have been a victory, a milestone in his life.[50][51]

Women's Work

Out came the weed trees. In went the long-awaited lilac bushes. Now that the house finally belonged to them, the family swung into action. For years, it seemed, Martha had been planning and visualizing what she wanted to do if only the house were hers. Ideas had come and gone, been tested and discarded. At night she must have lain awake plotting the changes as others would count sheep. Suddenly the future was here.

Down came the old fences. Up went wallpaper and drapery. Such a whirlwind of effort the family had never experienced. Soon their efforts to reshape the former white elephant earned the home a name: The Robertson Place.

While the women had their work, Robert was setting up an office in an outbuilding on the property. It was a barn-like structure which had space for a horse stall and a buggy, should the family ever acquire one. These things would have been important to a nineteenth-century gentleman farmer from Virginia.

Inside the house, Martha had her own concerns, the greatest of which would have been all the bare floors and windows. She probably enjoyed the idea of outfitting their residence, but to do so would require many shopping trips to Chillicothe and many hours—no, days and weeks—at her sewing machine. Bolts of organdy and damask, yards of mattress ticking, and bags and bags of feathers came home with her, and from them Martha produced curtains, mattresses, pillows and table linens for the home. Some of her work is still in evidence these 150 years later.

On one of her shopping trips, Martha must have purchased a lamp. Shiny and new, the ornate brass kerosene lamp held aloft a tall, glass chimney. To light it required a match and some kerosene. Replacing a candelabra, this lamp was given a place of honor in the front parlor where its graceful and powerful light filled all four corners of the formal room.

Martha's daughters, eager to assume responsibility for the newfangled light source, might have divided up the chores. When dusk overcame the house on the hill each evening, perhaps it was the eldest, Margarite, who adjusted the cotton wick and set the kerosene aglow so that the family could read or do hand work. Its light was equal to that of three candles. Virginia, the night-owl, would have been the natural choice to blow it out before going to bed. And on the following morning, the least glamorous job of washing soot from the lamp's glass chimney may have fallen to Sally, the youngest child.

Sally probably took on her task with good nature because, according to those who knew her, she was always in good spirits. And despite the fact that she was the family's pet, she remained unspoiled. As she matured, this youngest daughter seemed to relish work. The Robertson family had always honored work, but for females of Sally's generation, this meant the never-ending tasks of the nineteenth century household: cleaning, cooking, sewing, gardening, or caring for the sick and frail.

But things were about to change. In the war just ended, many courageous women had served as nurses. Depicted in the engravings of the family's copy of *Women of the War; Their Heroism and Self-Sacrifice*, these women might have been a source of inspiration to the young Robertson girls. But the book's heroines were self-taught. At the time, there were no schools to train and certify nurses. Nearly all girls were trained to care for their family members, but very few worked to serve the world at large. Yet such valiant caregivers as Clara Barton, by ministering to soldiers during the Civil War, had sparked a movement that would not end until a new profession of nursing was created.

At the same time, other powerful female personalities were attracting attention on the world's stage. Even in the previous decade, Martha Robertson and her young daughters might have followed in the *Gazette* the daily adventures of the sensational young singer Jenny Lind, who thrilled American audiences with her nightingale voice while touring with P. T. Barnum's circus. And then there was author Mary Ann Evans, who masqueraded under the pen name George Eliot and seemed to flaunt her independence by leading a flamboyant—some would say immoral—life style.

Virginia

Maybe Virginia, the middle sister, would be the first of the Robertson women to break tradition and look for satisfying work outside the home. Would she be one to take the other road? Perhaps those who watched the Robertson family could have predicted that this particular daughter might stumble as she crossed the slippery passage into adulthood, because when it came to the friends she saw and the hours she kept, Virginia often challenged her parents' rules. Now, at the age of twenty-one, Virginia was straining under the parental roof.

As if to accentuate her independence, Virginia's unusual looks set her apart. Her features, though not unattractive, were spare. As a young lady her high cheekbones, sensitive slim nose and crescent eyes resulted in a look of exotic refinement. Her lips were minimal, and yet there was something appealing and pert about Virginia. When she cocked her head to listen, one sensed a bright intelligence; however, if one challenged the strong-willed Virginia, a combative nature—not unlike that of her father's—might surface.

Being somewhat delicate in stature and preferring feminine pursuits, Virginia rarely exposed herself to the weather; as a result, her skin glowed with the light of porcelain. And out of nowhere, it seemed, came those green, almond-shaped eyes. Actually, when Virginia dressed herself carefully—and she had a flair for this—she could be almost breathtaking.

But perhaps the middle child thought herself to be unbeautiful. Despite the fact that she was a Robertson, Virginia was surprisingly shy. This trait may have given the middle child a reputation for being somewhat standoffish, which in turn would have kept her just outside the ring of rough and tumble horseplay. Virginia was the type of young person who at church gatherings would slip away to meet privately with her friends. Such behavior no doubt concerned her mother and caused her father to raise his eyebrow. No doubt her older sister Margarite was often called on to serve as mediator.

Shortly after the war's end, Tom Steadman showed up at Robertson Place, and the veteran was given a warm welcome. It was clear he was very interested in Virginia, but whereas the middle daughter obliged her parents by receiving Mr. Steadman's visits and accepting his invitations to socials or church outings, there seemed to be little pleasure in it for her. In fact, Virginia began to make excuses.

Nevertheless, before Tom had left to join the 188th regiment, Squire Robertson had called upon the Steadman family and made known his approval of the courtship. Having served the township as tax appraiser, Robert knew how to size up a farm, and the Steadman farm in Bainbridge was prosperous and well-tended. It would be handy, Robert must have noted, to have a farmer's son in the family, one who could take over when he himself was no longer able to manage Robertson

Place. Tom might even be able to help with fencing and planting and any number of jobs Robert had to supervise now that he was owner of over three-hundred acres. A man with no sons tended to think of such things.

But now, when the veteran's name was brought up, Virginia fell silent. She and her father began to disagree about her future and who should decide it. Hadn't he shaken hands over the agreement? In any case, Margarite should be the first to marry. Everyone would expect the prominent Robertson family to follow convention, and Margarite had a serious beau. Her prospects were promising.

In the spring of 1871, at a time when rain showers erupted with frequency throughout the valley and sent thunder rumbling through the foothills, the atmosphere at Robertson Place was charged with tension. Doors may have been slammed; meals missed. Outside, the air hung humid and heavy. Inside, Margarite and Sally found themselves tiptoeing through the chambers, fearing an explosion between their moody sister Virginia and their stern father.

In retrospect, someone should have paid more attention to the sudden calm that befell Virginia in the days before her disappearance. Robert might have better kept up his guard, for on what seemed to be just another morning, dawn breaking with a rooster's crow, Sally came rushing into Margarite's room.

"Where's Virginia?" she blurted out. Something was awry because Virginia Robertson never rose early. Margarite bolted upright, her stomach tightening, her mind going blank. For on that ominous day, on a day which would never be recorded but which would alter the Robertson family lives as no other, normality came to an abrupt end. Throwing off her covers, Margarite leapt to the doorway between the two bedrooms, then, diving back into her own four-poster in shock, she buried her face in her pillow. In her brain was seared the vision of Virginia's empty bed.

During the secrecy of that moonless June night, Virginia Robertson had climbed out the window, down the still-standing ladder and into the unknown. Margarite's mind flashed back to last night when the household had lain awake listening to the sounds of tree frogs and crickets and the occasional cicada. They had all been lulled by the familiar sound of the birds settling into the towering cottonwoods in the lower grove; they had drifted off to sleep hearing the soothing call of the whippoorwill. It was into this night, Margarite realized, that Virginia had stolen.

Please God

What had her sister been thinking? If only Margarite could turn back the years to when the three sisters would flit about, cart-wheeling across the lawn and catching fireflies. If only she had been privy to her sister's plot so that she might have saved Virginia from plunging into a life that would surely be marred by shame and regret.

Please God, don't make me have to break the news. It was all Margarite could think, because of one thing she was certain: Michael McCord had been at the bottom of that ladder. Michael McCord was the only person who could have persuaded her sister to cross her father, to escape from the safety of her bed, the only one who could have persuaded her to turn her back on her rightful inheritance. It had to have been the McCord boy.

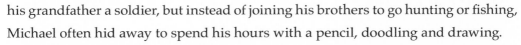

Racing back in time, Margarite's mind may have lit upon a vivid image of Virginia when she was just fourteen or fifteen. Margarite had caught her younger sister blushing in the presence of one of the few village boys who had not gone off to war. Michael McCord was barely thirteen at the time, but he was handsome. And when it came to girls, he was precocious.

Like Virginia, Michael McCord possessed a sensitive and reserved nature. His father was a farmer, his grandfather a soldier, but instead of joining his brothers to go hunting or fishing, Michael often hid away to spend his hours with a pencil, doodling and drawing.

Across Michael's broad and tanned forehead was a flop of casual blond hair, and below his strong brow were a pair of the most languid, pale blue eyes a mother ever looked upon. A fine physique and downy, smooth skin were Michael's as well, but the young girls dreamed and wrote florid poetry not about his skin but about his full, kissable lips. Even she—Margarite Robertson!—had flirted with the boy.

Surely it was this Adonis who had whisked her sister away. Past intrigues were no longer mysteries. The late night outings, the stash of provisions under her bed, the interest in learning how to darn a man's socks—even Virginia's calm before this storm—they all fell into place now.

Minutes were passing. Margarite had to act quickly, but how would she tell her parents? How could she prepare them for the blow they were about to receive? A mother's empathy was all she could hope for. Michael McCord was the heartthrob of just about every girl in Bourneville. Any one of them would have traded places with Virginia in a flash. Besides, her sister was old enough to marry. Maybe she was truly in love!

Margarite hesitated. She would have to pull herself together. Shivering from fear, she caught the reflection of her sober visage in the mirror above the washstand. Smoothing back her hair, she then braced herself with a splash of cold water from the porcelain pitcher and pulled on her chemise and petticoats.

It is likely that Martha collapsed in disbelief when Margarite announced that Virginia was gone, but Robert was a realist. In a split second he pictured the escape, and the force of truth jettisoned him from the house. "Robert?…Robert!" One can hear Martha calling after him as he disappeared into the barn.

Grabbing a pitchfork, Robert began to hurl great batches of hay from the stall. Brain afire, his own past unraveled before his eyes. Once again, he was that poor boy arriving in Ohio aboard a covered wagon. For more than forty years, the Virginian had done all he could to establish himself and his family. He'd poured his life into this new land, helped turn the raw settlement into a law-abiding, civilized place. Now one of his own flesh had ruined it. Ruined it. How dare she!

Surely everyone in town knew that he had promised Virginia's hand in marriage to the veteran from Bainbridge. How humiliating! Never would she and that new baby-faced lover of hers get *his* sympathy!

During the long nights and days that followed, Robert Robertson continued to burn. Rumors of Virginia's whereabouts began to surface, but revenge overpowered him, and he could not erase its demand. His anger had no expression save the idea of banishment.

Days grew into weeks, weeks into months. Regrets began to gather in the corners of Robert's mind. Had he done the right thing? Should he have forced his own standards upon this independent-minded twenty-two-year-old daughter? Had he overreacted to her disobedience? At some point the anguish became unbearable and Robert turned back to the earth for solace. A renewed interest in his corn fields served to put some distance between him and his curious constituents. Even though he was a successful businessman and keeper of the law, the boss farmer pulled on his work boots and took to the fields to bury his problems and numb his senses.

But alas, it seemed that all Robert's attempts were in vain. In haste he had made the vow. There seemed no way to reverse it. His pride was so hurt that after all these months he could not find it in himself to forgive.

Never again would Robert see his daughter Virginia. Never.[52]

Life Goes On

While her husband brooded and wrestled with his mind, Martha turned to her own garden where the pungent smell of soil, wet with rain and earthworms, promised new life. She too was wounded. And when she had finished thrusting the blade of her shovel into the earth's crust to uproot its noxious weeds, the gardener knelt down to sow a small packet of seeds. Planting a garden was Martha Robertson's way of starting over. Like her husband, Martha then watched the skies, but not for marauding crows; she was waiting for rain to return beauty and order to her life.

Meanwhile the Robertson girls tried to pick up the threads of their own lives, but the house on the hill felt odd. It had been so lively when the three of them had filled its rooms with sewing projects and visitors, laughter and chatter. Music and writing may have brought a measure of solace to Margarite. Sally, still the family's baby, pretended to ignore her sister's sudden disappearance by filling the vacuum with humor. But in the unnatural silence of the house on the hill, those attempts fell flat.

As for Virginia, she did not return, did not show her face at the door. Instead, she and Michael settled in the little hamlet of Massieville, just south of Chillicothe. From Mollie Hathaway, a friend of Sally's, came an occasional letter in which she mentioned having seen Virginia and Mike. Other acquaintances told of seeing Virginia in Chillicothe, and, what's more, they said she was thinking about testing the waters back in Bourneville.

Rumors of Virginia's return would have upset Robert Robertson. Perhaps it was his parents-in-law, Mary and Henry Poole, who were able to reassure or council him. The quiet pair often welcomed their son-in-law when he rode by their cabin on Lower Twin. Sitting side by side on their porch swing, on that late afternoon in autumn, Mary might have been the first to speak. Having been the daughter of a strong-willed father, she admitted that she could relate to Virginia when she took flight. Henry might have too, but his is a story spun from the grim facts that I was to discover almost two-hundred years later at the Poole cemetery, which is located very near the site of their cabin. If true, it is a story which a modest man such as the senior Mr. Poole might have carried to his grave.

Rebecca

Rebecca was her name. Henry continued, forcing himself to say her full name aloud. "Rebecca Norwood." Across the road and up steep Teter Hill to its wooded top, there lies an unmarked graveyard. Today, the locals call it the Poole cemetery. But there are no tombstones bearing the name Poole here. Instead, under the fallen maple and ash leaves is a row of child-sized shallow depressions, marked with small natural stones bearing the crudely carved—some might say hastily carved—names of Elenor, Nancy, and Clarissa Norwood.

Back in 1819, when their mother Rebecca Norwood was twenty-six, she befriended the Poole family from Maryland. The Poole boys, Hezekiel and Henry, were motherless. Their widowed father, John, was a blacksmith, and their kid brother Walter had just died. With her honey-hued skin, her bouncing tresses and plump figure, Rebecca showered charm over the male household. Before anybody knew what was happening, John Poole was announcing plans to marry the young widow.

But Rebecca was so young—closer in age to Henry Poole than to his father John, and she had children of her own—three little girls. Yet there was no changing John Poole's mind. Sitting on the cabin stoop listening to Henry's version of Rebecca's tale, Mary Poole nodded in agreement. She remembered having danced the reel at Rebecca and John Poole's wedding.

Henry continued, but at this point in the story, the mere thought of Rebecca brought a slight carmine flush to the cheeks of the sixty-seven-year-old. Suddenly he was fourteen again living with the father who had brought his boys over the mountain to start a new life. Henry closed his eyes, remembering how awkward he had felt watching this new woman romance his father. To make himself scarce he had stolen away to fish in Paint Creek or to hang out in Haller's Bottom where there were Vinsonhaller boys to play with.

Over the days and weeks that came, the atmosphere in that dark cabin changed. Things came to life. Did Henry become accustomed to Rebecca's home-cooked meals and the cozy setting charged with love? Finished with schooling, Henry was free to strike out on his own. But what was the hurry? If the cunning Rebecca had asked Henry to help her start a new garden, he might have responded with a broad smile. If she had told him to jump off Copperas Mountain, he might have considered it. Nothing would have been too much to please the bonneted and barefooted Rebecca. But having grown up in a male household, Henry would have known almost nothing about women. He wouldn't have recognized the pregnancy that began to affect his stepmother, and even when Rebecca's figure began to change, the youth may still have remained oblivious.

When the moment of comprehension finally arrived, Rebecca and Henry's eyes would have met in a flash of recognition. Under his tangle of disheveled curls, his face flushed bright red, making him shove himself away from the table, upturning his chair, to flee from the cabin. How embarrassing not to have known! Even more embarrassing to know!

While racing from the cabin's stifling air, an unspeakable truth seared itself upon Henry's brain. He loved Rebecca, but in an impossible way. He loved her in the way that his father loved her. What a terrible situation! He would have to leave home. There was no other solution.

But before he ran away, Henry thought to pen a note in his schoolboy English to his father, requesting that he be notified when Rebecca delivered her baby. The birth announcement, however, never arrived. In its stead, in a saddle bag that left Twintown on a fresh horse headed for Chillicothe, was a brief note addressed to Henry Poole bearing the following news: "Rebecca and baby lost. Funeral tomorrow."

Two years after Rebecca Norwood Poole's own death in 1820, her three remaining daughters died.

Even if Henry Poole had thought it fitting to tell his son-in-law Robert of the time he had run away from home, the tragedy of what followed gave him pause. In that same bleak year of 1820, Henry's own father, John Poole, at the age of fifty-three and in the depths of bereavement, would himself die.[53]

By the time Robert Robertson's visit to the Poole cabin drew to a close, the shadows on Spruce Hill had turned from azure to indigo. While preparing to leave, half-listening and half-dreaming, Robert Robertson paused to reflect upon his own life. He too had known tragedy, beginning with his own father's premature death. Loss of baby Jane had been too painful for words. Now there was his daughter Virginia to worry about.

Love Comes to Margarite

*B*ack in the house on the hill a new reality was taking shape. In the air hung both expectation and trepidation regarding news from their daughter Virginia because in all likelihood she would soon be pregnant. Though the remaining daughters were still in their father's good graces, Margarite and Sally were still walking on tiptoes, afraid of setting off their father's temper.

In a way, the Robertson girls may have benefited from their sister's scandalous elopement, for if their father had been so burned in his attempt to arrange an advantageous marriage for Virginia, perhaps when it came to their own suitors, he would be reluctant to meddle. Were this the case, it would especially suit Margarite, because a while ago Margarite had taken up a tentative correspondence with her distant cousin. Although Margarite had barely brushed elbows with Erskine Anderson while the two attended the Salem Academy, she knew a bit about him because Erskine was an upperclassman and his name nearly always appeared at the head of his class.

That her beau was unlike her father may have been part of Erskine Anderson's allure. Erskine was not so bold. He was not so driven. He did not exude confidence as did Margarite's father. Instead, Erskine was more retiring and sensitive.

At a tender age, he had joined his friends to fight for 100 days in the war: and those who knew Erskine remembered that he had been captured and force-marched 150 miles to the notorious Confederate Libby Prison, there to be plagued by hunger, rodents, insects, dysentery, stagnant heat and suffocating humidity.[54]

War had altered Erskine Anderson, but he was lucky. Along with his tiny pocket diary and a ring carved from a scrap of ebony, he had managed to escape with his life.

Back home in Ohio in the bosom of his large missionary family and under the tutelage of his uncle, D.C. Anderson, a prominent banker and himself a veteran of the war, Erskine steadily regained his health and found a place in the Frankfort community. The mild-mannered Anderson son appeared to be settling into a secure, if modest, life.

A cautious approach toward romance was Margarite Robertson's way. Quite the opposite of her impetuous sister Virginia, Margarite would be thoughtful and deliberate in her search for love. She would need time to understand this son of missionaries, this veteran of war.

Their courtship began casually. In a letter dated Sept. 24, 1870, Erskine wrote:

Coz Margarite,

If it suit your convenience and pleasure [I] would be happy to meet you at home on Wednesday Eve, Sept. 28th.

Yours,
Erskine

Margarite considered herself reserved, even-tempered, and mature. However, despite her determination to remain unflustered, she might have felt a burst of excitement when Erskine's black horse mounted the crest of the drive. No doubt the encounter threw Margarite off balance. For even though the young man who stood between the columns of the front stoop was her distant cousin, in this new frame, he was transformed into a suitor. It could have been an awkward moment, but I can picture Margarite drawing a deep breath and leading her guest into the back parlor where he could be seated on the small tufted divan. Sitting on the piano stool, Margarite might have spun herself round to the upright to place her slender, trembling fingers on the keys before she began her repertoire of songs.

Because it was late September, and the side door onto the terrace was open, beckoning breezes may have prompted Margarite to think of inviting Erskine outdoors to see the last of the summer's flowers. Margarite could show off her horticultural vocabulary: Lamb's Ear and Moses-in-the-Basket. And then, should she lead him through the orchard to see if the Grimes Golden apples were ripe?

Once through the gate and across the field, Erskine may have offered his arm to Margarite as they prepared to negotiate the roots and rocks of a steep incline to another pasture, this one lower than the first and hidden from view of the house. Lush with mint, a thick carpet of green ran along the creek bed. Cast in shade by a grove of giant cottonwoods, it was a place for lovers to chase one another and to leap in the air to catch the falling leaves. Behind the massive tree trunks, on that balmy evening in September, a tender romance may have been born.

In time, Margarite would discover Erskine's artistic bent, his deep piety, and he her refined intelligence and passion for nature. At the time of their courtship, it was their mutual love of poetry that proved to be the magnetic force. The two began to compose sonnets to one another. Slowly, Erskine bared his heart and soul to Margarite.

Just what did Margarite's father think about the pairing of his eldest daughter to the boy from Frankfort? When Erskine came to call, the squire may have tried to maintain a polite distance, but the temptation to loom near the parlor's pocket doors would have been powerful. Had he given in to his curiosity, Robert's furtive behavior would have made the shy suitor even more reticent, which in turn would have made the squire even more suspicious.

No doubt the male posturing exasperated Margarite. An artistic soul such as Erskine could not be compared to the dominant figure cut by her father. From Robert's point of view, did the pleasant young man from Frankfort have what it would take to achieve stature in this world? Could he accrue enough money to care for his daughter and maintain her standing in the community?

For decades Robert had worked to lift his family above the common plight of settlers. His little girl had run around barefoot on the dirt floors of their Bourneville cottage, but now she was accustomed to a bedroom of her own, nice clothing and occasional delicacies such as fresh oysters and Spanish chocolate. Would she be satisfied with less?

Signs of Wealth

Robertson Place was gaining a reputation for its grace and refinement. When guests entered the columned entrance, they found a pair of parlors which Martha had carpeted with patterned rugs and hung with heavy drapery and wallpaper from England. Martha could serve them teas from India or coffee from Java. In her pantry cupboards were rows of store-bought tins from far and wide, thanks to the train tracks which now crisscrossed the American continent.

For years Martha had stitched nearly all the family's clothing. She had released pleats, lowered hems, let out tucks and added darts to keep up with her daughters' growing physiques. At last, she was able to indulge the family by hiring an itinerant seamstress to come to the house. Along with her professional skills, the seamstress brought a suitcase full of new patterns and ideas from the latest copies of *Godey's Lady's Book*. Keeping up with fashion was an extravagance that set the Robertson women apart. How, Martha must have worried, would a bank clerk such as Erskine hope to provide such luxury?

Plush times were indeed in store for the Robertsons during the years following the war. Income from their farmland was making the family prosperous beyond their dreams, and to help work it and provide support for their comfortable life-style, the Robertsons needed extra help. Into the small cabin across the creek, Martha and Robert settled a family of ex-slaves. Although their names are not known, in exchange for use of the cabin and some land to farm, this family provided work which, in turn, provided the Robertson family with another important luxury: leisure time.

Fancy lap work, such as tatting and tapestry, began to show up during this period. Margarite executed an elaborate quilt with colors of red and green and salmon. She stitched her initials M.M.R. along its scalloped border, and of all the handmade quilts in the house, this is the only one bearing initials—which I take to mean that Margarite was especially proud of its bold design and intricate handwork. Reading for pleasure was another important leisure activity. Among the many gold-lettered titles which remain in the house's glass-doored bookcase are collections of poetry and a five-volume set of *Macaulay's History of England*. A copy of Louisa May Alcott's *Little Women*, with its March family of four daughters, was certain to have been popular.

A more tangible symbol of wealth was sitting down in Robert's barn—a new carriage, all shiny and black. For riding on horse-back, each member of the family had a hand-tooled leather saddle. When dressing for church, it is likely that the squire tucked into his suit's breast pocket his own small but personal token of success—a shiny rose-gold timepiece with matching fob.

Despite their new riches, it is likely that Robert remained somewhat humble in public, for the painful experience of their daughter's defiance was now part of his identity. The scandal stood as the great equalizer in his life—and was probably never far from the minds of his constituents.

Nevertheless, the squire continued to carry out his elected duties as church superintendent and justice of the peace. Despite his indisputable success, in the end, Robert understood that he was a poor boy from Virginia who had made some smart land deals and had worked hard at being a good merchant and facilitator of the law. As proof of this attitude—even though he had reached the status of the most substantial citizen of Bourneville—there would be no etched portrait of Robert Robertson in the fancy leather-bound volumes of Ross County's history, published in 1880. This proud but down-to-earth man would do no business with the obsequious salesmen who scoured the countryside looking for men and women willing to pay for their portraits to be made and their histories published for posterity.[55]

On the other hand, it would be wrong to conclude that the Virginian did not thoroughly enjoy the results of his efforts. The earthly pleasures which he had earned for his family were a source of satisfaction and pleasure every single day. No wonder Robert worried about his daughter's future. Yes, the young Erskine had potential, but what if his expectations about a future in banking did not materialize? The Anderson boy did not have land to fall back on. It made Robert's stomach queasy to observe the tenderness mount between the timid suitor from Frankfort and his most capable daughter, his Margarite.

The Marriage Proposal

It was Squire Robertson's habit to stop every day at the village post office. Housed in the home of Mr. Boswell, one of the town's founders, the post office served as one of the town's daily meeting places. Neighbor met neighbor and exchanged news or comments on the weather. Most of Bourneville's 150 inhabitants would receive no more than four or five pieces of mail per year. Of course, Robert's professional responsibilities would have necessitated considerable correspondence, but today, on the morning of April 2, 1871, he spied a tiny envelope in his mail slot. And this particular envelope, with its three-cent stamp and Frankfort postmark, most certainly piqued the squire's interest. He recognized the distinctive, elegant script. Yet despite the friendly setting, he might have pretended that nothing was amiss, tucked the envelope into his breast pocket, and made a hasty return up the gravel lane.

One look at her husband made Martha drop whatever she was doing to escape with him to the privacy of their bedroom. Once there, Robert carefully opened the letter addressed to him as Robt. I. Robertson, Esq.

Respected Sir and Madam,

In few words I shall attempt in this to make known to you as the parents of Margarite my objective thus addressing you.

The long standing acquaintance that has existed between your daughter and myself has ripened into an attachment. And as you are doubtless aware we now bear toward each other relations more than those of friendship.

It now becomes my duty and privilege to solicit your united consent to our union at some future time in those holier and more sacred relations.

Anxiously awaiting the result of your consideration, I am

Very Respectfully Yours,
W. E. Anderson
Frankfort, O, March 31/71

Why the pang in their hearts? Sentimentality was a rare emotion for the rugged settlers who had steeped themselves in self-discipline. Even Martha, known for her soft heart, was a stranger to tears. Still, their firstborn, the light of their home for twenty-five years, would be leaving the nest. Martha had certainly known it was coming. With a mother's clairvoyance, the tenderness between the two young people had become palpable. Perhaps, balanced on the edge of their four-poster, Martha sighed and whispered to her husband of many years that she was indeed thankful for the match because Martha must have realized that in Erskine, Margarite had found a soul mate.

Three days later, with considerable formality and restraint, the Robertson patriarch seated himself at his desk to write their reply.

Bourneville April 3rd 1871

Mr. W. E. Anderson

Dear Sir,

Your kind note of the 31st [was] duly received and its friendly contents well considered. We now reply, and in thus doing permit us to say [that] the laws of nature are so arranged that the affection of parents and children in general are strong and deeply rooted, and especially for those who have always been kind and obedient to their parents, and to part with such from the old parental roof naturally touches a very tender cord of the heart. Still when we remember that those same laws sanctioned by the divine teachings of our Savior approves of the pledges of holy matrimony and seals such sacred union as you referred to in your note, and when we further remember that you (as we sincerely believe) are a good kind Christian young man in whom we have unlimited confidence, we mutually join in giving our consent in the union you propose with Margarite. Trusting that in such union your days on earth may be bright, lengthy and peaceful and your titles for a home in heaven indisputable,

We are
Very Respectfully
R. I. & M. Robertson

Setback

All of this happy anticipation occurred in the spring of 1871, setting into motion a gentle buildup to a summer of engagement parties followed by a year of sewing for a bridal trousseau. But this was just before the family was shaken to its core and before Robert took to his room. All of this was before Virginia Robertson, in her haste and desperation, climbed down the ladder of her bedroom window and ran off into the night.

And so it was that Margarite's plans for marriage were suddenly jettisoned, dashed between the disbelief of an embarrassed family and the curse of a father's outrage. Virginia had upstaged her older sister, and there would be a long year of second guessing, a year of smoldering. Not until the following spring was the Robertson household sufficiently healed to begin again making plans for Margarite's nuptials. When at last their thoughts were refocused, a flood of pent up ideas came rushing forth.

To bolster her husband, Martha tried to involve him at every turn. Would he see to the grounds? Would he engage the minister to perform the ceremony? And would he decide where the guests should park their buggies?

Buggies? If things did not improve, there might not be any horses to bring guests to Margarite's wedding. In 1872 the region's transportation system was paralyzed by a nationwide influenza epidemic among horses, and most of the horses in Ross County were sick.

Nevertheless, Martha prepared herself for the task of making a wedding dress. However, before the ladies of the house could take scissors to the mountains of white organdy, the family must select a date for the wedding. To guide their decision was a sing-song ditty known to all young women:

> Monday for wealth
> Tuesday for health,
> Wednesday the best day of all,
> Thursday for losses,
> Friday for crosses,
> And Saturday no luck at all.[56]

In her mind Martha imagined that by eleven o'clock on a Wednesday morning in September, the mist would be rising from the valley's floor. Sugar maples tinged with orange and sumacs blazing scarlet would color the haze. And on such an autumn morning a string of shiny black buggies, slicing through the brilliant woods on their way to the Robertson Place, would create a glorious sight.

On to the guest list. Yet here lay the dilemma. Everyone in the family was loathe to tackle it because of the painful decision that lurked therein. Virginia. What was the

Margarite's Wedding Invitation

family to do about Virginia? The thorny issue of Virginia's estrangement had been festering for a year and now the family would have to face its consequences.

If Virginia were not invited or allowed to attend, the family schism would deepen. Like it or not, Margarite's wedding was sure to be tainted by the missing sister. Yet for Virginia to attend would force the squire to swallow his pride and retract his vow never to see her again. What's more, the appearance of his banished daughter might steal the spotlight from the bride. There was simply no good solution to their quagmire. Virginia's presence or absence on September 18 would serve to embarrass the family anew and provide the family's detractors with nothing short of an invitation to gossip and speculate.

Nevertheless, by midsummer of 1872 the front hall of Robertson Place was impassable, the kitchen strewn with recipe books, the dining room table covered with pins and patterns and the library piled with wedding invitations. All available surfaces had disappeared under the weight of wedding paraphernalia. Curious relatives were streaming to the back door with offers to help. Martha's sister Asaneth and her Aunt Ada stopped by. And like moths to a flame, Sally's girlfriends were drawn to the bustle in the house on the hill.

Still, something and someone was missing. If Sally had pleaded her big sister's case, Martha's resolve might have wavered because each time she came across a garment, a drawing, or a gift made by Virginia's hand, its unexpected appearance thrust a tiny stab into Martha's heart.

Since the elopement, Sally had kept up a constant correspondence with her older sister. Did any of the Robertson ladies visit Virginia in Massieville? A thirty-mile round-trip journey by horseback or buggy would not have been an insurmountable obstacle. It would have been easy to rationalize. Father had not actually forbidden Virginia's presence in the house, he had simply said that he never wanted to lay eyes on her again. Pressure was mounting. Martha was tempted to consider a furtive plan. Would her loyalty be questioned if she merely withheld the particulars of a certain clandestine visit until later—much later—after September the 18th when the father of the bride would be in a mellow mood, softened by the wedding's afterglow?

Respect for her husband had grown exponentially over the decades, and Martha could not have risked her husband's ire. It would have been close to anathema to go against the will of her husband. In retrospect, I think it highly improbable that Virginia was allowed to return home to see her sister get married because in an essay written many years later, his great-granddaughter was able to state that Robert never again saw Virginia. So in the kitchen of Robertson Place during that summer of 1872, instead of furtive whispers or the sound of Virginia's excitable voice, it is likely that the soft chatter of women's voices filled the air with the seductive talk of wedding plans.

Margarite Marries

For those who received an invitation to the wedding at the stylish Robertson Place, a surprise was in store. Most of the women attending the affair expected an elaborate gown for the family's firstborn, perhaps a satin one with a thousand tucks of silken gauze or a veil of imported lace. Instead, Margarite Robertson chose a dress of relative simplicity. Perhaps she harbored a bit of prudery left over from the days when the local Methodists had thought the least ornament to be "folly and wickedness."[57]

So there was no costly beading or embroidered flowers for Margarite, just a wide ruffled border to serve as trim for the modest dress of cotton organdy. The seamstress had fitted and pinned the garment to Margarite's small frame, which, on her wedding day, was squeezed still smaller by a corset supported with stays of whalebone. That Margarite should wear such a cinching apparatus under her wedding dress was understood because it was a symbol of a lady's self-discipline and social status.

Yet even without this conceit, there was a dignity and confidence about the way Margarite Robertson carried herself. She exuded a sense of well being. Elegant clothing and striking looks were not necessary—nor were they her style even as a bride.

On any day other than today, no one (with the exception of the groom or the bride's family) might have considered Margarite to be particularly beautiful. Her pale hazel eyes and straight mouth were set in a face rather too long for her proportions. And it was questionable whether the painstaking effort required to crimp her bangs with a curling iron and to roll the rest of her straight brown hair in damp strips of fabric had accomplished any improvement to her plain appearance. What did add some whimsy and ornament to her otherwise serious face was a pronounced dimple in the center of her chin. When Margarite smiled, it was impossible not to smile back.

Yet below the calm visage Margarite presented to the world, deep down there glowed a small ember. Although this young lady was a model of decorum and self-discipline, within her soul was the spirit of her father. Nascent in Margarite there lay a flicker of ambition.

But let us not conjure the bride's future. Instead let us imagine the day's festive occasion for its innocence, its beauty. The family was keyed to its highest notch, their home at its finest and the food and staff were ready.

The sound of gravel crunching under horses' hooves and metal-rimmed wheels announces the arrival of the first carriage. In it are the groom and his brothers, John and David Anderson. Close behind comes a second buggy, carrying Erskine's parents along with a swarm of Anderson daughters. Among them is the most recent addition to Erskine's family, his baby sister Hattie, who is asleep in the arms of her mother. In their wake another handsome carriage arrives, this one bearing more Andersons. The groom's uncle, D.C. Anderson, alights from his horse-drawn rig to stand with majestic bearing on the bright green of the squire's freshly mowed grass. Adding drama to his appearance is his long white beard, which cuts a swath down the stark, coal black of his suit. From the dark cavern of his conveyance, nearly hidden by a voluminous bonnet, Erskine's grandmother Elizabeth slowly unfolds herself and emerges into the bright sunshine. Today the matriarch is attended by her great-granddaughter, Grace. It is a shame that Grace's mother Clara (Erskine's sister) is away in Boston studying art, for more than anyone else, Erskine's sister could have been counted on for her elegant attire—perhaps a dress of taffeta—and there would have been a mass of ringlets piled atop her head and delicate chandelier earrings swinging from her earlobes.

Next to arrive are the bride's relatives. Today's gathering is bittersweet for the Poole family because the last time it convened was for the funeral of Margarite's grandmother, Mary Poole. Just weeks before Erskine penned his letter asking for Margarite's hand, Mary Poole had died. Mary Vinsonhaller Poole, the paper said, crossed over on April 13 due to "a variety of afflictions" at the age of sixty-eight.[58]

Clockwise from the top: Elizabeth Anderson, D. C. Anderson, Sarah Anderson
John Anderson, Laura Anderson, Grace Andersson Muse

Today her widowed husband, Henry Poole, arrives at the Robertson Place on the arm of his son Major Poole, the war veteran. Two of his daughters accompany them. Margarite's grandfather is now in his seventies and has known a world of grief in his time—so many untimely deaths—starting back in Baltimore with his young mother, followed by his father and Rebecca. Four of his own babies had died in infancy, and then, ten years ago, his daughter Eleanor died of diphtheria at age twenty-five, the same age as today's bride. But for this one day, for his daughter's and granddaughter's sakes, the widower has gathered his strength, put his grief aside. On this day he will focus on the celebration at hand, the marriage of his daughter's firstborn.

Robert has but a single blood relative as witness for his daughter's nuptials on September 18. His uncle Joseph died in 1865, but his sister Emily and her husband are soon to arrive from Frankfort. Several of the squire's business partners and acquaintances—among them the co-owner of his store, Mr. Nathaniel Core—arrive from the village, and joining the family's local friends, they now congregate in clusters near Martha's rock garden while the polite chatter of the assembled guests fills the air and the crunch of horseshoes and buggy wheels against gravel gently fades away.

A hush descends. From the piano in the parlor arises the plaintive strains of *Aura Lee* (the same tune recorded in 1956 by Elvis Presley as *Love me Tender*.) Whispers spread over the lawn as guests surrender themselves to the nostalgia of the Civil War song. "Aura Lee, Aura Lee, Maid of golden hair. . . ." Guests strain in anticipation to catch their first glimpse of the man Margarite Robertson has chosen to wed. "Take my heart and take my ring, I give my all to thee."

From a side door of the brick estate, a young man of average stature emerges. Well-proportioned and fair-skinned, his wavy hair is the color of cider. But note that the most distinguishing feature about William Erskine Anderson is his red goatee. It grazes the stiff white collar of his formal wear and occasionally vibrates with his nervous cough. Though the groom carries himself with ease, he appears a bit shy, or, at the least, mild-mannered. As he stands locked in position beside the minister and casts a dreamy gaze above the crowd, a few on the lawn think they detect a rather wistful look in the eyes of the groom.

To some of the assembled guests, it might seem unlikely that Erskine could ever live up to the bride's esteemed father. But for anyone aware of the Anderson family's prestige, this is not a forgone conclusion. Erskine's parents are illustrious missionaries. Their home, known to everyone as Mount Nebo, is a center for religious activism. While the groom never accompanied his father to distant lands,

Erskine's childhood was colorful and rich. Aside from religion, the Anderson clan is known for its enthusiastic support of education; its men stand as pillars of the Salem Academy. Perhaps the most important factor about the family is that D.C. Anderson, the groom's uncle, is a prosperous merchant and a well-respected civic leader throughout the region and will be in a position to lift the prospects of his nephew's future.

While the guests jostle for a better view and exchange their bits of information in hushed tones, perhaps some of them readjust their opinions about the day's match. As Margarite, on the arm of her father, comes into view in a cloud of white organdy, Erskine's gentle blue-gray eyes glow with affection. Well-wishers nod their approval.

During the ceremony, Martha and Robert are standing side by side on the lawn of their gracious home, drinking in the beauty of their eldest daughter and absorbing the significance of the momentous occasion. On this brilliant fall day in 1872, the bride's father might himself be re-examining his earlier misgivings about Margarite's betrothed, might even manage to suppress his embarrassment over the missing daughter; for this day is to the Robertson family a most precious gift. Long after the last carriage departs, the wedding bouquets wilt, and the glassware and linens are all returned to their cupboards, Martha and Robert will undoubtedly continue to ride the wave of their euphoria.

But when the house grows quiet and their elation dissipates, the parents will discover that in its place is an ache, an ache not to be explained by the mere departure of their beloved Margarite nor by the diminished energy within the house. Their daughter will soon create a home of her own making, not in Bourneville, but in Frankfort. No doubt their last daughter, Sally, will soon follow her lead. Robertson Place will become an empty nest.

Virginia Returns

As for Virginia Robertson, that Wednesday in September 1872 was excruciating. For in her naïveté Virginia may not have contemplated the eternity of banishment. On that fateful moonless night when she lay awake, listening for the pre-arranged signal from Michael McCord, she had intended to inflict a sting of revenge upon a father whose control she resented. As she waited in heightened excitement, petticoats tied up and ready to place her bare foot on the top rung of the ladder, Virginia may not have foreseen that her father would cling to his fury, that he could be as obstinate as she. No, by now the middle child probably expected to be allowed—if not invited—to return to the family circle and certainly for her sister's marriage.

Yet even without her father's blessings, a homesick and determined Virginia decided to return. Two years after her elopement, Virginia and Michael McCord moved back to the town they'd grown up in and set up housekeeping in a small cottage next to the McCord homestead. It stood directly across from the Robertson & Core general store.

No doubt, in the days to come, Robert tried to avoid coming face to face with his daughter, but Virginia Robertson's presence in the middle of his village would have made the feat nearly impossible. And what about Martha? Did she feel obligated to join in the shunning? Would her husband's ban forever poison her relationship with the free-spirited Virginia?

Evidence indicates that Martha devised her own route to reconciliation. Perhaps she did not wear a path up and down the hill from her house to Virginia's cottage, but once Virginia took the first step of returning to her family's turf, Martha began making her own overtures. Despite their efforts, for weeks and months—even years—a tension would certainly have brought discomfort to the Robertson household.

Relief from all this turmoil, however, was about to arrive. In the post office at the bottom of the hill lay a tiny letter from Frankfort, the envelope of which was addressed in Erskine's now familiar looping script. On a morning in early March, perhaps just as a late spring snow posed a threat to the early crocuses in Martha's garden, Robert arrived at the kitchen door with the little missive clutched in his eager fingers. After stomping his boots to release the snow, he settled himself by the kitchen stove before giving full attention to word from Margarite's world. "Good news!" he cried after breaking the seal. "A baby's coming!"

Sadie is Born

Oh, these were the best of times for the newlyweds Margarite and Erskine Anderson. Surrounded by friends and family and immersed in their own optimism, the couple flourished in the groom's hometown, and as long as the protective Anderson umbrella held, their future was secure. Indeed, everything was in place.

How miraculous to think that ten years ago in 1864, while the nation was still fighting its bloody war, Private William Erskine Anderson had been left to die amidst the putrid squalor of Libby prison. His desperation of old was but a distant memory now. The prospect of fatherhood filled him with a new vigor. All was well. Or so it seemed.

A distance of twenty miles, or a five-hour buggy ride, now separated mother from daughter. Margarite would no doubt have preferred to be nearer home during her pregnancy. Instead of her own family, her husband's people would have to watch over her when her confinement drew near, when it would be unseemly to appear in public.

Erskine's family was a gentle lot, but in-laws can be judgmental. Margarite's letters home worried the point, but Martha assuaged her daughter's fears with daily letters of reassurance and advice. As the ordeal of labor and delivery loomed ever closer, women on both sides of the family made their needles fly with dizzying speed as they quilted coverlets, knitted booties, and wove blankets.

Just as day broke on the morning of October 11, 1874, in the bedroom of a small cottage in Frankfort, a baby girl was born. All the Anderson women hurried to catch a glimpse of the newborn and to bask in the glow of her ecstatic parents. She was named for Margarite's grandmother, Sarah Robertson, but the baby soon won her own endearing nickname: Sadie.

Sadie's Bourneville grandparents, having anxiously awaited word by telegraph, harnessed the horses to their carriage and sped through Porter Hollow to greet their new grandchild. Their animals knew the way by heart now. Down the lane, turn east, left off the pike past Grandpa Poole's cabin, right through the towering red maples in the hollow, left past the giant pin oak, then slow to a trot through Roxabell and finish the journey with a saunter into Frankfort.

In the days that followed her labor and delivery, Margarite's doctor instructed her to refrain from nearly all activity. She was not to put her legs over the bedside for ten days, not to begin walking again for two weeks. Bedridden though she must be, Margarite slid into her maternal role, nursing and falling in love with their infant Sadie. Margarite had passed her first test and was optimistic about having more children. Fatherhood seemed to suit Erskine as well. Head in the clouds, he was in love all over again. It seemed that the tiny object of their affection performed a new miracle each day: making her first smile, rolling over, tugging at her daddy's curly red beard. So much to treasure, to fix in one's memory. If only time would stand still.

In the future, however, it would become apparent that in the bedroom that held Sadie's cradle beside the matrimonial bed, not everything was right. Erskine's cough of old, the one that was so mild and insidious that even Margarite had become deaf to it, began to worsen. It wakened him at night, demanding notice. And there were night sweats which went undetected at a time when slumber was already interrupted by the urgent cries of a newborn. Erskine's ebullient nature was flagging; more and more, he was drawn to the couch.

But all focus was on baby Sadie. The volume of her lusty cries was gaining even as her father's own strength was waning. Adrenaline kept Margarite going, but underneath her optimism was a mounting, if silent, panic. Erskine was running a fever and complaining of chest pain. Friends and family began to whisper. Aunts and cousins tiptoed in the back door of the young family's cottage to offer help. Could they take Sadie out in the carriage? Could they run an errand for Margarite? Covered dishes and Christmas cookies arrived on the front stoop.

Doctors came and went, but by Watch Night, the final eve of the year, a silent gloom had settled over the little cottage in Frankfort. The doctors had laid down their verdict—consumption. Into the Anderson residence had stolen the "Captain of the Men of Death."

Erskine's body was slowly, systematically, self-destructing with tuberculosis. Back in 1864 when the war between the states had nearly run its course and this young soldier lay in the filth of Libby Prison, the germ had invaded his lungs. Rallying to his body's defense, Erskine's youth and spirits had staved off the immediate threat, and when comrades tunneled an escape out of the hellhole, the Anderson boy had run for his life. But, unknown to Erskine, his chest cavity would continue to serve as host to an invader. Now, some ten years later, after returning to Ohio where he would put together the pieces of his life and again gain happiness, the stealth germ reasserted itself. With diabolic precision, it was now exploding into action to destroy its very home in the lungs of this new father.

Doctors and scientists were yet to identify the source of tuberculosis. At the time, tuberculosis was the leading cause of death around the globe. It would be seven years before they would understand that Erskine's incessant cough might have been infecting the others in his cottage. It would be seven decades before an antidote for the suffering could be found.

And so the physicians who tended Erskine could only suggest bed rest and fresh air. Desperate for a miracle, as the weeks wore on, the family turned to prayer.

Keeping vigil over the listless limbs of their gentle husband, brother, nephew, grandson and son, the Anderson kin stood by helplessly until, on the afternoon of July 12, 1875, just nine months after the birth of his daughter Sadie, Erskine drew his last, labored breath.

Tragedy Strikes

The seismic drama that ended in Erskine's death took only a few months to play itself out. Margarite, having spent her reserves on encouragement and false hope, was exhausted. Sadie was now nine months old, crawling around their small quarters, slapping her wee hands on the kitchen floor and playing peek-a boo around the corner.

In Bourneville, Margarite's father was marking his own fifty-seventh birthday on the July afternoon in 1875 when a postman arrived with a telegram. Though he and Martha were anxious about the deterioration of their son-in-law's health, the finality of this blunt message from Frankfort struck a stunning blow. Such a short time ago—just yesterday, it seemed—Robert had given his first-born in marriage to the man who now lay under a sheet on his death bed. What would this mean for Margarite or for little Sadie, so tiny and vulnerable—too small to have etched the lines of her father's face into her memory? His daughter Margarite had barely gotten used to being a wife, a new mother. Now, suddenly, she was faced with widowhood. And she was only twenty-seven-years-old.

Scarcely would the squire have put the telegram in his pocket before a dire image flooded his brain. Margarite would be in shock. Important decisions could not wait; the business of death would soon envelope his daughter.

Indeed, at that very moment back in Frankfort, a phalanx of men in black suits were lining up to have a word with the newly widowed Margarite. Doctor, lawyer, undertaker, church officials—they all found their way to the shuttered Anderson cottage on that sad day. Easing past the in-laws who were milling around on the front porch, the men waited their turn to enter Margarite's darkened parlor. How could she face them in her queasy state? Except for periodic uncontrollable shaking, her body was numb, her mind spinning. Only by rote had she been able to make her fingers lace the high-topped shoes and fasten the long row of buttons on her waist-cinching bodice of black. Sequestering herself in her bedroom,

Margarite postponed the inevitable and sat cradling her face in her hands.

First to be dealt with was preparation of her beloved's body for burial. To embalm was not yet an option in the region; it was a new process, one that had been developed during the war in order to preserve the bodies of the soldiers so that the cadavers could be sent home. A process such as this would have helped, especially if the Anderson family planned to hold a viewing in the middle of July. Instead, Erskine's grandmother Anderson instructed the women of the family to cleanse the corpse, which on this day was the body of her own grandchild.

No doubt John Anderson was on hand to ready his brother's clothing for burial. With care and deliberation, the sibling closest in age to Erskine brushed clean the suit Margarite had laid out, the same suit Erskine had worn on his wedding day. Perhaps it was at this time that Reverend Galbraith introduced to Margarite a stone carver. In her daze, she gave a nod when the man showed her an etching of a white marble pedestal. Atop the pedestal lay an open book, and on it Margarite instructed him to chisel the words, "He was precious."

High on a hill in Lattavile sits the old Concord Church, the simple, white-frame church which Erskine's grandfather helped to found back in 1803 and which had been the scene of Margarite's and Erskine's early courting. Hidden in the attic are the twenty-six cots which were put to use during the days of the Underground Railroad. Today, under the blistering July sun, the Anderson and Robertson clans will gather for a funeral.

From town and countryside, the mourners arrive in their formal black clothing—much of it wool—which without mercy gathers and traps the brutal heat of the midsummer sun. Seeking relief from its hot rays, the mourners step into a sliver of shade in the churchyard to watch a team of glistening black horses labor up the long gravel hill. Behind them is the hearse-wagon.

As the mourners file into the historic church, they adjust their sun-blinded eyes to the darkened sanctuary. For their son's funeral, Erskine's parents have asked their old friend, Reverend R.C. Galbraith, to conduct the ceremony at Concord. Having known the Anderson family for almost three decades, he took the assignment with a heavy heart. Now, on this mid-summer afternoon, he mounts the low stage to address the crowd below, which is posed in grief on narrow, high-backed pews. Above a sea of fluttering paper fans, the reverend raises his voice to deliver what will be his final service for a young man whom he baptized, confirmed, married, and whose child he had just one month ago christened. He reminisces about appointing Erskine to be deacon, and, as the Lord's "willing servant," to lead the other church elders. Now he speaks of the fact that Erskine died "without a murmur,...believing God doeth all things well."[59]

Under her long veil, Margarite's tears mingle with beads of perspiration before dropping to stain her tightly fitted, cropped, jacket; other droplets find their way onto the lap of her skirt, heavy with crinoline and bustles. Sitting on either side of her, elderly mourners fan themselves to avoid fainting in the stifling heat. If little Sadie were to have been brought to her father's funeral, she would have been fidgeting and fussing and pleading with one of her aunts to be taken outside.

A mournful dirge rises from the upright piano behind the podium signaling the end to Reverend Galbraith's sermon. As if in a trance, the gathered crowd pulls itself up and begins to pour out of the chapel into the searing light. John and David Anderson lead their parents and Margarite to the freshly-dug grave.

The cemetery, hugging the hill below the church, stands bare and treeless in the heat; the tuberoses, overly sweet with fragrance, are withering in the sun's glare. Margarite begins to feel woozy and closes her eyes against the surreal scene. When the family draws its circle around the gaping hole, Reverend Galbraith gives his signal and the pallbearers lower Erskine's rope-cradled casket down, down into the earth.

Grieving

Margarite would find it hard to believe that she had gotten through those first dark days after the funeral. Somehow an unknown force had taken over, a force that pushed her forward making her body plod through the mandatory motions of mother and widow. Did she remember pulling the drapes in her Victorian cottage or hanging black bunting above the doorway? Or did she remember the procession of relatives arriving with offers to whisk young Sadie out the back door? Only as a blur did she recall the seemingly endless line of men in black who had come shuffling through her parlor, papers in hands, requesting her signature.

How comforting it was to hear her father's voice at the back door. He had been making the trip often those first weeks after Erskine's death, and his stalwart presence was helping to keep Margarite's world from falling apart. Having dealt with legal matters for decades as justice of the peace, Margarite's father was able to decode the pile of documents that awaited his daughter's attention. Margarite later mused in fond recollection, that, as fathers are wont to do, he had then begun the habit of quietly writing out his own checks to cover her mounting expenses. For years, Margarite Anderson's real estate taxes would be paid in this manner.

Grieving could have easily become a way of life for Margarite in the weeks and months that followed Erskine's death. Since England's Queen Victoria had lost her beloved Albert in 1864, the social custom of mourning had become popular, so popular that it now passed for high fashion. Socialites were dressing themselves in black. Dark interiors were the rage. After the royal funeral, Victoria, the undisputed arbiter of Old World society, had secluded herself, and for twenty-six years the queen did not appear in society. In shrouded rooms on both sides of the Atlantic, women took to crafting mortuary art. With needle and thread, they embroidered canvases which depicted their loved one's tombstone under a weeping willow tree. They wove the hair of dead relatives into memorial wreaths, and on every lady's dressing table sat a jar for collecting strands of her hair which might someday become an adornment when jewelers worked them into broaches or bracelets.

Mourning and death were further popularized by the newspapers. Editors serialized tales of the macabre and saved space on their front pages for poems about death. During the late 1800s, in an era when death was so glorified, in any small community the specter of Margarite's diminutive figure dressed in mourning would have evoked sympathy. A widow's black silhouette with a baby carriage was a loaded combination.

At the same time Americans were romanticizing death, they were making a cult of motherhood. To be pregnant and to attain motherhood was the ultimate goal for most young women in Victorian America. Preachers preached it, teachers taught it. Society exerted pressure on females to remain nearly sequestered in their homes, and the only world most women would ever truly know lay within the domestic walls. Home was considered a sanctuary from the dirty streets, a bastion against all that was corrupt or evil, a place in which the gentle sex could fulfill her job as the world's civilizing force. And like it or not, in her small Frankfort community, Margarite would have captured and held center stage as she unconsciously played out the convergence of two national obsessions: motherhood and death.

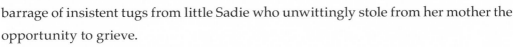

After the town's heroine had ushered the last businessman or church elder offstage, she did not—as a playwright might have scripted—throw herself upon the divan in a swoon. Instead, there was a barrage of insistent tugs from little Sadie who unwittingly stole from her mother the opportunity to grieve.

During the weeks leading up to Erskine's death, others had answered the baby's cries with sugar tits or glass bottles and had happily cared for Margarite's infant daughter. But now the baby's need for a mother's attention trumped any temptation the young widow might have felt to give in to self pity. As a result, a slim ray of light seeped under the curtains of their darkened stage. For Sadie's benefit, Margarite would postpone her sorrow. In a future not yet imagined, in a manner not yet conceived, Margarite Anderson would one day honor the memory of her husband.

Doom and Gloom

*W*hile Margarite struggled to realign her emotions in the microcosm of that bungalow in Frankfort, other dramas played out beyond the threshold. On her mother's side of the family, the Poole family was reeling after cousin Walter, Jr. had died at age twenty-six after losing four children and his wife Peggy Ann. On the Anderson side, Erskine's younger brother John was now becoming the subject of worry. The cough that he had been trying to suppress was beginning to sound eerie and all too familiar. Of the seven children born over the last twenty-two years to Erskine's missionary parents, Mary Heiser and William Harrison Anderson had already lost three (and would lose three more.) In a last ditch effort to stem the tide, his parents loaded their son John onto a train heading to the mountains of upper state New York for treatment at a health resort dedicated to those suffering from tuberculosis.

In 1870 massive floods had ushered in the decade, creating chaos throughout Paint Valley. Boats navigated the streets of Bourneville. Drought followed, and after the horse epidemic came the crop-damaging locusts.

In the South, violence marred reconstruction efforts, and rebuilding stalled. The nation's economy was faring no better. Right after Margarite and Erskine's marriage in 1873, the nation's banks had closed their doors in response to a financial panic. Hard times and depression lasted five long years.

As a result, Americans were increasingly willing to pull up stakes. Many passed through Paint Valley in their migration westward. Hungry for land, the migrants—soon to reach twenty million—swelled the route and caused problems for the United States government. To make room for them in the West, the army was assigned the task of pushing the Sioux and Cheyenne tribes onto reservations, and in June of 1876, Americans read with horror that in Montana, 262 of their soldiers, led by General George Custer, had been massacred at the Battle of Little Big Horn.

Distractions

Despite the newspapers' grim headlines, in the microcosm of daily living, babies could always be counted on to claim the limelight. Back in Bourneville, Virginia and Michael McCord were contributing their share of newborns. Floyd was now three years old. A second child, Lizzie, toddled along behind, and now that her husband was starting a carriage-painting business, Virginia was pregnant again. Despite the estrangement that silenced the air between Robert and his daughter, Virginia's children seem to have been somewhat immune to their mother's quarrel. They often visited their grandfather's store.

In 1877, Sally, the last of the Robertson daughters, was ready to claim a little of the limelight for herself. At twenty-two, she was engaged to be wed. Her fiancé was Henry Caldwell, a South Salem man who had served in the 149th division with Erskine. Before dying, Erskine had asked this lawyer friend to be co-executor of his estate. So, although Henry Caldwell had come to the Robertson Place on legal business, he had left as Sally's suitor. Perhaps Sally's marriage brought a bit of bittersweet consolation to Robert and Martha Robertson. They had much

in common with Henry's parents and favored their daughter's choice.[60]

On the morning of August 19, 1877, the gates of Robertson Place were swung open to welcome guests from South Salem, Frankfort, Chillicothe, Bourneville, Bainbridge, and Hillsboro. A "gala affair" was how the newspaper described the event. Sally appeared that day fitted out in an ivory gown of gleaming sateen, held close to her petite frame by rows of tucks and gathers. After a brief honeymoon in Cincinnati, as the new Mrs. Caldwell, Sally held a reception for forty-five guests back in South Salem, where "the tables were set with excellent taste."[61]

Now, from Sally, came happy news. She was pregnant. But meanwhile, over in Frankfort, Margarite was tussling with a major life decision. Perhaps it was inevitable that at some point she would dream of returning to Robertson Place. But how could she wrench her daughter Sadie from the affectionate bosom of the Anderson family? By then Sadie was familiar with all her father's relatives. They would have delighted in pushing her hither and yon on the streets of Frankfort in her elaborate baby carriage, and Hattie, Erskine's baby sister, was the toddler's current and constant companion. Three

years older than Sadie, Hattie Anderson was already legendary. Her flamboyant personality was known throughout the community, and she conspired in leading three-

year-old Sadie into and out of mischief. Together they made dolls of corn husks and hollyhocks. Together they dissolved into peals of laughter when, from the remains of wizened brown apples, they created their cast of comical contorted faces. Sadie lived a near storybook life in Frankfort.

Yet Margarite may have worried. Would the melancholy of her husband's family affect Sadie? Just what was going on beneath Sadie's translucent skin and those blond sausage-roll curls?

Margarite is Restless—Chautauqua

Where could Margarite go, if not back home? Considering her options in the year of 1878, Margarite Anderson might have thought about moving to Hillsboro. Her sister-in-law Clara Anderson—the one who had studied art in Boston—was there. Young women were flocking to the southern Ohio town for both its educational opportunities and its causes. The place was a magnet.

While Margarite was considering her next move, it was Lake Chautauqua in upstate New York that captured her immediate attention. Here, four summers ago, church folks had gathered under tents to hear lectures and be entertained. With an emphasis on education and the arts, the idea of these summer camp meetings were a big hit with the Anderson and Robertson circles, where learning and church-going were so important. Chautauqua was on everyone's lips.

Years ago there had been a Christian revival in Bourneville which had been of another sort altogether. It occurred just a few years before Margarite was born, during the winter of 1842–3, but folks in Ross County still talked about the historic Meharry Revival when a fiery Irish preacher reportedly saved 180 souls.[62] If that church meeting had been anything like what Conrad Richter described in his book *The Town*, it would have startled the sedate Robertson family. Richter writes:

> *The savage preaching, the gloomy singing, the violent praying, the threats…. One preacher would fall from exhaustion and another and still another took his place till a dozen had manned the pulpit. Under their unceasing fire, the people would sit and moan, cry out wordless things, throw out their arms, leap and wrestle with each other. Often a mighty jerk would go among the women like the plague, their heads snapping and their hair coming down to lash and crack like bull whips in hypnotic unison.*[63]

Chautauqua was nothing of the kind. It was refined and cerebral and ecumenical. Since it was highly touted by the nation's luminaries, Margarite Anderson's in-laws probably gave their wholehearted encouragement to the idea of Margarite's going east for the experience—although it is entirely possible that some of them disapproved of her leaving Sadie, who was four at the time. In any case, in the summer of 1878 and amidst much fanfare, Margarite boarded a train and off she went to a vacation devoted to self-improvement and uplift, one where fellow Christians congregated to discuss politics, to take courses in religion and literature, science or ancient history. Under tents beside a lake, or on blankets in shady groves, they raised their voices in hymns, listened to lectures by traveling speakers, clapped heartily for enactments and gazed in amazement at the lantern shows.

Chautauqua camp meetings became a phenomenon in American life during the late 1800s, and for decades to come rural Americans flocked to its tents. Chautauqua would be the centerpiece of Margarite's summers, and her enthusiasm for it was to trickle down through the generations.

But at the end of the summer of 1878 when Margarite returned to Frankfort, it seemed that sadness, like a recurrent bad dream, was lying in wait for her. Her brother-in-law John had returned from the sanatorium back East in order to die at home. His valiant letters had kept the family believing, but between the lines could be detected an unfounded optimism. Tuberculosis would take another of the Anderson boys.

From South Salem came a letter from her sister Sally informing Margarite that her tiny niece was in grave condition. At the same time, the sisters were beginning to have questions about the health of their father. While their mother, now 50, was in her prime, according to reports from the locals, Squire Robertson was beginning to lose his edge. He seemed docile, almost childlike, and Martha was starting to hire others to do the things that Robert had always done. Although Robert had never done the actual work of plowing and planting, he supervised his farm workers and made important decisions about the property. More and more, Margarite found her thoughts winging back to the house on the hill.

Maybe it was more than nostalgia and filial responsibility that caused Margarite to think about returning to Bourneville. At thirty-three, she was a single mother with no source of income, and remarriage did not seem to be on the horizon. Like it or not she and her child were entirely dependent upon the largesse of her parents and that of her deceased husband's family. If she returned to Bourneville, at least the big house could absorb them, and the farm would support them. It only made sense.

If she were to return to Robertson Place now, Margarite reasoned, Sadie could grow up in the house they so loved. Suddenly a flood of childhood memories came rushing forth. In her head she imagined little Sadie chasing through the parlors, swooping up the front stairs, flying through the bedrooms and scampering down the back steps. Her daughter would hide amidst the quilts in the old linen closet and have picnic lunches down in the lower pasture among the cottonwoods where Margarite and Aunt Asaneth had so often fished from the banks of the creek. And what child, when she reached a certain age, would not insist on playing Juliet from the upstairs balcony?

On the other hand, returning to Bourneville and Robertson Place would mean a small defeat for the widow because she would have to break up the little nest that she and Erskine had made of their cottage. She would have to blend back into the household of her parents and try to resist the tendency to become the child once again. More than that, leaving Frankfort meant leaving Sadie's daddy. Every day in Frankfort the omnipresent Anderson clan was making an effort to keep their son's memory alive. To leave his home was to admit that he was not returning, could never return.

Yet in the summer of 1880 Margarite prepared to return to Robertson Place. Sadie, now five, practiced for the big day by tucking her dolls into the black wicker doll carriage while her mother busied herself packing their dishes and housewares into barrels.

Return to Robertson Place

"Maggie's coming home!" It had been eight years. Martha flew from room to room opening doors and throwing back the shutters in Robertson Place. After the last of their daughters had left, Martha had made the decision to close off several rooms to make the house seem more cozy and to conserve heat. For someone who had grown up with a big family in a small cabin, the big brick house might always have felt a bit too large for Martha. Robert did not like the idea of closing off the stately front parlors, but neither did he relish the chore of keeping up with several hungry fireplaces. Over the winter the couple had managed to live in the back part of the house where heat from a generous fireplace and a big kitchen stove kept them warm and rose through a floor register cut in the dining room's ceiling to a back bedroom where they slept.

The Women of Robertson Place

With Margarite's return, however, they could once again open up the entire house. What luxury! Two more bedrooms, the front parlors, and the music room would again see the light of day. Robert called to his dog, fetched his cane and ambled down the lane to spread the news. "Maggie's coming home!"

Martha's joy was coupled with palpable relief, for it was a strain living in a household where the balance of power was changing. No doubt Margarite's presence would further shake up the family's pecking order, but little Sadie's arrival would soften the blow of Robert's decline and perhaps give him a new perspective on the time remaining. He would see that new and important projects were at hand. Yes, he might think, let Martha and Margarite deal with business while he teaches Sadie to play checkers.

Indeed, life in the big house did take on a different order when the eldest daughter returned. Martha gladly folded herself back into the matronly role as the head of domestic issues while Margarite stole away into the village to familiarize herself with her father's world. Meanwhile Robert rededicated himself to the role of grandparent and began to bond with his sweet-natured grandchild. On the back porch they played games and built little houses with blocks. And when P.T. Barnum brought his circus to Chillicothe, Sadie persuaded her grandfather to take her to see the elephants bathe in the canal.

A Grandfather's Role

Robert knew that there was much to see right here in Bourneville, and Sadie was now big enough to be interested in her neighbors. So one fine morning Sadie and her grandpa set out to explore the village at the bottom of the hill. Hand in hand they plotted their tour as they walked down the gravel driveway. They would visit each of the village's residents and establishments, except for the church and grandfather's store which Sadie already knew by heart. As the pair stood at the gate ready to cross the road, Robert made a quick adjustment to their plan. For there stood his pride and joy, the handsome new red brick church. They would just have to pay it a visit this summer morning.

His shoulder against the heavy front doors, Sadie's grandfather nudged them open into the cool, high-ceilinged sanctuary. The cavernous space smelled of wood and shellac; light streamed in from a single stained glass window, bathing the room

in amber. Since 1848, as its superintendent, Squire Robertson had been informing, cajoling and sometimes prodding the Methodists of Twin Township. Most recently, he'd persuaded them to raise $7,000 to build this fine new building with its slate-roof and distinctive spire. This was the third church on this site, the first having been destroyed by flames back in 1841 when on New Year's Eve the congregation prepared for their traditional "waiting for Christ's knocking."

Stiffened with arthritis, the squire led his granddaughter down the aisle between the empty walnut pews and up to the pulpit. Sadie stood on tiptoes, but when she could not see over the top of the lectern, she turned her curiosity to the upright piano. Out of tune, the keys sent a cacophony of mismatched notes bouncing against the high rafters of the nave. It was just a matter of time, Robert knew, until Sadie's eyes caught a glimpse of the heavy rope in the back of the sanctuary which hung from the belfry and lay coiled on the floor. "Just once, Grampa? Just once?" Sadie pleaded as she dashed down the aisle toward the rope. He knew that if he let her hang with all her weight on the rope, the brass clapper above would clang against the huge bell in the steeple, making all those for miles around stop what they were doing to wonder why on earth the church bell was ringing.

Sadie Tours Bourneville

Back outside in the bright morning sunshine, Robert pointed to the house next to the church. In it was Miss Walker, the spinster music teacher, who lived with her mother. Gentleman that he was, Robert tipped his hat to various old men who occupied the porches of the village and, for Sadie's sake, labeled them by the wars in which they had fought: this man's father fought for independence in the big war with England, that one was in our war with Mexico. There sat an elderly gentleman who fought in the War of 1812, and the man over yonder, the one without a leg, he fought in the worst one, the one between the states. Sadie knew something about this last worst war for in her family it was referred to in hushed voices.

"Morning!" called a voice that seemed to emanate from under a buggy in the carriage shop up ahead. Distracting the two from their rev-

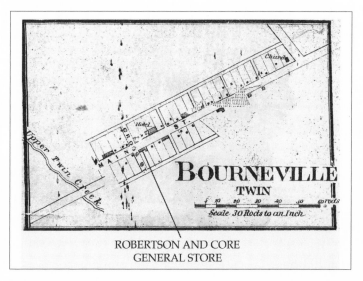

ROBERTSON AND CORE
GENERAL STORE

eries was the owner as he crawled from under the carriage where he was working on its springs. Across the alley from the shed sat the Methodist parsonage. Sadie looked up the long, sloping front yard to where Parson Evans lived. She tugged on her grandfather's sleeve to get him to pause so she could take in the parsonage's impressive size and admire its gabled silhouette against a summer sky of robin's-egg blue.

Mr. Shadford, a colorful character from England, lived next to the parsonage. He was one of the town's blacksmiths. Next to him lived a bachelor who befriended every child in the village and this morning promised to keep his eye out for the squire's tow-headed granddaughter. Over there, indicated Robert, lived the bee-keeper, Mr. Kernan and yonder was the cheese maker, Mrs. Fuller. She turned out the best cheese around, claimed Sadie's grandfather. In the spring when you wanted to plant vegetables, Robert advised, you could go to Mrs. Flora's door for seedlings and you could also get a new bread start because she was the keeper of the town's jug yeast. Chaney's big flour mill stood at the other end of Bourneville but here behind the Flora's house was a small grist mill and a complete threshing outfit.

Sadie's Aunt Virginia lived up ahead. It would prove to be an awkward moment for the pair because of her Grandpa's shunning of Aunt Virginia. Unconsciously, the child rose up on tip-toes as they passed by the house, whose clapboard siding seemed to vibrate with taboo sentiments.

Next was the town hall. Though undistinguished as an edifice, Sadie viewed the large white building in awe, since not only the town's elections and political rallies were held here, but also its box socials, pie socials, cake walks and fiddling contests.

Robert needed not to remind Sadie that this is where her mother came on Monday nights to meet with the other members of the Twin Township Literary Society.

Tucked behind the hall in its shadow was a small, newly built limestone structure. Its single unglazed window was lined with black iron bars. What, wondered the child, could this be? With a quizzical expression, Sadie looked up at her grandfather's face as he lifted her so that she could peer into the dark and empty space. "This is the town's calaboose—its jail," explained Robert. And as he set her down he explained that the squat building had already served its purpose because the man who built it drank too much whiskey, and when he finished the job ended up spending the night in the very jail he had just completed. Sadie thought this was pretty funny. But as she wrinkled her nose, she caught sight of the frown on her grandfather's face. The name of the stonemason was Sam McCord, relative of Michael McCord, the son-in-law who had caused the Robertson family so much grief.

Boughten Bread and Oyster Stew

With mild relief, Robert turned his attention ahead to the home and store of Abe Summers. Upon seeing the squire through his glass storefront, out bounded "Uncle" Abe. The merchants greeted one another warmly, for the root of their friendship extended way back to Rockingham County, Virginia. Serving periodically as postmaster since 1857, Uncle Abe was better known to the current generation of Bourneville's inhabitants for having sold the first loaf of "boughten" bread. From the store's doorway there wafted a unique and tantalizing odor. Lunchtime was near, and Sadie was tempted to leave the safety of her grandfather's side. After she crept inside and adjusted to the dark, Sadie wound her way around the long, sawdust-strewn aisles to the source of the aroma. When her grandfather arrived at her side, he hoisted the featherweight child up onto a stool and pulled from his pocket a dime. With crackers and catsup, Sadie Erskine Anderson enjoyed her very first bowl of oyster stew, the mollusks having arrived in a boxcar fresh from the East Coast. To Sadie's generation, Uncle Abe's store would come to stand for that rare and nostalgic treat.

Spooning his soup, Grandfather Robertson continued to regale his granddaughter with the stories of Bourneville. Next came the story of the Stanley family who lived just beyond Uncle Abe's store. Len Stanley had served in the last war with his brother, and when they returned home, the two had married a couple of local young women who were themselves sisters. Len and his wife had many children while his brother remained childless, so eventually Len offered one of his girls to his brother to raise. Sadie's eyes widened in disbelief.

Barbers and Butchers

Mr. and Mrs. Frederick Douglas Day, an African-American couple, were the town's barbers. They had turned the front room of their house into a barbershop.

Peering around the corner into the alley, Sadie was suddenly accosted by a blast of odors. Here was the town's hub. Amidst a complex of buildings stood the town's slaughter house. "Pee-uuuu," complained Sadie. Robert could feel his grandchild's grip tighten as they spied a glistening carcass of beef dripping with blood. Intermingled with the beef were pork, mutton and an occasional rack of venison. Presiding over the raw hulks of meat were three butchers from Baden, Germany, the brothers Frey and a son, Martin. With deft wallops the Freys cut their raw material into chops, roasts, or cutlets, and with finesse they smoked their pork for bacon or ground and stuffed it into an endless chain of links.

An ice house stood on the back side of the butcher shop. Behind lock and key and under bales of straw were massive chunks of ice cut from frozen lakes in the North. The heat of the summer made the brick walls feel cool to the touch of Sadie's palms, but come fall, when the supply of ice was exhausted and the door stood ajar, village boys would sneak inside to puff on their cigarettes of corn silk.

Horse Kicks and Whiskey Bottles

A stench of fresh manure stung Sadie's nose as she rounded the bend. Bordering an adjacent alley were the town's stables. Fresh horses were required by the stagecoaches that plied the highways through Bourneville, and here a supply of twenty or more horses could be sheltered. Robert reached for Sadie's hand as they approached the stalls, for, though the beasts were now quietly chewing their feed or napping, one could never be sure when an ironclad hoof might surprise with a swift kick.

Some local families boarded a horse here; others came to rent one to make a trip in to town. Next to the stables was a lot full of carriages, and at the end of the stables stood a room unknown to the five-year-old. Children were barred entry to the town's saloon. They soon learned, however, that this establishment was the source of a potent drink called a "Blind Robin," and that after election day the boys of the village could round up empty whiskey bottles to sell back to the saloon's proprietor for a penny apiece.

Mother would be wondering about them by now: it was well past Sadie's nap time. But Sadie was not the least bit tired, she insisted. Without a struggle, the squire gave in to the fair-haired child.

Dinner Bells and Hollyhocks

Picking up the pace, Robert pointed to the town's hotel. Sadie looked up to see a stairway leading to a dining room. Inside that second story room, Jane Flora and Jane Ford served the hotel's guests. From miles around, visitors made the journey to taste the Janes' delicious cooking. At dinnertime, one of the cooks would announce the meal by stepping out on the back porch of the dining room to ring the brass bell in the little belfry. With mockery in their voices, the boys of the village would call back, "Pig tail done! Pig tail done!"

Red and pink hollyhocks lined the fence that bordered North Alley, and as Sadie let her fingers run along the pickets, Robert tipped his hat to Noah Johnson, the craftsman who had built the fence. Beyond the fence Robert pointed out a woodworker who made cabinets and coffins, and at the end of the village there lived another blacksmith. A double log cabin was the last structure on the north side of the road and Robert waited by its front gate for the mail stage to pass before helping Sadie cross the Chillicothe-Cincinnati Pike, then a dirt-packed road, lined with trees arching to the mid-line and offering shade.

Politics and Religion

Dr. Chenoweth lived on the south side of the highway and Sadie recognized his home and office. The town's doctor had served as surgeon during the

Civil War for four years. Not every war veteran living in Bourneville had served the Union army; a few had served the Confederacy. As if by rote, as Robert passed by each home or business, he pointed out the politics of each inhabitant. Here lived a staunch Republican, there a Copperhead Democrat. One's religious persuasion was also common knowledge in the little hamlet. It served as a way to keep score between Presbyterians and Methodists. Silas Nessell and his family were prominent Methodists. The Purdums had no children and left their farm to the Presbyterian church.

No one in town could surpass the McCracken family for its longevity. As founders of Bourneville, they had built one of its earliest houses and now the McCracken heirs occupied the old homestead. To Sadie the preschooler, history and genealogy would have had only vague meanings, but as an adult Sadie would research her own heritage and collect vast boxes of clippings about the history of the region.

"T. J. Plyley, Hides, Leather and Tallow" read the sign above the next building. Built during the Civil War to house a tannery, it was L-shaped, sixty-feet-long, and now it stood vacant.

Lamplighter and Coffin Maker

At last! Grandfather's general store! Courtesy drew the two in for a quick hello, but Sadie's strength and interest were flagging. Robert hurried her by the next site which also was familiar; it was the little cottage in which Sadie's mother was born. Sadie and her grandfather were about to finish their tour, but they hadn't yet passed the cobbler in his Merkle Shoe Shop, the Lance home—where a misspelled sign read PIANTS for sale—and the Grand Army meeting hall. For years the village lamplighter lived in a small house in front of the hall and occasionally Sadie would be allowed to go there to watch and listen as the veterans practiced muster, held drills, built campfires, or played their fifes and drums.

Before the village had its first mill, people were forced to carry their grain to another township or to grind it themselves. Grinding was the worst job in any household, so folks rejoiced when Jones and Chaney built the mill near the eastern end of the village, (they would later mourn its loss when it burned to the ground in 1888.)

A hearse loomed into view as Sadie and her grandfather finally ended their tour. Here lived the village undertaker. Robert avoided either a glance or a comment about the ominous, black coffin wagon. Death of the child's father was a subject to be avoided.

In silence, the pair dragged their tired bodies up the gravel lane to home where each collapsed for a long nap. Robert was satisfied. He had introduced Bourneville to Sadie, Sadie to Bourneville. It was a town in which he had come of age, a town which he had helped to build. And now, seeing it through Sadie's eyes, he could see that Bourneville was indeed a gentle but lively American town.[64]

Work to be Done

Now that summer was in full stride, Sadie was ready to explore her grandparents' farm. Martha showed her where to look for eggs in the hen house, when to pry the shiny green peas from their jackets and how to plant potato eyes in the freshly tilled earth of Grandma's vegetable garden. As the earth warmed and violets made way for grass, Sadie unlaced her shoes and ran into the dewy pasture to watch Bossie be milked. The kitty Bluebell often bounded along beside her in hopes of a squirt of warm milk.

Cousins came from the village to play. Although Robert could not bring himself to forgive daughter Virginia, her children were welcome at Robertson Place. On long hot days they caught minnows in the shallow parts of the creek or sprawled out in front of an empty hearth in the cool shuttered house. They served tea and cookies to their dolls and played hide-and-seek behind their grandmother's curtains. And at the end of the summer, when the searing heat loosened its grip upon the valley, Sadie went to the cellar to retrieve her grandmother's canning jars. Martha instructed Sadie to sort and arrange the aqua glass jars in rows around the kitchen where they would stand ready for the juicy red pulp of tomatoes or the glistening amethyst nectar of grape jelly.

On just the right day in late August, when the sweet smell of Concord grapes beckoned to the bees, Robert propped a ladder against the arbor by the back door and allowed Sadie to scamper up to pick the succulent clumps. While Sadie hunted for the next bunch to pluck, her cousin Floyd, Virginia's boy, stood below to catch it in a pail. Soon Sadie would start school and Floyd was full of advice.

But winter would come, and as summer faded and the days grew shorter, Martha and Robert began their yearly preparation. They would need a little extra help this year so they asked a young man to help around the property in return for room and board. A son of the local Gragg family would turn the soil in Martha's vegetable garden, scythe the lower lawn and stack wood.[65] Aside from his presence on the farm, this particular autumn felt different. Through the gathering haze in his mind, Robert sensed his strength was ebbing. On mornings when his muscles moaned and his memory was clouded, in a deep and wrenching way the squire understood that his days were numbered. There was work to be done, and he must not delay.

Almost from the time he first spied this fertile valley from atop a seat in his mother's covered wagon, Robert may have been thinking about the end game, the time when a line would be drawn to tally his life's accomplishments. Over the productive years when his mind was nimble and he had energy to spare, Robert had often contemplated this final act. Now, having reached sixty-two years of age, it was time. All the surveying, bargaining, buying and selling, all the repositioning, managing and risk-taking were over. No more would he be taking his horse down the township roads looking for land to buy, no more would he be scripting contracts. There remained only the business of dividing.

It all came to a climax one icy winter morning when the rest of the house had yet to stir. After tossing and turning for hours, Robert roused himself and pulled on his woolen robe. Holding on to the banister for support, he eased his stiff joints down the winding staircase and made his way to the music room which now housed his desk and books. Hunched there at his desk, he drew out a clean sheet of linen paper and dipped his quill into the bottle of blue-black ink.

> *I, Robert I. Robertson, of the Township of Twin, County of Ross, and State of Ohio, do make and publish this my last will and testament.*
> *I give and devise to my beloved wife, Martha Robertson, during her natural life or while she remains my widow,..."*

Robert carefully wrote out the terms of his will. When he had finished the document, he drew in his breath and added:

> *I have hereunto set my hand and seal this 25th day of Dec. in the year A. D. 1880.*
>
> *Robert Isaac Robertson*

Satisfied, Robert slumped back in his chair. This task, so long postponed, so dreaded for its finality, was now over. He would probably never again be called to settle a dispute, record a deed or give an opinion. No one would ever seek him out for a loan or ask him to run for office. In the stillness of the dawn, Robert gathered a blanket around his slumping shoulders and allowed himself to contemplate the end.

Dozing off, the squire rested, and when he awoke he lifted his watery eyes to savor the sunrise. A peach-colored glow began to fill the sky beyond the wavy window panes. Each December 25, the sun rises in the exact center of the front room window and intensifies into a fiery ball. But on this morning of 1880, Robert shielded his weak eyes from the blazing spectacle and let his heavy head fall to his chest. There was a new and distant ache in his heart.

Christmas Morn

But wait. Someone is afoot upstairs. It is Christmas morning. Robert props himself up on his elbows to listen. Sadie will soon come bounding down the back stairs to make a beeline for her stocking. Here she is.

"Look Grampa Robbie, look!" She sees the yarn sock, full and lumpy and straining from its hook on the mantle.

Christmas day has begun. As it unfolds, a progression of familiar activities unfurl. Out in the kitchen the ladies will begin making the oyster stew, and Martha is

Mary Poole McKee

fetching her fruitcake from the attic of the wash house where it has been mellowing since Thanksgiving. No extra leaves will be needed for the dining table today. Sally will not be bursting in the back door laden with gifts because she is still feeling bereft after the death of their first baby. Virginia, always so lively and full of Christmas spirit, will not be herding her children up the hill to share in the holiday festivities because she is not yet welcome at the table. How many years has it been now? Nine. Martha lets out a muffled sigh. Of course there is Margarite, but her widowhood continues to cast a thin veil of melancholy over everything.

On that Christmas Day in 1880, along with the holly and candles, there was a nostalgia for the old days when the Robertson family was all together and in its prime. As she poured herself a glass of hard cider, Martha may have remarked that today was her sister Mary's birthday. Many years ago Mary had moved with her husband, Dr. McKee, to Iowa. So very far away. Would the sisters ever be reunited again? Martha longed to feel her sister's hug.

Breaking Martha's reverie might have been the sound of approaching sleigh bells had it not been for this year's winter weather. Brown ice covers the rutted roads between Robertson Place and the Poole cabin where Martha's widowed father still lives. He and two of his children, Martha's unmarried siblings, would have to miss Martha's Christmas dinner and her mincemeat pies. Thank heaven for Sadie! She will soon be flitting from room to room, unaware that she carries the spirit of Christmas on her own tiny shoulders.

The Unthinkable

Another Christmas such as this would pass before the end came for Robert Robertson. There were two more years of bonding with Sadie, of gradually giving up the reins to his eldest daughter. However, in the fall of 1882, the patriarch sank into a debilitating senility.

Margarite saw her father's decline with clear eyes, but how would she deal with the task ahead? Soon her father would become an invalid. Could she act as nurse to the somewhat formal man she so revered? The very thought of it made her uneasy. It was a different story for Martha. Caring for the man she had once called Master Robertson, the man who had been her husband for thirty-five years, would be her duty and her privilege. And once she came to grips with her husband's imminent death, Martha rode a bolt of adrenaline into action.

Still, she would need help. For this Martha turned to the family living in the little cabin across the creek. In exchange for help around the farm, the former slave family had been cutting timber, caring for the horses, and washing heavy farm clothes in Martha's great copper kettles. Martha remembered a time nearly twenty years ago when her husband had offered the cabin to runaways and when she was shaken with fear as she swung the old hand bell to alert them of bounty hunters. These days, Martha merely crossed the foot bridge and knocked gently at the door of the log house.

Yes, they would come to help in what they called the "big house." Under Martha's supervision a makeshift bedroom was created on the first floor in the seldom used east parlor. Large pieces of furniture on porcelain casters were swung into position and fresh linens brought from upstairs. A crackling fire was built and the shutters flung open to let in the swarming southern light.

Soon a routine emerged from the initial chaos. Margarite took over the running of the kitchen while Sadie ran errands to the village for groceries or tonics and tinctures. In silent acknowledgment of the efforts made by his caretakers, Robert may have clung a little longer to what was left of his life, but as the days drew shorter and the holidays loomed near, Robert's mind and body slipped further and further. A kerosene lamp, turned low, glowed in the hallway outside the sickroom while the two women took turns keeping vigil until finally, on the second day of December 1882, Martha Robertson could not awaken her husband.

How enormous was the difference between life and death. Without a word, Margarite bundled up against the cold, picked up a lantern, and set out to notify the coffin maker.

By noon the word was out. Robert Robertson is dead. The town's squire, the justice of the peace, the church superintendent, the store owner, the boss farmer, the owner of Robertson Place is dead.

Margarite, her hand shaking, scripted an announcement to be delivered the next day in both of their churches. As was the convention, they invited the mourners into their own home for the viewing and service. The weather was foul and the roads still pocked with standing water, but despite the bad weather, a steady stream of in-laws and neighbors, former students, customers and clients, fellow worshipers, businessmen and competitors managed to arrive at the house on the hill to pay their respects to the squire's family.

The Funeral

It is the day of the funeral. In the front parlor of the Robertson Place lies Robert's shrouded, recumbent figure in a coffin. The room is crowded with mourners. When at last the service is over and the coffin's lid lowered, a sea of black woolen dresses and suits begins to part, allowing the Robertson women to precede to a waiting carriage. Climbing aboard, Martha pulls an old Scotch plaid blanket across her lap. It is the one trimmed with horsehair, the one she made years ago as a Christmas gift for her husband. Now, seeing the initials R.I.R. that she had embroidered with her own hands so many years ago, tears sting her eyes as she arranges the woolen lap robe across the three generations—Sadie, Margarite, and herself. A whip is cracked and the horses obey the signal to fall in behind the coffin wagon on this last, ponderous journey to the graveyard.

Back through Porter Hollow over twenty miles of chuck-holes and ruts, the horses carry Robert's casket and his mourners to Concord Church. Near where his son-in-law Erskine lay, the pall bearers, shivering in the damp cold, wait to unload the coffin. But when it comes time for them to lower the casket into the cemetery's cavern of orange subsoil, Martha cannot bear to look. Beneath the net veil she clamps her swollen eyes shut. She is not ready to have such an image of finality be etched into her brain. Yet deep in the widow's heart is a truth which she cannot deny.

Never again will her world be the same. A force of energy such as Robert Robertson's is nowhere on the horizon. It is the end of an era.

The Reckoning

In the days that followed Robert's funeral, Martha bolstered herself against the numbing work that lay ahead. As tonic against the visions of Robert's last days, she returned to the attic of her memories. What a dashing school teacher Robert had been when she and all the other school girls had fallen in love with him. In vivid flashbacks Martha brought back visions of her husband as surveyor, tramping the bottoms with his brass quadrant and compass; as judge, settling the town's quarrels; as proud father ushering new visitors into their beloved home. He had swept her away with his skill and daring when he saved the town's store from bankruptcy and stunned her by crafting a deal to buy the house of their dreams, the house she could never imagine leaving, Robertson Place.

But then the newspaper arrived with its obituary. "Softening of the brain," it said, was the case of death. This must have caused Martha to well up in tears. But to her great relief, the Bourneville correspondents to the (unnamed) newspaper followed with an apt description of the man she knew.

> *Mr. Robertson was in the truest sense a self-made man. In intellect he was more than ordinary. As a Justice of the Peace, which office he held for the period of over thirty years, not one of his decisions was every over-ruled by a superior Court. He had a well-disciplined mind, the result of long years of almost uninterrupted study. He had a wonderful energy and struggled through the hardships of poverty in his youth and early manhood, accumulating a large fortune. He was proud of good name, which was to him of far more value than "much fine gold."*

The daughters converged at Robertson Place to shore up their mother and to help her navigate the cruel dealings of death. Sally brought her attorney husband from South Salem and a tentative knock at the back door announced the arrival of Virginia. To settle an estate, law required that inventories be made for tax purposes. In the spring of 1883, the following list of chattels belonging to the estate of Robert Isaac Robertson was filed in the courthouse:

> *One sewing machine*
> *Books*
> *Three stoves*
> *Five beds and bedsteads*
> *One lounge-bed*
> *One cupboard*
> *Cooking utensils*

Table ware and service
Three bureaus
Three sets chairs
Four tables
Four rocking chairs
One clock
One side saddle
One wash stand
Two candle stands
One settee

The inventory noted that there was no cow, but that there was coal, meat, and corn for a year's use. The tally continued:

One dun horse
One carriage
One Piano Brake, There and Son, NY
Surveyor's compass and chain
One wheelbarrow, three saws, two hoes, one mattock
Five augers and old irons, rake
One step ladder
Two scythes
One iron scraper
Two double-barrel shotguns
An old crock cupboard
One man's saddle
Three office desks, table, one ax, one sledge
One 15 gallon brass kettle
One iron kettle
One sausage grinder
Two baskets and one box[66]

Redressing a Wrong

$\mathcal{B}$efore the sisters began to sort through their father's things and to rearrange the house for its female inhabitants, Sally's husband Henry insisted that the family convene for a reading of his father-in-law's will. Robert had assigned Henry Caldwell and Margarite to be co-executors. On January 23, in the front parlor of the Robertson Place, the balloon-backed dining chairs were assembled alongside the settee and platform rockers. Virginia, her fourth baby in arms, looked for a seat where, if needed, she could nurse her infant. Named for her grandmother Martha, baby Mattie was but a few months old.

A decade had passed since Virginia's elopement had provoked her father's anger and caused her to be cast out of the family's inner circle. Over the years she had braced herself against the possibility, even the probability, that she would be left out of her father's will. Was she about to receive that final punishment? Hushed, the family members seated themselves in self-conscious silence, eyes averting one another as they waited for Henry to rise and clear his throat.

> *In the name of the benevolent Father of all, I, Robert I. Robertson, of the Township of Twin, County of Ross, and State of Ohio, do make and publish this my last will and testament.*
>
> *I give and devise to my beloved wife, Martha Robertson, during her natural life or while she remains my widow, all the real estate, and personal property of every description, including all moneys, and effects whatsoever, that I may die seized with, and own and possess at my death, excepting so much thereof as may be necessary to pay all my just debts, burying expenses and excepting Lot No. 53 in Frankfort, Ross County, Ohio, and excepting the legacies I herein devise, and enough for taxes.*

So far there were no surprises in the text of the will read by Henry Caldwell on that cold day in January. Robert's sister Emily would get the lot in Frankfort and the inventory of his store would go to his current business partner, Joseph Burgess. What held the family members rigid in their seats was to learn the legacies of the rich farmland. With no son as the natural heir, there was a question of how, or if, the land would be divided. As Henry continued to read, Margarite brought hand to heart and exuded an inaudible sigh of relief. For upon Martha's death, along with the small farm that accompanied it, the prized house on the hill would pass to the eldest daughter. Margarite would receive the homestead, Robertson Place.

Henry read on. Sally was to inherit a farm next to the homestead, where underneath the rows of corn lay a giant concentric earthwork mound. Virginia would receive the one next to it, and it was the biggest! All eyes riveted to Virginia's corner. Suddenly it was clear to all those assembled that, from his grave, Robert intended to redress a wrong. To the defiant Virginia, he had been generous.

How could this be? wondered Virginia. Her father's act of generosity stunned her. Did he have a premonition that she would soon find herself in dire need? In the year that he penned his will, Virginia had just given birth to Daisy, her third child with Michael McCord, and to most observers her future looked reasonably solid. How could a father who kept himself at such a distance have known any different?

As other family members struggled to absorb the far-reaching implications of the will just read, Virginia strained to remember her father's long forgotten softer side. When she had been desperate for her father's advice and empathy, might it have been there for the asking?

Regret came in floods. Had reconciliation been possible after all? Too late now. So alike one another, it was pride that had kept them apart. She had made the first move by returning to her father's village, but for some reason, that proximity had not helped matters. Not until her father had written his will was he able to show his compassion.

Virginia fought back the urge to cry while the rest of her family looked on. Finally the tears sprang unbidden from her eyes and coursed down her cheeks. Limp from emotion, Virginia rose and offered her baby to Margarite, then met her mother's outstretched arms in the center of the room. How both of them ached to turn back time!

But there was no turning back. Virginia would have to live out the rest of her life without any chance to make amends to the man who now offered her an olive branch. She would have to make of her life an apology.

Robert's intentions were clear. Martha would continue to own and manage Robertson Place and retain title for all his land until which time she died and the daughters inherited their individual farms. Meanwhile, they would serve as stewards of the land. They were to farm it and harvest the crops. And according to their father's will they were to pay rent to their mother for its use. By this mechanism Robert Robertson was able to provide income for each of his heirs while binding the family together.

From the start, Margarite's inheritance of the homestead would change her future. It ended up defining not only her life, but those of generations to come.

Margarite's Dilemma

*M*argarite was flattered to receive her father's mantle, elated to think she would eventually be the sole owner of the Robertson Place, but there would be a price to pay. For when it came to his eldest daughter, Robert had been very specific. On that Christmas Day of 1880 he had written, "...it is also my wish and desire that my said daughter Mary M. Anderson (Margarite) occupy said premises with her mother, as a renter, during the life of her said mother, paying her said mother yearly, as rent for said premises the sum of One Hundred and Fifty Dollars ($150.00)."

Eventually, Margarite would realize her quandary. Truth was, the land left to her was a farm of only seventy-five acres and by itself could not possibly support the big house. In tandem with her sisters' rent, yes, but after their mother's death when she alone would have to keep up the place—then what? Nor could this land, or any part of it, be sold; for upon her own death, Margarite was to pass the Robertson Place on to Sadie. (Though not in his will, his last stipulation appeared to be understood and accepted by all.)

How on earth was Margarite to come up with all the money required to pay rent while living the sheltered life prescribed by her father? At present Margarite had no outside source of income, which was why she had come back home in the first place. If her mother were to live to be the age of her Grandmother Vinsonhaller, there could be forty-one more years of rent due.

Three-hundred dollars in cash was what Robert had allotted each of his daughters to get them started. But aside from questions about income, Margarite was wrestling with another issue. Was this how she *wanted* to live out the rest of her life, sequestered and cosseted by her father's money and her mother's oversight? Could she lay claim to no more than her family's legacy?

Margarite was too like her father to settle for the passive life he had prescribed. Ever since Erskine's death, it had seemed that people were always trying to come up with a plan for "the talented Robertson daughter." Whether it was the stuff of dreams or the subject of animated conversation, whether it was planned in secret or encouraged by others, there seems to have been growing in Margarite an urge to carve out her own future, to define herself by her own capabilities.

Big decisions lay ahead for the young widow. In her time it was the custom of wealthy families to shelter their daughters. Those daughters were not supposed to work, especially not in public view. Yet how was she to earn any money while staying at home with her mother?

Margarite was not alone in her dilemma. It was a pivotal and confusing time for women of her generation and socio-economic class. Many, like Margarite, had lost their husbands or fathers as a result of the Civil War, and yet few avenues were open to them if they wanted to work. Since the 1850s, women could find jobs in factories, but factory work was never a choice for educated women. A few single women became teachers, still fewer, nurses, and virtually none were clerks. Here was the double-bind: even if women needed or wanted to work, society told them to stay home. From press and from pulpit, women were told to dress and act as if they did *not* have to work. Resist the temptations of cities, of fame and of glory. Stay home was the constant drumbeat; stay home to nurture babies and glorify the nest.[67]

In the Robertson home, wedged between Shakespeare's sonnets and numerous Bibles in the huge walnut bookcase, stood biographies and testimonials by women who dared break the mold. There were books touting the bravery of contemporary women, such as *Women to the Rescue*, a story about women who fought for temperance, and *Women of the War*, an account of women who followed the Civil War troops as nurses. Sitting behind the bookcase's glass doors, was another book whose title begged the question, *What can a Woman Do?*.

So what *would* Margarite do with the rest of her life? If ever Margarite were to step outside her family's cloister, writing would be the likely route. She may have been inspired by two authors whose books she had read: the wildly popular Louisa May Alcott and Harriet Beecher Stowe. Margarite did try her hand at writing fiction, and perhaps she was one of countless women who poured themselves into sonnets, novels and tales of romantic adventure over dainty writing tables in the privacy of their bedrooms. But it was rare for a woman to take her art seriously.

An exception to the rule was painter Mary Cassatt, who was now exhibiting her paintings in Philadelphia. Back in 1866, when she had wanted to further her study of art in Europe, her socially prominent father famously declared that he would rather see his daughter dead than to see her live abroad as a bohemian. Such was the prejudice against women displaying their talents in public.[68]

Along with other housewives across the nation, the Robertson women subscribed to the *Ladies' Home Journal* and later to *The Delineator*, which were among the earliest of periodicals to be published for a wide and exclusively female audience. Women had been doing some writing about themselves and things female, but they were more likely to be the recipients of a massive amount of advice. The elegant *Ladies' Home Journal* carried its share of advice, alongside instructions for such practical things as washing curtains and getting rid of flies. It published patterns for dresses and handiwork such as doilies and antimacassars, and it depicted the latest hairstyles. Mothers got ideas for children's games and new recipes, and the journal even published an occasional song. Along with such domestic subject matter were stories. Fiction written both by and for women was for the first time finding a vast new audience, and that writing may have been what most interested Margarite.

However, the florid prose made popular by such magazines backfired on readers and potential writers such as Margarite Anderson. Preachers and teachers pounced on the idea that fiction was a threat to the feminine mind. It would corrupt young girls and their mothers. Yes, reading novels was bad for their brains, pontificated the scolds. It was not only their brains that were jeopardized, announced spokesmen like Henry Ward Beecher. The nation's wives and mothers were becoming weaklings as a result of spending time reading instead of doing housework or exercising. A popular health writer of the time, S. Wier Mitchell, went so far as to suggest that, "future womanly usefulness was endangered by steady use of her brain."[69] In 1870, it was thought that "stimulating emotional reading could create uterine congestion, weak backs, painful menstruation and leukorrhea."[70] The worriers wondered aloud: Where are the hardy pioneer women who can pack a deer, chop wood for the fire, walk miles to town? The brave pioneer, the bearer of many children, man's constant helpmate on the farm—they are disappearing! What is to become of this nation?

If Margarite and her contemporaries had heeded the alarmist preachers and social conservatives, they would have shunned public exposure and avoided the polluted and immoral cities. Instead of pursuing their dreams, her generation would have stayed home to study the classics, strengthened their bodies with exercise, redeemed their souls with Bible study and pious living, and served the nation by having many babies. In the late 1800s, this was the nation's ideal.

A year would pass before Margarite decided what to do with the rest of her life. In the spring of 1883, Margarite Anderson, widow of Erskine and daughter of Robert I. Robertson, decided to leave home to become a teacher. Though she would go no further than thirty miles and would choose a path already blazed by others of her gender, it was the turning point in her life. What's more, she would become a role model for the women in her bloodline.

Breaking the News

How did Margarite tell her mother of her plans to leave home? Was it after the dishes were washed and the chores completed that mother and daughter, handwork in their laps, settled into the wicker rockers on the side terrace of Robertson Place to enjoy the waning light? Sadie, innocent of the pending announcement, might have been wending her way through a sea of nodding blue-bells on her way down to the big lower lawn to catch the twilight's first fireflies. Martha's rimless spectacles would have been in their usual position on her nose at just the proper angle to enable her to knit while glancing up to follow the slow progress of the cattle as they ambled back toward the barn.

Was Martha surprised to hear of her daughter's plans? For quite a while now, the vibrant town of Hillsboro, just thirty miles west, had been attracting idealistic young people like Margarite. Things happened there. It was in this southern Ohio town that ten years ago, on Christmas Eve, 1873, Eliza Jane Thompson led seventy of the town's socially prominent women from saloon to saloon singing, praying, and demanding that barkeepers sign a pledge not to serve alcohol. The actions of these women sparked a renewed interest in the Women's Temperance Movement.

On the other hand, there was little Sadie to think about. What was all of this to her? No doubt Erskine's sister Clara, the one who had studied art in Boston and was now teaching in Hillsboro, had told her niece all about the town's Music Hall, the fancy Clifton Hotel, and its three female colleges. No, Margarite was certain that the child would love Hillsboro.

Sitting on a dresser upstairs was a letter from David Anderson, Erskine's older brother, offering Margarite a job teaching at his boys' school. His school turned out to be at the Hillsboro College which also held classes for younger children on the premises. And what about transportation? A train from either Storms or Dill Station near Bainbridge would take them to Hillsboro.

Big changes were ahead for Martha who would be left to live alone in Robertson Place. Together she and her daughter had shared their widowhood; together they had faced the world. Martha Robertson had lived her entire life within two miles of the Robertson Place. The same was true for her mother, Mary Poole. Many of her acquaintances had never once made the four-hour trip to Hillsboro, the seat of Highland County; they thought of it as the other side of the world. After all, beyond Hillsboro lay Cincinnati, the gateway to the West.

Yet how could the little community of Bourneville hold a bright spirit like Margarite? Few professionals lived in the village: a doctor here, a teacher there, maybe a smattering of businessmen. Young people with ambition were looking elsewhere to fulfill their dreams. Some headed out West, most simply moved to the nearest city. Even those inclined to farming were leaving because none of the township's good land was available for purchase. It was no use, realized Martha, to try to dissuade her daughter.

A feeling of loss may have crept over Martha as her thoughts catapulted back to the tearful scene of her brother's departure for war, or back further to the dramatic leave-taking of Uncle Lorenzo when he rode off with Colonel Fremont to explore the West. Martha could remember her own grandmother Vinsonhaller's story about wrenching herself from her mother's embrace before climbing aboard the wagon which would take her across the barrier mountains. If Martha had compared her loss to that of her great-great grandparents who stood on the shores of the Old World waving farewell to children who would never return, Margarite's plan to move to Hillsboro did not merit even the slightest whimper. After all, her daughter was now thirty-five, and it was not the first time she had left home. What's more, the destination was a mere thirty miles away, less than a day's journey. However, there was another issue about Margarite's leaving that was a bit unsettling. She was planning to go to Hillsboro without the protection of a man.

And yet, Martha likely raised no opposition to her daughter's plan. It was not her way. Martha herself was growing sturdier and sturdier as she aged, and she and her husband had reared Margarite to stand on her own two feet. Why not encourage this move? Besides, there was no way to stop her.

Bolts of fabric were unfurled across the table among dress patterns, buttons, and lace. In no time at all, the dining room in Robertson Place was transformed into a dressmaker's domain. Martha was not about to miss out on her daughter's adventure, and she was never happier than when embarking on a huge sewing project.

Years ago Margarite had shed her mourning clothes of black, but her current garments now came under scrutiny. Could a tuck here or there, perhaps a new collar, transform the tired clothing of widowhood? In this way, Margarite's wardrobe was remodeled. By separating the worn tops from their stiff skirts and adding fresh ruffled blouses of white lawn or batiste, a fashionable new look could be achieved. Dressed in her new clothing, Margarite resembled one of the Gibson Girls whose images would soon grace the covers of the nation's magazines. And while mother and daughter worked on Margarite's attire, little Sadie gathered up her own pinafores and frocks to be modified or let down. But, please, could she have a sailor-suit?

At summer's end the preparations culminated in one last trip to Chillicothe where Margarite became enamored with an elaborate traveling trunk. Its rounded top was striped with oak slats, its sides covered with pressed tin. Likewise, Sadie would choose a smaller trunk whose tin top was embellished with bas-relief roses. Martha herself might have been too practical for such decoration, but there was no resisting when it came to buying them for her daughter and granddaughter.

A New Setting

The minute Sadie Anderson's feet hit the boardwalks in Hillsboro, she could feel its urban energy. Busy with commerce and culture, in the late 1800s the county seat of Highland County was a vibrant place. Its population numbered five-thousand. Electric light bulbs hung from wires strung across its intersections, and Hibben's Dry Goods, Ayres Drug Store, two grocery stores and a stationery establishment lined its main street. The thoroughfare was one of dust and dirt or slippery mud, depending on the season, but even so, folks dressed up more than they did in Bourneville or Chillicothe. There was no need, Margarite told Sadie, for the two of them to feel at all embarrassed about their altered clothing because their new wardrobes were quite in style. Martha had risen to the task. The Anderson ladies could hold their own on the boardwalks of Hillsboro.[71]

Where the Andersons found lodgings in Hillsboro remains an enigma. Perhaps Margarite and Sadie lived with Erskine's sister, Clara. Boarding houses were popular at the time, and many large and ornate three-storied houses were being built along the leafy main streets. Was it in the top floor of one of these grand edifices that mother and daughter found a room to rent? Looking down through the tree boughs to the street below would have been a novel experience for a nine-year-old used to country living. How odd it must have felt to sleep on a cot under the gables, to live among other boarders, to take one's meals with strangers.

Everything about their lives was new and different. For one thing, Margarite would, for the first time in her life, have a real paying job. Awaiting her inspection was a stack of books she had pre-ordered from a bookseller in Cincinnati. From these texts Mrs. Anderson, whose qualification for teaching was the completion of a four-year course of reading with the Chautauqua Literary and Scientific Circle, would teach English, literature, music and religion.

While teaching of Faust and Burns, an energized Margarite enrolled herself at the Hillsboro Female College and Conservatory of Music. Advanc-

THE HILLSBOROUGH FEMALE COLLEGE.

ing her own education had been part of Margarite's plan, and since the 1850s, this school had been a bastion of education for women, attracting students from several surrounding states.

According to its catalog, the school professed that it could provide "a thorough mental and moral culture at such rates that young ladies, unable to pay large bills, could have the privileges of a finished education."[72] Margarite would study here for seven years, during which time this college (as well as others in Hillsboro) "flourished scholastically and languished financially."[73] Two years before Margarite graduated in 1890, the college dropped its female designation and took in male students. In May 18, 1894, the building went up in flames, and although it reopened the following year, the school was doomed by financial problems and soon thereafter closed its doors forever.

However, while Margarite and Sadie were in Hillsboro, the college was in its prime. It provided not only classes for adults, but those for children as well, and it was here that Sadie was enrolled in the fourth grade. During class Sadie wrote notes back and forth to her girlfriends and kept a tiny diary in which she and her friend counted the days until Christmas. From this diary it is clear that the child did not excel in penmanship, but Sadie's sunny and exuberant nature soon made her popular with classmates.

Music recitals punctuated their weekends, and mandolins were all the rage. At one concert the mother and daughter attended, dozens of suited-up young men filed onto the conservatory's concert hall stage bearing the popular eight-stringed instruments. Margarite became an enthusiast and bought a gourd-shaped mandolin. Plucking its strings back in her bedroom, Margarite began to compose a little music. Before she knew it, she was creating the lyrics.

Fever Strikes

Life in Hillsboro was not always fun and exciting. As did towns everywhere, this one harbored disease. At the age of nine, Sadie contracted scarlet fever, the childhood killer. Panic gripped Margarite as she applied cold compresses to her feverish child.

In Bourneville, Margarite's telegram triggered Martha into action. Wasting no time, she boarded the train to Hillsboro with a hastily assembled satchel of medicinal aids. More important than her remedies for a sore throat—even than the new doll or tiny music box tucked into the side pocket of her tapestry valise—was the confidence she would bring to the strange boarding-house room that passed for an infirmary. Grandma's presence would help to make everyone sleep better and Sadie to get well.

Even so, Martha had the wisdom to stay on after the fever broke because after the rash subsided, the worst part was yet to come. Sadie's hair began to fall out in loose clumps. The loss of those coveted, cosseted blond curls shocked even Martha, and the adults tried to hide their dismay at the sight of the lifeless, gold ringlets lying in disarray upon the child's pillow. When Sadie caught sight of herself in the mirror, she covered her face and shrieked. The combined powers of two generations were necessary to calm the mortified, sobbing child. When Sadie got well, promised her grandmother, they would make a trip to the dry goods store for that little bonnet and the muff lined with rabbit-fur.

Graduation was a joyous event. Both mother and her high-school daughter received diplomas from their respective schools in the spring of 1890. Returning to Robertson Place they brought with them souvenirs of their life-changing adventure. Scarlet fever left Sadie with a head of tightly curled hair which would remain her signature throughout the rest of her life. Tucked under her arm was a prized possession, given by her teacher upon high-school graduation. It was the book, *Girls Who Became Famous*.

A degree in literature was Margarite's reward for the seven years spent away from home. The diploma from Hillsboro College declared Margarite a "Mistress of Liberal Arts." Along with her certificate,

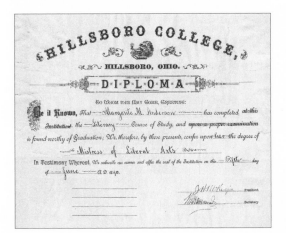

cradled in a leather case lined with crushed blue velvet, was something she would never again be without: her precious lacquered mandolin.

Homecoming

O ver the years, Margarite was to find solace in her books and her mandolin. She was to dedicate a good part of her life to producing poetry and music, and she would pursue these arts far from home in Washington, D.C. But in 1890, when Margarite and her daughter Sadie returned to their home in Bourneville, they resumed their comfortable lives with Martha at Robertson Place.

Chautauqua filled their summers. By now Sadie was a willing accomplice, and in 1891 the Robertson women were instrumental in establishing the First Annual Chautauqua Encampment at Concord Church. No longer would Margarite trek to Pennsylvania or New York in order to attend Chautauqua. From Bourneville, it was just eighteen miles. Although the country church was far from cities, six trains arrived daily at the train stop in tiny Roxabell to disgorge passengers from Cincinnati and Dayton.

Men slept outdoors in tents, female participants in the church's manse. Horses were fed, conveyances cared for, and police and sentinels stood guard. There was always a guest speaker to draw interest, and one year a traveler from Persia electrified his audience.

Margarite served as president of Chatuaqua's Literary and Scientific Circle, and over the years she participated in many of its committees. Inspired by its goals, she continued to learn—and possibly to teach—for many years.

However, during the seven years that Margarite and Sadie were away at school or Chatauqua, much had changed in Paint Valley.

Someone is Missing

S omeone is missing. In Aunt Virginia's house in the village of Bourneville, there is no man to fix things and to be father to her four children. There is no Michael McCord residing here. After Margarite and Sadie had left for Hillsboro, her sister Virginia's life took a dramatic turn. As winter broke and the first green pips of snowdrops poked out from under the skirts of the lilac hedge, Martha Robertson began to suspect that something other than colic was wrong in the McCord household. Mattie, the new baby, was especially fussy. Virginia was acting strange, and the children were misbehaving. Indeed, there was gossip. Spring was about to burst on the scene, and when the maples begin to sprout their red fringe and mourning doves take up their cooing, when the first calf of the season bawls for its mother and the bottom is flooding, no one has time for gossip. But that particular year there *was* gossip. Where was Virginia's husband? Everyone wanted to know.

Years later, Virginia would tell a judge that her husband had abandoned her in February of 1884 and that she "had to support herself and [her four] children by her own means." In the divorce filing, she claimed that Michael had become intoxicated and struck her, but the stated reason for their separation is in doubt.[74] In a society where manners mattered so much, divorce was rarely discussed or even considered. The law made it so difficult for those wanting a legal separation that those who actually filed for divorce had to fabricate reasons, making their conditions sound more dire that they actually were in order to impress the judge. Perhaps Virginia and Michael simply drifted apart. However, no matter how one painted it, no matter whether one or the other spouse had been at fault, their separation would have only added to the stigma Virginia already carried as a result of running away from home. It had proven hard to erase that seminal event from people's memory, even though in 1873, a year or so after she had run away, the couple had arranged for the itinerate minister Samuel McAdow to make their union legal. Still, people liked to remember the drama of elopement. Although it was Michael McCord who left, it was Virginia's shame to bear. And it would be her mother's too.

Virginia's marriage to Michael had lasted a dozen years, long enough for her to give birth to four children. By the time that Margarite and Sadie returned to the valley in 1890, he'd been errant too long to hope for reconciliation. Michael McCord had moved on. He would resurface in Chillicothe with a new wife, more children, and a business whose advertisement in Wiggens' 1894 *Chillicothe and Ross County Directory* read "painters of fine buggies and carriages, ornamental signs, dec. wk, fresco, inter. finishing and landscape ptg a specialty."

Looking back, I suspect it was Margarite, newly returned from the city, who persuaded her younger sister to put the past to rest, to get a divorce. Virginia had

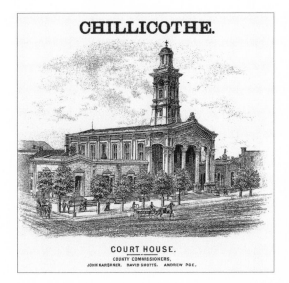

CHILLICOTHE.

COURT HOUSE.
COUNTY COMMISSIONERS,
JOHN KARSHNER.   DAVID SHOTTS.   ANDREW POE.

been living on her own for six years, but until now there had been no reason for her to undo the law that legally bound her to the impatient lover who had helped her climb down a ladder to run away. Now, there was a reason. The middle child of Robert Robertson was ready for change, ready for adventure. She would summon her courage and go to the court house in Chillicothe to file for divorce. How about this for the gossips to chew on!

Adventure for Virginia

A man stood knocking at Virginia's door. Framed in the doorway was a stranger to her children but a face known to all the adults in town. Mr. Robertson had shaken hands with him when the two had discussed marriage with his daughter almost thirty years ago. News of Tom Steadman's return astonished everyone because after Virginia's elopement, this native of Bainbridge had vanished. Jilted and heartsick, he had pulled up stakes and headed north. He went far away to Manistee, Michigan, which was known as the summer home to Chicago's lumber barons. But in 1872, it was a town still in ashes after the great fire. Manistee needed to be rebuilt, and the man from Bainbridge spent the next twenty years there as a telegraph lineman and, after the town got back on its feet, as a house painter. He also become a husband. Twice over. Lasting love seemed to elude the Civil War veteran, but perhaps he and his former sweetheart could ignite a spark.

The newspaper was kind. Deferring to the Robertson family's reputation, it never mentioned the couple's divorces. Instead, the scene it depicted in Virginia Robertson McCord's cottage on New Year's Day, 1992, was innocent enough.

New Year's Nuptials at Bourneville
One of the quiet but none the less enjoyable holiday weddings deserving of
mention, was that in which Mrs. Jennie McCord, one of Bourneville's highly

respected ladies, and Mr. Thomas P. Steadman, of Manistee Michigan, were
the contracting parties, the ceremony which joined them hand to hand, being
performed at the bride's cosily furnished residence in that village Friday eve-
ning of last week, at eight o'clock, with Rev. F. M. Evans officiating

The article went on. It predicted success for the marriage based on the following:

...their affection is not altogether of sudden birth, but of long standing,
their having been engaged to be married earlier in life, at the time of Mr.
Steadman's return from his service in the army. But providence ordered
otherwise, and their union was not consummated until now.[75]

Sadie, her mother, and grandmother—all three were in that cozy cottage to witness the couple's wedding and to wish good luck to their exuberant Virginia. On the
following Monday, while the rest of the world returned to its business, the middle
Robertson daughter, now forty-two, bundled up her four children, closed down the
house, made arrangements for her farm, and headed
north to begin a new life among the snow-covered
pines of Michigan.

Slowly, life in Paint Valley returned to normal.
Martha and Sadie picked up the pieces of their lives:
Margarite continued writing, did church work and
helped run the household. Periodically, she received
mail from Michigan. Virginia's eldest, Floyd, missed
his girlfriend. Lizzie and Daisy, fifteen and twelve,
raved about ice skating on Lake Michigan. Know-
ing Mattie, she was bound to have a gaggle of new friends. Everyone kept fingers
crossed, hoping that Virginia herself would be happy in the new marriage.

But it was not to be. Within two years of their departure, the newly formed family began to fall apart and to trickle back to Ross County. As for her husband, Tom
Steadman seemed determined to live the married life, but it would not be with Virginia that he would find marital bliss. Virginia was his third wife but would not be
his last. Her son Floyd, now seventeen, was the first to leave: he returned to marry
his sweetheart Ona Marie Maughmer and to settle down in Paint Valley. Soon it was
Virginia herself who yearned for home and the hills of Southern Ohio. Had she been

impetuous or too optimistic when she ran off to Michigan with Tom? Maybe she had been foolish to think that as an outsider and a third wife she could easily make the transition into Manistee society. It didn't matter any more. Deflated, but certainly not defeated, Virginia would pack up the remaining three children and head south. She would go home.

Sitting in a Row

*I*n Virginia's mind was a plan. She would build a house on the 164-acre tract she had inherited from her father, on land whose soil had been so generous. She would live in it just the way she wanted to. No man would lure her away; no man would spoil the rest of her days. Siting her house on a rise east of Robertson Place, the middle daughter envisioned a sturdy house. No common little farmhouse would it be, no sir! Up would go a fashionable Victorian-style house. Replete with gables, it would have a broad porch from which Virginia could view the rich bottom land that would support her for the rest of her life. On October 2, 1894, according to a note found in the family Bible, a foundation for that house (which still stands) was laid, and six weeks later, on November 12, a jubilant Virginia moved into it.

No sooner would the echo of hammers die away than her younger sister Sally in South Salem would catch the fever to return to Paint Valley. In between the old brick homestead and Virginia's brand-new Victorian house, Sally and her husband would break ground for a modest two-story frame house on her inherited land. It would sit atop a knoll near the earthworks of an ancient civilization, and would serve as home for the rest of Sally Caldwell's days.[76]

So it could be said that by the end of the 19th century, Robert Robertson's wishes will have come true. Sitting in a row, on land cut from the original Nathanial Massie survey, would be the homes of three Robertson heirs.

But when Sadie returned to Paint Valley after graduating from high school in in 1890, there was only one house on the Robertson property. And it was here that Sadie Anderson would come of age.

Coming of Age—Halcyon Days

Gregarious and full of life, Sadie enjoyed visiting her neighbors. She made her rounds to the village by tucking up her skirts and hopping on her bicycle. What a nuisance it was to keep one's voluminous skirts out of the bicycle's chains and spokes. The Robertson household never lacked for ladies' magazines and pattern books illustrating the latest fashions, and with no males in the house to object, Sadie was probably one of the first in her crowd to sport bloomers.

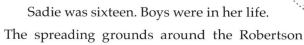

Sadie was sixteen. Boys were in her life. The spreading grounds around the Robertson Place where Sadie used to chase fireflies, now became the setting for Sunday socials and house parties. Carrying a butler's tray full of sandwiches and cool drinks down to the lower front lawn, a spirited Sadie joined her friends in games of croquet and badminton. And there was even a tennis court in her dreams.

A lawn court would be just one in a string of changes that would enliven the Robertson Place during the later part of the century. At last the women were free to pour all their attentions and creativity into their property, and a sizable amount of money was expended on its alterations. Without anyone to check their fancies, the three ladies came up with what must have seemed to the villagers an endless series of expensive projects.

Italianate arches and Victorian cupolas were on the minds of Margarite and Sadie when they first returned for summer breaks from Hillsboro. Robertson Place already had fancy corbels and a front stoop with an overhang that verged upon the fanciful gingerbread style. But the ladies were thinking of other improvements, and inevitably, their infectious enthusiasm wore down any of Martha's reservations. A cadre of roofers, carpenters, and painters descended on the stately old Robertson Place and near the end of their alterations a reporter from *The Scioto Gazette* remarked in his article of Nov. 10, 1887:

The residence of Mrs. M. M. Anderson, of Bourneville, has just been remodeled and painted to such an extent that persons who formerly knew the place would hardly believe it was the same.

A new roof was their largest undertaking. Years later I would discover evidence that a fire might have destroyed some of the house's original wood shingles, and perhaps this was the impetus behind the remodeling efforts. Vents, meant to cool the upstairs bedrooms, had already been cut across the front of the house in a space below the roof's overhang. For further cooling, Martha now added an awning over her front bedroom window. Though a little out of keeping with Robertson Place, the striped awning would provide shade until a newly planted maple tree took over. Finally, a fresh coat of somber grey paint was applied over the homestead's brick facade.

The single most dramatic addition to Robertson Place, however, took place in the front yard. Into the broad expanse of grass, the ladies carved a new carriage way in the shape of a teardrop. Buggies could now circle the teardrop, dropping their riders at the granite walkway that led to the front entrance of the house. Or, at the entrance to the teardrop drive, a lady visitor might tie up her horse at the hitching post and, using the tall stepping stone, there dismount. In the center of this teardrop, the ladies marked out a circle. It was this, their first attempt at landscape design, that was to become the centerpiece of the front yard for generations of gardeners.

Since the mid-1800s, increasing numbers of Americans had been discovering the pleasures of growing things; they were turning the garden from a necessity into a hobby. Even new city dwellers found a corner of their postage-stamp backyards in which to dig. Seeds and plants from all over the world began to show up in the nation's flower beds. Even so, Martha and Margarite placed in the center of their circle an urn containing what would have been to Midwesterners a very odd choice: a single cactus. In fact, the cactus was very fashionable. During this period, a similar planting was in front of the White House in Washington.[77]

During the halcyon days of the late 1800s, not only did the women alter the exterior of the house on the hill, they also set about modernizing its interior. Where did the ladies do their everyday cooking up until now? The answer remains illusive. But just a few steps behind the house was a low-ceilinged building—a one-roomed frame structure which, at the very least, served the Robertson household as a wash house and summer kitchen.[78] As late as the year 2000, the walls of this building were lined with shelves sagging under the weight of earthen crocks and wooden bowls; on its dirt floor sat empty barrels and copper tubs. In the loft above, alongside the family's valises, were rafters where Martha could have dried her herbs.

The Wash House

In the dim light of this low-ceilinged out-building, at least some of the cooking and laundry chores required to run the large household were carried out. Up until now these jobs were performed by the same family Robert had resettled in the log cabin after the Civil War. Its family members were well-versed in the idiosyncrasies of the kitchen's brick fireplace with all the long-handled, forged-iron utensils which hung from its mantle. It was in this small space that the helpers pressed apples into cider, stirred mush over the fire, and poured wax into candle molds.

Each day of the week had its particular job. Monday, for instance, was wash day. Early in the morning, someone had to start a fire to heat the wash water. After pumping the water from the well, the helpers would have carried it by buckets across the yard to the enormous tubs which hung in the large open fireplace. By now the fire was roaring and steam and lye soap stung everyone's eyes, but, only after numerous washings and rinses which consisted of stirring and lifting the heavy linens and garments with long-handled wooden forks, would the women begin the herculean task of wringing the steaming rinse water from the weighty cloth. During the cold season it would have challenged the women to work in a space so dark and cramped, and then to lug the dripping garments outside to dry.

On Tuesdays the women brought out the heavy irons for another hot and steamy day in the confinement of the crowded room with its two small windows and short door.

Big changes were coming. In the late 1800s, the women of Robertson Place added a kitchen to the main house. From this time forward (except for seasonal activities such as the making of cider and applesauce or sauerkraut) the old cabin-like structure functioned primarily as a wash house.

In their new kitchen, the women installed several luxuries which made their lives easier. They mounted a countertop pitcher-pump beside the sink. The current well was in the back yard, although deep in the cellar of the main house are the remains of an earlier well; out on the south lawn there is evidence of a yet another wellhead. Back in 1858 when they reoriented the house to face south-east, they must have abandoned the southern one and dug a new well in the back yard where the household performed its daily work.[79]

Before now, a cellar provided cold storage for wintering fruits and vegetables. To get there, one had to go outside and open a heavy storm door before descending below ground. Some twenty paces from the back door, stood the milk house, where the family kept its dairy products. There was always the worry of spoilage or freezing, so a convenient icebox would have been a delightful addition to the new kitchen.

In the midst of their new kitchen, the women installed a massive, wood-burning cook stove to replace the fireplace as a source of heat. The range dominated the space with its modern presence of iron. Softer aesthetic elements also began to permeate the Robertson kitchen. On the western side of the new addition, the ladies created a cozy eating area from which they could watch the sun set or view the creeping

phlox in their rock garden. To top off this space, they added leaded-glass transom windows with inserts of marbleized green glass, and above that, a slate-roofed turret made of fish-scale wood shingles—all of which gave the space a light-hearted touch.

Yes, remodeling the kitchen in the late 1800s brought sweeping changes to the Robertson household. Not only did it improve the house's function, it brought modernity, luxury, and, most importantly, youth. A change of staff was in order. Sisters Edie and Fanny, a pair of girls from the village, were hired to replace the departing family of freed slaves. These sisters would go on to serve several generations in Robertson Place, nearly becoming part of the family.

Sadie's World

During the last decade of the nineteenth century, this feminine world was home to Martha, Margarite, and Sadie. Representing three generations, these women formed its emotional core and left an imprint that would last more than a century. They took care of it without the benefit of husbands or fathers. Beyond its gate were men, of course. Skirting the periphery, they entered for the occasional meal or to perform the specific jobs which made life possible at Robertson Place. One exception was Aunt Sally's husband Henry Caldwell, the farm's boss farmer, whose presence would have been somewhat regular since he managed the farm operations. But, other than this single male relative, one can only imagine the various types of masculine characters who approached the house, from the roughest grave digger (dressed only in bib-overalls) who arrived at the back door to split wood, to the refined and courteous preacher (dressed in a black suit) who showed up at the pillared front door. Years later, my mother would recall in an essay about her youth, "The minister would come to call from time to time, and when one of my mother's dogs chewed his high silk hat to bits, the episode was such a highlight in their lives that it was retold many times through subsequent years."[80]

Did the ladies keep farm animals? It is not certain, because—other than riding and work horses, a few chickens, and a milk cow—none have been mentioned in their writings. What is certain is that the ownership of Robertson Place would have forced the women to make decisions concerning its upkeep. Whether it was a broken-down well, a malfunctioning chimney flue, or an ailing tree, they would have been the final deciders. A myriad of seasonal chores would have been theirs to supervise such as cleaning out the wood gutters, getting in firewood or plowing up the vegetable garden.

The villagers still had plenty to talk about during the years after Squire Robertson's death; it seemed there was always something going on at the big house. Yet aside from the occasional extravagance or flight of fancy, everyday life at Robertson Place was based on frugality and self-sufficiency; the bottom-line had to be carefully guarded. During the summer, Sadie helped tend the massive vegetable garden and learned how to preserve its produce. She became an avid seamstress under her grandmother's guidance, working the treadle of her sewing machine as she created clothing and household linens.

While it is true that their life was self-sufficient, it could best be described as genteel, reasonably secure, and entirely feminine. Summer at their country home was especially bucolic, except during a drought when farm owners, be they male or female, fretted about the crops. An exception occurred in the summer of 1893 when the Robertson ladies decided to make an excursion to Chicago to see the World's Fair. Otherwise, warm weather brought on for the women a season of picnics and bicycling, one of blue chicory in the pasture and berries on the vine.

Chautauqua still ruled the months of June, July and August. All three generations attended its outdoor sessions, saturating themselves in literature and the arts. Although summer at Robertson Place could be gentle and verdant, winters could be harsh and isolating. When the skies darkened and the weather turned, Martha stayed home and was content with her domesticity. Sadie, like her mother, was high-spirited; she played the piano, sang, and among her friends was the instigator of plays and musicals. Before winter was over, Margarite and Sadie inevitably looked beyond Paint Valley for stimulation. At first, Margarite and Sadie moved together, north toward Columbus where they rented rooms or an apartment, but later Margarite traveled alone, east to Washington and south to Atlanta. Sadie's destination, however, would be west to Cincinnati.

Finishing School for Sadie

*I*n the Queen City of Cincinnati, Sadie found a rooming house on Belleview Avenue in Walnut Hills, quite near the University of Cincinnati. In the late 1800s, men still dominated university life, and Sadie began to attend classes at an adjacent institution. Miss Katherine's was a finishing school for young women. Cincinnati art historians, Cece Scearce Chewning and Mary Alice Burke, believe that it was here at Miss Katherine M. Lupton's School for Girls, a school offering classes in the arts as well as academics, that Sadie likely pursued her interest in painting and wood sculpting.

Carving of wood furniture was becoming a popular pursuit among American women in the later part of the 19th century. As one particularly droll historian put it: "Now women began to carve in wood—and though it seems an unheard of, impossible, and almost outrageous thing for a lady to do, they took to their tools like ducks to water and became utterly engrossed by their newfound sport. For a time, there was scarcely a mantel or a door jamb which was safe from the attack of a chisel in the hand of some wife or mother, intoxicated by art."[81]

The craze originated in England amidst the Arts and Crafts Movement, and was intended to counter the "vulgarity" of the products of the machine age. Its founders hoped to teach poor and unemployed women to create hand-crafted items of beauty for the home. But when the movement was introduced to America in Cincinnati by Englishman Benn Pitman, it attracted women from the other end of the socio-economic class—educated young ladies who, like Sadie, who did not need to work but who wanted to pursue the arts.[82]

Sadie was in the Queen City during the heyday of art carving, but during that time she also learned to paint. Her oil paintings were executed with a progressive level of skill, but they held no candle to her work in wood. On easels and picture frames, fire screens and mantelpieces, the student from Paint Valley sculpted the natural world she had grown to love. With her tools and mallet, she chiseled an array of delicate wild roses and ferns on the top side of a heavy scroll-legged library table. In deeper relief, on two separate walnut mantel pieces, Sadie carved snowball bushes and meandering trumpet vines, the beloved flowers of home. To this day Sadie's mantles grace the fireplaces of Robertson Place.

Having developed such a talent gave Sadie satisfaction and a certain amount of pride, but in the Victorian world in which she lived, a lady's artistic output was still seen as having special value only to her family and close friends or to a potential suitor. Seldom would the products of a lady's talent be displayed and never sold. As a result, it was not for many decades that any of her work was documented, and not for a century when in 1996 Chillicothe held a bicentennial exhibit in its Pump House Art Gallery that any of it would be seen by the public.[83]

Artistic skills set Sadie Anderson apart from her peers. But to what end? Once home from school she might try to keep up her painting and carving, but at heart Sadie was neither a career girl nor a scholar like her mother. She wasn't a social-ite either. Her enthusiasm for life had carried her far, but she too was caught in the same dilemma that faced many women of her class. Would she remain a talented but cosseted young lady of privilege, or would she strike out on her own uncharted path?

Delano was Different

The answer came to Sadie in the form of a suitor. Certainly, a pretty young lady such as Sadie would have attracted attention. At lawn parties at the Robertson Place there had come numerous young men as guests. But not until she met Delano Butler did anyone capture her serious interest. Delano was different.

Focused and serious, he was a student of law. He was a man who could handle himself with calm dignity, yet at other times he could be quite jovial and hurry along at a spirited gait. A crop of light-brown wavy hair, gray-blue eyes, classic—almost patrician—features made him nearly dashing. Yet there was much more to this man from Adelphi than his gait or his good looks.

Adelphi was a typical small town on the other side of Chillicothe, but from the start, Delano's journey to manhood had not been easy. In fact, his early life had been interrupted by a stunning tragedy. When Delano was only thirteen months old, his home had caught fire. His parents, trapped inside the frame house, perished in the flames.

Little Delano was rescued, and he had the good fortune of being taken in by a neighbor family. The Wittwers were not only welcoming, they were well-to-do, and, by some standards, exceptional. Delano and his sister were adopted, and along with the Wittwer children, John and Edward, Delano would receive all the trappings of a privileged male childhood.

Delano's new father, Edward Wittwer, had his hands in many endeavors. He was a prominent merchant, a developer of coal property, and a bank president. His own father was a Swiss diplomat, his wife's father a judge. He was multi-faceted and a colorful character who later in life distinguished himself as a noted archaeologist. Upon his return from Egypt, the local newspaper published a picture of him riding a camel. An advertising brochure entitled "A Glimpse of Europe," declared that Mr. Wittwer delivered his talk seventy-five times around the region for the price of twenty-five cents admission.

As a parent, however, Delano's father could be strict. Delano did not always see eye-to-eye with his adoptive father, and in a surviving letter, Delano wrote that Mr. Wittwer told him, "…if he were willing to follow their ways, he could ride with them; if not, he would have to go it alone." Delano later reflected that even though he did not always agree with the ways of his adoptive family, as a youth he'd sensed that he was better off staying with them. Upon graduation from Adelphi High School, Delano, the class historian, chose for the subject of his commencement address the theme of adversity. "Like some herbs that need to be crushed to unlock their sweet-est odors," he recited, "some natures need to be tried by suffering to evoke the excellence there is within them. The battle of life is in most cases fought up hill, and to win it without a struggle is perhaps to win it without honor."[84]

Indeed, after fate thrust him into the arms of the Wittwer family, Delano flour-ished. He showed so much promise that the Wittwers offered to help send their adopted son to college. Ohio Weslyan University was the natural choice; all the Wit-twer men had attended the institution. Over those college-year summers, it was understood that Delano would work side-by-side with brothers John and Edward baling hay or hauling lumber for their father.

After graduation Delano began to teach school in Hallsville, a small town near Adelphi. His teaching certificate qualified him to teach Orthography, Reading, Writ-ing, Arithmetic, Geography, English Grammar, History of the United States, Phys-iology, Hygiene, and a course in Stimulants and Narcotics. But Delano wanted to study the law. In 1894 he entered the Ohio State University's new law school in Columbus and became a member of its second class to graduate.

Perhaps Delano and Sadie knew one another while Delano was at Ohio State. It appears that at about this time Sadie and her mother began to spend their winters in Columbus where they could participate in the university town's culture. It is also possible that Sadie and Delano met each other in Ross County. What is certain is that for several years prior to his courtship with Sadie, Delano had been dating someone else. She was from Chillicothe, and she, too, was talented. Her name was Sylvia Reedy and she was an accomplished pianist. Sylvia was hopelessly in love with Delano. In fact, she would never forget him.

What was it that ignited the spark between Sadie and the eligible bachelor from Adelphi? One wonders whether beneath Sadie's outgoing personality there may have been a latent melancholy which caused her to seek a kindred spirit, a soul which had experienced a little loneliness and loss. At age five, Sadie had written to a pen-pal, "I have a papa in heaven, no brothers or sisters."

During Delano's final year of law school, he and Sadie were seeing more of one another, and upon his graduation Sadie hosted a birthday party for him. It was at Robertson Place, and judging from the favors, it was quite elaborate. But in the fall of 1897, when the parties of summer were over, instead of looking for a job in a law office, Delano made plans to go West. Maybe this was the traditional last fling. Maybe Delano was inspired by his adventurous step-father who, in his youth, had ridden to and from Des Moines, Iowa, on an old style high-wheel cycle. There may have been another reason for Delano's trip. Dry air in Colorado was thought to be curative, and since Delano suffered from recurrent bouts of ear and throat infections, he may have gone to the mountains in an attempt to improve his health. It seems likely that Sadie and her mother encouraged the trip, because the premature death of Erskine had taught them of life's fragility. We may never know the reason, but in the fall of 1897 Delano headed west. At first he stayed in Boulder to teach courses in civics and history at the University of Colorado, but when the session ended he took to the road. He rode a bicycle and occasionally hitched train rides. He wrote in his diary about sharing a meal with hobos, sleeping in barns and camping his way into the Rocky Mountains.

Faithfully, Delano wrote letters to his dear Sadie. In each town along the way he posted his outgoing mail and sought news from home. In one of those remote locations, an eager Delano found a letter addressed to him in care of general delivery. It was in Sadie's handwriting. Would he like to spend the holidays at Robertson Place?

Unconditional Love

On a chilly December evening, Delano arrived back in Ohio. Bursting upon the scene at the Robertson Place, his pent-up energy instantly transformed the sedate scene. His manly voice filled it with new life as he strode from room to room. While open fireplaces crackled and popped with fresh logs, the scent of pine mingled with the stringent aroma of oranges and cloves. Margarite and Martha pretended to be engrossed in their Christmas baking while Sadie showed Delano to his bedroom upstairs. He would be sleeping in the room across the hall. Like the master bedroom, it had its own fireplace, and Sadie showed him where the coal was kept in the black metal coal bin, a container which she had decorated with a tole painting of blue roses. In December the brick walls of the house were cold to the touch but this room would soon feel cozy.

In January of 1898, an elated Delano wrote this to his stepbrother John:

> *Of course you know I was over at Bourneville. Went Friday before Christmas and came back to Chillicothe Monday, Jan. 3. Suffice it to say I had a delightful time—and—well, it is all over. I have admired the girl from the beginning in many ways—though I had supposed that her training and the life she had been used to would never permit us to be very intimate friends. I found I was mistaken in this—she is a girl that has had the best of everything always—college education, the best of social and etc. She is just where I would have her, having gone through it all and found what I have also found—that it is a blank and does not satisfy.*

Despite their privileges and higher learning, Sadie and Delano seemed to have sensed that their lives were somehow lacking. Furthermore, because of his chance upbringing, Delano may have felt that the love he received from his adoptive family was conditional. The thought of loving Sadie and being loved by her in return may have held for him the promise of a love deeper than any he had known.

Yet he worried about providing for Sadie.

> *When I asked her [to marry], I did not know she had a penny [of her own]—in fact she had taken the pains to give me the impression she had nothing. But I made up my mind after deliberation that I could not find such qualities combined—though I searched for them. Though I also knew it would be a struggle, I made up my mind to try to do the best. I was quite willing to wait until I could make things more comfortable. This she refused—saying if she could not be permitted to help plan, work, save and etc., that half her pleasure would be taken away from her.*

Delano spoke of a possible job in Toledo but went on to tell his step-brother John the following:

*3 days later Sadie casually remarked that Old Robertson Home Place and farm had been left to her by her grandfather and she would get it upon her grandmother's death—said she thought she would tell me and perhaps I would be interested in keeping it up, making changes and etc.......
so she is not poor by any means— though it made no difference to me—I loved her before I knew she had anything.*

The idea of ownership of the Robertson Place passing over Margarite to Sadie upon Martha Robertson's death is a bit puzzling. Perhaps there were tax advantages or a feeling that without a husband Margarite could not hope to maintain it financially or physically. However, as it turned out, her influence over the running of the place would continue until her death—sometimes at odds with her son-in-law.

In his understandable euphoria, Delano ended the jubilant letter by telling his brother of Sadie's gifts:

She gave me a handsome gold watch for Christmas, doubly valuable to her because it was her grandfather's. It is very fine and must have cost

The Women of Robertson Place

much. She said it was to be mine someday and I might just as well have it now. Also two fine volumes of Robert and Mrs. Browning.[85]

On the Eve of the Century, Sadie Weds

Sadie and Delano's engagement lasted an entire year. With parties to plan and attend, the time flew by quickly. Sadie posed for her photograph with an ivory comb in her hair and Delano took that law job in Toledo. When summer was over and the days grew shorter, Margarite and Martha flew into action.

Margarite was an enthusiastic entertainer through-out her life, but her daughter was a little more conserva-tive. Sadie asked her mother for a small wedding, one for family and a few close friends. Margarite complied, and when the invitations went out, she had every in-tention of keeping the celebration simple.

> *There will be a quiet home wedding at "Rob-ertson Place" on Wednesday, January Twenty Fifth, Eighteen Hundred and Ninety Nine at half past Ten o'clock when our Sayde Erskine Anderson will be united in marriage with Mr. Delano Wilgus Butler.*
>
> *We will be pleased to have you with us at that time.*
>
> *Mrs. Mary Margarite Anderson*

But as the day drew near, none of Robertson ladies could resist the challenge and pleasure of dressing their beloved home in all its finery. In an account published two days after the January 25th event, *The Ross County Register* described it thus:

> *Flowers of Spring Bloomed in the House,*
> *While Outside Lay the Snows of Winter*
> *The broad old reception hall of Robertson Place was transformed into a*
> *wedding chapel. The stairway was draped with tarlatan and vines, the large*

newel posts becoming white pedestals upon which were placed jardinieres of cut flowers.

The article noted that a relative played…

sweet old strains of Annie Laurie, after which pretty little Ethel Caldwell, the bride's cousin, descended the white stairway and untied the ribbons that guarded the sacred enclosure of the marriage scene. Then through avenues and archways of white and green came the official clergyman, accompanied by Hon. D.C. Anderson [Erskine's uncle] and the bridal party. The former taking their positions at the bottom of the stairway and the bride and groom halting at the third step from the floor. The white fur rugs upon floors and steps and the airy grace of the surrounding draperies formed a most fitting background for the charming picture which the young couple presented. The fair face of the bride looked especially sweet in her costume of white spray de chine, made over a lining of white silk with satin crystals and having a white lace bodice of rare value and pattern which was also worn by her mother. The lower edge of the skirt was bordered with lilies of the valley.

After describing the carved ivory fan carried by Sadie, the reporter went on to comment that the groom looked…

unusually distinguished and handsome in a dark suit relieved by a cluster of the bride's flowers upon the lapel of his coat.

After the ceremony,…

little Miss Caldwell parted the floral curtain and led the way for the bride and bridegroom to their dining-room. The bride's table was arranged with a center piece of white pressed silk and flowers above which was suspended a floral bell and above that a floral star. The guests' dining-room was profusely decorated with flowers and vines, the center decoration being a floral fountain.

Where, one might wonder, did all the flowers come from in midwinter in a world where everything had to be transported by train or horse-and-buggy? *The Register* notes that the bride's flowers were sent in from Columbus, Springfield, Chillicothe and elsewhere—presumably from greenhouses. Another excerpt from *The Register* listed items from the wedding menu:

Breakfast toast with broiled figs, orange salad, sliced turkey with steamed dressing, candied sweet potatoes, pressed chicken, oyster macaroni, celery slaw, stuffed bananas tied with ribbons, cream bread, Bavarian cream cake and coffee.

Wedding gifts were described. There was an embroidered table linen from Mrs. D.C. Anderson and a cut glass and silver set from Attorney P.S. Karshner. Margarite gave the couple a Bible, art works, china and silver. A popular gift was gold coins. Finally, there was a description of the bride's going-away gown—"blue and gray camel's hair with gray English walking coat, hat and gloves to match."

According to the *Register*, the couple headed south for their honeymoon. However, a letter sent just a week later indicated that the newlyweds did not stay long; they seemed eager to get on with things. Ending their brief tour back in Columbus at the newly rebuilt Neil House, located directly across from the State House, on hotel stationery a euphoric Sadie declared that every day was "...far happier than the last."

Part 2
1899–1945

Life in the Capital City

It was on the eve of the twentieth century that Sadie and Delano Butler began their lives in Columbus as a married couple. Delano landed a job with a law firm, and the newlyweds settled themselves into the capital city. His brief stint in Toledo had given him some initial experience in the field of law, but he never intended to put down roots there. Competition was stiffer in Columbus, but the fact that Delano was an early graduate from Ohio State's new law school made him a prime candidate.

Columbus was fifty-five miles from Robertson Place. Back then the trip would have been a major undertaking. By horse and buggy it would have taken a day; the train would not have been much better. However, it went without saying that Sadie would want to go home frequently, and her mother would expect no less. Or so Delano thought. But Margarite surprised the newlyweds—and maybe a few of her contemporaries. Soon after the wedding, she boarded a train, and headed south. Mother and daughter would not see one another until springtime when warm breezes beckoned everyone back to southern Ohio. Margarite, now past fifty, began to spend her winters in the South. For many years she stayed in tourist homes, such as the Gillis House in DeFuniak Springs, Florida, and sent her personal laundry back and forth by train to Sadie. (This habit of sending personal laundry back and forth by train was not uncommon at the time.) She also sent frequent missives to her hometown newspaper, *The Scioto Gazette*. Writing with enthusiasm about the charms of the South, she became something of a travel writer.

Martha held down the fort back in Bourneville. During wintertime, she did not like to budge. Her daughters, Sally and Virginia, stopped by to check on her from time to time, but when snow socked them in for weeks at a stretch, they relied on the village girls, Fannie and Edie, to trudge up the icy hill to check on Martha. In 1904, a telephone was installed on the wall of the dining room at Robertson Place. Its wires were strung to the road from a pole in the front yard and from then on, calls were made back and forth every day. Martha's little granddaughter, Ethel Caldwell, asked the operator to be connected to Robertson Place so that she could entertain her snowbound grandmother by playing a piece on her piano.[86]

When the wind howled and the skies were a permanent gray, Martha closed off the front rooms. In the cozy back rooms, she kept a fire going. "Bluebell jumped up in my lap just now, " she wrote to Margarite.[87] Youth was wonderful, she might have mused, but age had its advantages. Solitude on a winter's night after a bowl of soup in front of the fire, a kerosene lamp to shed light on her quilting—these were times to be savored.

From her back door Martha could see the homes of her other daughters. A reassuring light glowed through the night from Sally's house; just beyond, on Virginia's hill, Martha could just make out the steady light of a lantern. Martha sighed as she ruminated about Virginia's wedding and the marriage that had caught everyone's imagination, but turned out to be bittersweet. Leafing through the family Bible, Martha paused to read the newspaper clipping from the event. It was too bad her middle child could never settle into married life. Martha missed her own loyal and dependable husband more and more as the years passed; she missed having a male companion.

Not much of a writer herself, Martha was nevertheless treated with a steady barrage of wordy letters from her prolific daughter, Margarite. From Sadie, Martha received the occasional bit of breezy news—not about what type of household they had chosen, but about "going to housekeeping." The young bride had thrown herself into setting up her house with enthusiasm, exclaiming over the most mundane detail. She made curtains, arranged and rearranged her few pieces of furniture, and did whatever it took to establish a home away from home, all the while working to create a social life.

With ease, the newlyweds seemed to fit into the local Columbus scene, and Sadie found their new life invigorating. Though smaller in 1900 than either Cincinnati or Cleveland, the metropolis in the center of Ohio was expanding rapidly. It had no natural boundaries such as Cincinnati's Ohio River or Cleveland's Lake Erie, and on every corner was noisy construction. What would become the legendary Lazarus De-

The Women of Robertson Place

partment store was already in business and on its way to becoming a mecca for the region's shoppers. Further north of town rose the Ohio State University where educators and students gathered. At the heart of the city stood the statehouse, a Greek Revival magnet to all things political. Lawyer that he was, Delano followed politics, both local and national. William McKinley was presiding in the White House, and the nation had just extricated itself from the Spanish-American War. A mood of anti-imperialism was detected by some, but on the whole, at the turn of the century, the American spirit was one of optimism. The image of a bespectacled and vigorous Teddy Roosevelt atop his galloping horse became one of the era's icons. Most of the nation's seventy-five million residents were still involved in farming, but those who weren't tied to land were as restive as ever, striving to improve their lot by moving westward, forming new states as they went—Idaho, Wyoming and Utah.

Even so, Paris, France, continued to maintain its position as capital of the western world. Exciting things were happening there; electricity and movies were the talk of the town. Automobiles were in the developmental stage; indoor plumbing was coming to the big city; coal furnaces would soon become a prestigious luxury; and women were on the move.

In this country, just as Sadie and Delano were easing into married life, the social status of women was undergoing intense scrutiny. During a time of accelerated change—or perhaps because of it—the arbiters of American society were making it their business to remind people that a woman's place was still in the home. Never, they said, has it been more important for women to stay sheltered inside their homes because—despite the allure of city life—cities were thought to be unclean and tinged with evil. Home should be a woman's temple, especially if she had children.

Simultaneously, there appeared on the international scene a brilliant Austrian doctor named Sigmund Freud, whose writings would eventually help shape the thinking of the twentieth century. His studies of the subconscious mind revealed new and disturbing relationships between mothers and their children, focusing even more interest on this generation of energetic young women.

It is doubtful that Sadie Butler, just taking her place in society as a married woman, was influenced—or even *aware*—of such thinking. Did she consider leaving the house to work? Did she ever toy with the idea of taking her art beyond the family circle? Even during the frenetic days leading up to Sadie's wedding, she had found the time to chisel ferns and wild roses into the surface of a walnut library table. That table now sat proudly in the front hall at Robertson Place. In the parlor, in front of the hearth, stood another testament to her training, the carved fire screen on which Sadie had painted a scene of swans swimming and swallows swooping over a pond of cattails.

So why, I often wondered as I was establishing my own career as an artist, did Sadie drop her carving after she married? A contemporary of hers said she never heard Sadie even talk about her work as an artist. But then I am reminded that even though Sadie possessed far more skill and formal education than most Americans (the average level of education was only fifth grade), no one in the Butlers' sphere would have expected a lady of her standing to use this education or training for purposes outside the home. Mary Cassatt had been exhibiting her paintings in public since 1880, but to her parents, the exposure was said to have been deeply embarrassing.

I don't think Sadie was either a crusader or a pathfinder. Instead, as a young bride, she appears to have set aside her chisels and brushes and put on an apron. Perhaps she would do some charity work. In her era, more than anything else, it was important that a young matron display her skills in the domestic arts. Cooking and entertaining were essential. However, charades on a Saturday night and a roast in the oven on Sunday would pale in the light of her greatest responsibility; it went without saying that Sadie was to bear children. And as she was soon to discover, once she started a family, there would be little time for anything else.

Homecoming

As if on cue, Sadie was pregnant with their first child. Such joy she felt. Such elation the two experienced. How proud they would be to present Margarite and Martha with a grandchild. Their excitement could hardly be contained.

Everything was wonderful, except it wasn't. Delano was happy about marriage, happy about the prospect of parenthood, happy to be living in Columbus, but he was not happy at work. Perhaps it was the pressure of working for a big firm. Or maybe there was a personality clash at the office. In any case, the newly-minted lawyer wasn't thriving. With a baby on the way and before they got too ensconced in Columbus, they had better make a decision.

A plan emerged that appeared natural to most onlookers, but to their detractors it may have been interpreted as a step backward. Delano and Sadie would move back to their home territory. Letters were written and interviews set up. With connections and luck, Delano was quickly taken in by a prestigious law firm in Chillicothe.

Sadie was well along with her pregnancy by the time they moved, and not eager to traipse around in her floor length, loose-fitting garb. How lucky were they to find rooms for rent in the heart of Chillicothe! The Foulke Block stood across Main Street and just south of Ross County's impressive limestone courthouse, where Delano would soon spend countless hours. His law office at No. 7 Union Block was one block from their apartment. Directly across the street was the turreted and equally massive Carlisle Building where other lawyers had their offices. The Butlers could not have found a more convenient arrangement.

Cozy is how Sadie described their new surroundings. Despite the nature of its furnishings, the apartment would indeed have been cozy because living with them was someone they called Auntie Dunn. (I could find nothing about Auntie Dunn; perhaps she was a hired nursemaid.)

Aside from the shared space, everything else about the Foulke Block edifice was grand. Built in 1896 to replace the old Commercial Row, it was state of the art. The red brick Romanesque building spanned a full half block on South Paint Street, the main north-south business street in town. On the street level were shops, but in the lobby were ferns and chandeliers and an elegant staircase which led visitors to the second floor where doctors and other professionals rented offices. Coiled neatly in decorative brass buckets along the wide hallways were canvas fire hoses. Breezes flowed gently through transoms above each door, and on the third and fourth levels were the apartments where Sadie and Delano would make their home for several years. These apartments were the premier addresses for folks who wanted to live in downtown Chillicothe.

After the holidays, Margarite remained at Robertson Place, postponing her usual trip south in order to help Sadie when the baby arrived. Twelve miles still separated mother and daughter. Margarite probably wished she were closer to town, because during the winter, horse and buggy travel was not always possible. Still, she would stay close to home until summoned. Sadie hoped to deliver her baby right there in their apartment unless, at the last minute, the doctor needed to send her to Chillicothe's new Emergency Hospital where the delivery might cost ten dollars.[88]

A Boy Baby

On January 25, 1901, Philemon Delano Butler was born. He was the first male to be born in the family for three generations.

Lasting proof of that winter's jubilation took shape in an elaborate work of art. It was a baby quilt, and one can imagine Margarite and Martha arranging with great care the cacophony of colors into bands of chevrons, alternating them with strips of lavender silk damask. All around the perimeter, the women attached a flurry of ruffles. No timid quilt was this!

Eleven months later, Sadie seems to have settled into motherhood. "Wasn't it amazing?" she wrote her mother. "Auntie D retires early so D and I sit and read by a bright electric light while Puddin sleeps."[89]

Adjustment

As winter receded and the snow turned to mud, Sadie's and Delano's euphoria began to slacken. In the shadows, something was causing the new parents to worry. Just as was the case during Sadie's own infancy, it was the baby's father who was showing a failure to thrive.

Was it their imagination? Delano didn't seem to be hearing their son's every little coo and whimper. Sadie had to repeat herself. And over the clang of the electric trolley and the racket of the new construction, Delano was forced to cup his hand behind his ear to catch the drift of conversation. At first the couple was in denial, but by spring it was apparent that Delano was losing his hearing.

Too many untreated throat infections were beginning to take their toll. Delano had taken good care of himself, but no home remedy or doctor could have helped. A tinge of adrenalin coursed through his veins. How could this be? There was so much he planned to accomplish. Delano knew that a hearing deficit would jeopardize his ability to practice law and to argue his cases. He must go to Colorado for its curative mountain air. Quickly. If it sounded like a desperation move, it was.

Painful though it was to think of leaving Sadie and the baby, Delano knew that without his hearing their lives would be dramatically altered. All the family agreed.

Colorado, however, held no cure, and when Sadie met him at the train station, disappointment was written all over Delano's face. His condition was worse. Sadie must have found it hard to imagine, hard to accept that doctors had no cure for deafness. Together, she might have hoped, they could and would surmount this obstacle.

In reality, everyone merely adjusted. Sadie spoke a little louder, Delano listened more intently. He began to read lips. At work there was enough good will among his colleagues that the young lawyer from Adelphi was able to continue practicing law, at least for now.

During Philemon's infancy, everyone worried over his health. Margarite even persuaded Sadie to bring her grandchild south for a part of each winter. It was hard on Delano. Upon returning from the South, Sadie wrote to her mother on December 22, 1903 that she was "so glad to be home. Delano so handsome and lonely." No wonder he had missed her; Sadie could light up a room with her warmth. According to a family friend, "Sadie was the force in the marriage."[90] While down South, Sadie had missed her hometown. "I love the hustle and bustle of the North," she exclaimed. "Even in the sleet and snow, Chillicothe looks splendid."

Once again, Sadie and Delano began to dream. On Church Street where some of the city's stately brick houses stood, a developer had bought up additional property and was starting to sell modest houses on small lots. He was trying to attract first time buyers, young families like the Butlers. Sadie and Delano began to save for a house.

"Won't it be fun?" Sadie wrote to her mother. "We'll hang wallpaper in the living room and there'll be a bedroom for the baby." Well, the baby was no baby by the time the young family moved into their new house at 309 Church Street. He was five years old and ready to start school.

Summers in the Country

Letters between mother and daughter continued to go back and forth even when Margarite was in Ohio. Robertson Place was just twelve miles away, but no train tracks connected the two. In the spring of 1904 Sadie promised that when the roads were dried out she would "get a horse and come out for a visit." It would be too expensive ($1.00) to hire a horse and buggy, she said.[91]

When summer arrived in full force, Sadie's trips evolved into more than mere visits. She and little Philemon moved into Robertson Place. Philemon played with family pets, Colonel the dog and Grim the cat, while the women busied themselves with sewing, gardening, and canning. Delano joined them for weekends, and sometimes they hosted house parties.

Going to the farm meant going back in time. Sadie and Delano's new house on Church Street was plumbed for an indoor bathroom; it would soon be modern. At Robertson Place the family would continue to use the outhouse or chamber pots for another thirty years. In the city their house was fitted for electricity; at the farm the women fed wood to the old cook stove and lit the evening with kerosene lamps. Another three decades would pass before giant towers would be erected across the region's croplands in order to string the wires that would bring electricity to the countryside.

At Robertson Place, when Margarite retired after dinner to write in her bedroom, it would have been convenient for her to switch on an electric light. Instead, it was the soft glow of a kerosene lamp that continued to illuminate her copious pages of leftward slanting script.[92]

In that east bedroom, the writer slept in one of its two Victorian beds, beds that dominated the room with their tall arched and carved walnut headboards. At night, out of the room's south facing window, she could view the moon rising over Spruce

Hill. However, during the heat of the summer Margarite kept her shutters closed. Her mother had allowed ivy to envelope the exterior surfaces of the house, and the thick vegetation helped to keep it cool. If windows were raised, and if there were a breeze to billow the organdy curtains and provide the sleeping chamber with cross ventilation, Margarite could be comfortable. However, across the hall Martha suffered on nights when the heat and humidity were oppressive. They bothered her more now that she had put on some extra pounds. Oh, how Martha wished for a good night's sleep!

In 1900, people could only imagine such a luxury as a sleeping porch without the nuisance of insects. At the Robertson Place, off the dining room was a long covered porch which faced west and looked over Martha's rock garden. Wicker chairs sat lined up across its length. If the air were moving, it was here that the ladies could catch the breeze as they rocked back and forth. But at dusk the dynamics began to change. Insects dominated the night. Not all were pests, however. Cicadas filled the dark void with their steady buzzing, and although their crescendo could be deafening, these insects were benign and so much a part of the farm that, even today, the first indication of their mating season brings on a rush of nostalgia. Lightening bugs have always been welcome because they provide entertainment for the children. It was mosquitoes and June bugs and horse flies that made the Robertson ladies pick up their knitting and scurry indoors. Screens, once they were introduced for use in homes, were an instant success.

Suddenly, a sleeping porch for Martha became a possibility. Sadie, a student of the Arts and Crafts Movement, took upon herself the job of designing the room, and she began by placing four pairs of craftsman-style windows across the twelve-foot-long space. Decorative hinges and brass handles were mounted on the tall divided windows so that Martha could open the windows into the room. Then screens were custom built to fit each section and the next generation would later add storm windows.

To connect the sleeping room with the outdoor porch, yet another exterior door was required. Now every room on the first floor of the Robertson house had at least one exit, and all of them would be fitted with screen doors. These entries were not only convenient; many considered them a safety feature due to the frequency of house fires. Because of the difficulty of raising and lowering large windows for ventilation, the screened doors soon became an element of comfort and ease.

Renovating the hearth in the adjoining dining room was Sadie's last task of the summer. Already in place was one of her carved walnut mantles, this one depicting the trumpet vines which in early summer opened their orange throats along the fence lines. For the perimeter of the small coal-burning fireplace, she selected ceramic tiles of brown and gold, emblazoned with a heraldic pattern which harkened back to the medieval influence of the Arts and Crafts Movement.

Clyde's Proposal

Despite the clamor and disruption of the current remodeling project, it is hard to imagine a setting more bucolic than summer at Robertson Place during the first decade of the twentieth century. It was here that three generations now combined their efforts to care for the new male child, Philemon. But all was not calm; an outside influence was bearing down on the women. While the barefooted little boy begged for more cookies or snuck off to explore the creek bed, the aproned ladies stood about wondering, worrying.

A big decision loomed over their heads, one that would affect the Robertson Place for the next hundred years. Now that warm weather had arrived, an answer was needed. For months they had been weighing and discussing the offer that had come to Martha over the winter.

Clyde, Sadie's younger cousin, was a fixture around the place. His parents, Aunt Sally and Uncle Henry Caldwell, were attentive to Martha's needs when Margarite

and Sadie were away, and Uncle Henry was taking care of Martha's farm. It now appeared that young Clyde had designs on Robertson Place. On February 22, 1904, at the age of twenty-two and about to graduate from The College of Wooster, he sat down to write a letter.

Clyde explained to his Grandmother Martha that he must soon make a decision about his life— whether to live and work in the city or in the country. Friends were telling him to stay in the country: they say life in the city is hard and not as pleasant. Clyde thinks he would have to travel a lot to make a living. Clyde has studied agriculture in college, and he reiterated to Margarite that he is indeed serious about his request to rent and manage the Robertson farm. (Clyde had posed the idea in an earlier conversation, but apparently his grandmother has not taken the offer seriously.)

After breezily chatting about the long and cold winter weather, Clyde spelled out his terms: 1) He would lease her land (forty-seven tillable acres) for $300 per year for five years and have complete control over it; 2) For $100 per year he would have use of all six front rooms of the house—furnished. (This would include the dining and front parlors—which Clyde claimed his grandmother rarely used—the library, front hall and the two large front bedrooms, leaving his grandmother with just two smaller upstairs bedrooms and the kitchen below); 3) For an extra $50 he would get the outbuildings—barn and cottage, plus pasture and orchard; 4) He promised not to keep stock around the house, "save a cow or two, a horse, not over ten hogs and a few chickens." He also agreed to let Grandma have use of the above outbuildings, pasture and orchard for her own individual needs. Oh, and he would just use the cottage (Robert's former office and carriage barn) for storage. In addition, he asked for $25–35 yearly allowance for repair money, and he promised to "keep up the yard"—unless he decides to change it.

Margarite was furious. The arrogance of it all! Clyde's justification for his sweeping proposal is that his family's farm is next door, and he and his dad will work the two farms in tandem. He also hints that he might be getting married soon and would need assurance of income and residence. Reasoning that since Martha didn't much use the front part of the house, the arrangement he has proposed shouldn't inconvenience her. And, since his Aunt Margarite doesn't like to leave her mother there alone, but wants to go off to Washington and the South, his plan should solve everyone's problems. He is adamant, though, that there would be no deal unless he gets the use of the main part of the Robertson house.

When Margarite first heard of the offer, she had fired off letters to her mother and to Sadie. Should she return from Atlanta immediately? Must she take matters into her own hands?

Incensed as she was, Margarite did not rush home; neither did Clyde get all his requests. But Clyde's proposal jolted Margarite into rethinking the future of both the farm's management and of her mother's predicament. Martha was in her mid-seventies by now. How long would she be able to live alone at Robertson Place?

The Robertson women needed no convincing that their land needed a full time farmer and that Clyde's father Henry Caldwell was the man for the job. He was doing the job now, but as he grew older, he would need help. Delano was no farmer, and my father was later to tell me that Margarite and her son-in-law did not always see eye-to-eye on things around the homestead. Maybe Clyde, under his father's watchful eye, could be entrusted with their land, but this house deal was just too much!

The Awkward Addition

*I*t is now 1907, and workmen are standing around, leaning on their shovels, awaiting instructions. Margarite has born the onerous responsibility of making the final decision. For someone who reveres her father's memory as much as she does, the order to plunge that shovel into the earth feels almost sacrilegious. She knows an addition to the house will become an invasion of the family's privacy; an end to the old order. But she can see no other way.

Wagons laden with new wood and gravel begin to rumble up the hill. Hammers fly and saws jerk back and forth. On the east side of the Greek Revival house, carpenters construct a frame addition—a two-room apartment for Clyde and his bride. This, plus the adjoining front parlor of the main house, will comprise their home for a number of years.

From an aesthetic standpoint, the addition was a complete failure; it was a conglomeration of period styles which no self-respecting architect could have condoned. Although the main house was not pure in architectural style—its Italianate cornices were there from the beginning—it retained a coherent sense of design and dignity. But as the apartment took shape, everything seemed to fall apart. Although it was set back from the main house's brick facade, and its entrances out of view, a long sloping shed roof spanning front to back was a quizzical choice and strangely incongruous. Furthermore, to disguise this unattractive feature, the builders added a false front, the kind that reminds one of dusty towns out west where the boardwalks are lined with cowboy saloons. Then, as an afterthought, or perhaps as a nod to the parent house, someone thought to add matching Italianate corbels under the shallow eaves of the false front. The overall effect was nearly comical.

In the end, it mattered not so much what the addition looked like or how many rooms it had. Here is how a society columnist from the *Gazette* described the changes: "Old Robertson Place, long the retreat for college girls and boys, has been refitted and furnished by Mr. Caldwell, the wall paper forest scene in the east parlor being especially attractive."[93]

To Margarite's relief, the newlyweds, Clyde and Wilhelmina Hemphill, brought their youth and charms to bear on the management of the Robertson Place. They were college sweethearts. She came from South Charleston, Ohio, and brought a sense of style to the union. Clyde was full of confidence. And when Margarite was away, Martha was relieved to have someone else take the reins. By 1910, when a census worker knocked at the door with a clipboard in his hand, he was told that Clyde Caldwell was now the head of this household.

On a Roll

Clyde's enthusiasm spilled over into his father's realm, and the young man soon convinced his father to build a new barn. Since they were farming three farms with a total of nearly six-hundred acres, Clyde pushed for a big one. Finished in 1908, the barn was situated across the creek on Caldwell property, but it would tower over the land. People took notice. There was plenty of work for Clyde, but the young man's energy and enthusiasm seemed boundless. He was always coming up with innovative new schemes.

Selling baby chicks was one of those ideas. At Robertson Place, Robert's old cottage/barn became the headquarters for Clyde's new enterprise. Ordered by mail, dozens of fertilized chicken eggs soon arrived in boxes at Bourneville's post office. Clyde lit a kerosene heater to warm the eggs to the ideal temperature of one-hundred degrees, mimicking the warmth of the mother hens. Exactly three weeks later, the suspense was broken. First one, then another, and suddenly the entire box was alive with the sound of cracking eggs. Tiny, high-pitched peeps filled the air as the chicks broke from their dark chambers into the light. Dozens, then hundreds, then thousands of chickens gulped their first breath of air, took their first wobbly steps in Squire Robertson's former law office.

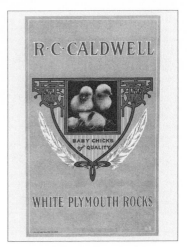

Clyde was on a roll. He told the census taker he was a poultry farmer, made up a brochure with pictures and pep talks, even hired a stenographer. As his secretary, Anna George, age twenty, would board with the family and keep up with the business records.

Disaster hit in the spring of 1911 when the incubators overheated, killing thousands of unborn chicks. In frustration and disgust, Clyde dumped the ruined mess over the hill. Decades later neighbors claimed they never forgot the stench.

It was an ignominious ending to a glorious run, and Clyde, the college graduate, became the butt of country humor. Jokes sprang up about the futility of book learning. While Clyde was scratching his head and coming up with his next scheme, Wilhelmina was having babies. One after another, they came: Louis, Wilson, John and Philip Caldwell. All four boys are thought to have been born in that small apartment attached to the Robertson Place.

Baby Sister, Shooting Rats, Family's First Car

Back in the city, Sadie and Delano were also adding to their family. On April 13, 1908, and just as the couple was about to move into their new home on Church Street, Sadie delivered a baby girl. In Bourneville, the thrilling news set Margarite and Martha to work again on another baby quilt. In contrast to Philemon's, this one was pieced together with a field of richly colored tiny silk cushions bordered by a row of pink triangles. To her doting family, Marian was a princess.

Shooting rats was what interested her brother, not a baby sister. Unlike the delicate newborn, Philemon, now seven, was all boy. He could play the role of

big brother, but in his letters to Martha, whom he called Grandma Robbie, he wrote not a single word of his new sister. Instead, he bragged of his exploits and regaled his grandparent with tales of capturing rabbits and toads.

Meanwhile, during that year of Marian's birth, 1908, Henry Ford introduced his Model T car. So while Sadie occupied herself with the new baby, father and son poured endlessly over newspaper ads of the Model T. As it turned out, Delano Butler could more than dream about owning such a wonder because at this time lawyers were earning even more than physicians.

In a photograph of Robertson Place made some three or four years later, Marian and her bother are pictured in the family's first car. Delano is seated nearby with the family's Spaniel. Friends are posed on a twig-style bridge that led over a gully to the creek. Philemon is smiling from ear-to-ear as he holds on to the steering wheel. Has he just been squeezing the rubber ball to make the horn go "ah-ooo-gah, ah-ooo-gah?"

A horseless, open carriage is what the family's first car looked like. It had neither a hard top nor doors. What it did have was a motor. However, a great deal of skill was needed to master the new-fangled contraption. If Delano did not crank the handle correctly, he risked injury. The motor, struggling to ignite, would sound like the low growl of some unknown farm animal. Over and over it would strain to produce combustion, but if Delano did it right, after a series of sputters, clicks and cracks, a spark would finally ignite and the engine would rumble into life. Once started, the Model T could go most anywhere. It carried its passengers over rocky dirt lanes, steep hills, muddy roads and shallow streams.

Owning a car marked a change in the Butlers' life, as it did for many Americans. After Mr. Ford perfected his assembly line, it wasn't long until cars were quite affordable and considered a necessity. So fast did people abandon their horses that the Ross County Humane Society had to protect many of the animals from neglect. American culture would never be the same.

Family Portraits

A time-honored way to mark a family's affluence was the family portrait. As soon as Marian was able to hold still long enough for a photographer to expose his glass plate, the Butlers took their children to a studio. Against an ethereal landscape painted in oil, the photographer arranged them into a formal pose.

Domestic life in the Butler family continued to intensify. Once again, Sadie was pregnant. Wilgus Anderson Butler, born May 23, 1911, proved to be a hearty child. He

loved the out-of-doors—especially the farm. He became particularly close to his father, and the two made their rounds in the Model T when big brother was in school. Soon after Wilgus began to talk, he sensed that in order to be heard he must speak directly into his father's ear. It became the little boy's habit to stretch his arms up to Delano to signal that he had something to tell him.

"The Noblest Woman I Ever Knew"

Martha Robertson embraced her new great-grandchild with a natural love and curiosity, but Wilgus would prove to be her last. On August 23, 1911, only three months after Wilgus was born, Martha did not awaken. From her obituary, friends learned that:

Mrs. Robertson seemed to have been in most excellent health on Saturday and Sunday and when she retired Sunday night. It is supposed that an attack of heart failure caused her death during the night. It had been her custom to arise very early in the morning, and when she did not arise, her daughter suspected something was wrong, and going to her room, found her mother dead.[94]

Martha Poole Robertson had lived a long life—eighty-one years. Born in a log house on the other side of the creek, this grandchild of pioneers took her first steps before Bourneville came into existence. When Mr. Bourne arrived in the settlement with his saddlebags of surveying tools, Martha watched from her father's arms as the man from Pennsylvania plotted the little town that was to be her home. Bourneville grew until it sprouted a hotel and a saloon, but Martha lived long enough to see her township vote that saloon right out of business. (In 1910, eight years before prohibition was enacted, Twin Township voted itself dry and would stay dry for over a century.) Martha could not vote for the nation's president, but she watched one of her daughters graduate from college.

During her lifetime Martha never lived more than a mile from her birth-place. She navigated her world by foot, traveled a little further by horse and buggy or train, and perhaps took a ride in Delano's motorcar. By just one year did the octogenarian miss seeing an airplane fly over Chillicothe.

As a child, Martha was on hand to watch the masons set the first bricks of what would eventually become Robertson Place. She knew the house when the ill-fated Prather family lived in it, back when it was a simple four-room house that faced west. After cholera struck down the Prather family and left only two standing, Martha watched in awe as a swarm of masons began to add more rooms and two sets of columns. Suddenly the house faced south and was a large and stately country home.

Then came the vivid years, when Robert was in his prime and her family moved into the big house. She'd held weddings for two of her daughters on its front lawn and hosted many a church social under the trees. Only just recently had the controversial apartment been added. What an effrontery! How, she had wondered, would that ever turn out?

Even though she identified herself with the property, if truth be told, Martha might have admitted that the best years were those she spent in the first little house, the one that sat right on the pike in Bourneville. Those were the days when her mother-in-law, with her soft Southern accent, lived with the family and set the tone in the Robertson household. It was in that simple clapboard house that Martha had started married life at the age of seventeen, run barefoot, and given birth to three daughters. Four—if one were to count little Jane.

After Martha's death, her sister Asenath had this to say in a letter to Margarite: "Your mother [Martha] was the noblest woman I ever knew. When I was a child I was in her home so much, [and] as a home maker she was perfect. I never heard a cross word ever spoken in the Robertson house."[95]

Queen Victoria was the icon people conjured up when they pictured Martha Robertson. In the thirty years after Robert's death, Martha wore her hair in a no-nonsense style, cut short and combed down each side from a central part. The simple hairstyle revealed Martha's forehead, just as it had the famous queen's, and might have misled strangers to think she was a bit stern. Small spectacles were always perched on Martha's nose. A short woman, Martha had grown stout over the years until she was forced to alter her clothing. At first she let out her skirts and petticoats to accommodate her expanding girth, but when that was not enough, she added sashes to breach the gap. Martha lived most of her life after the industrial revolution, but of the garments she passed down to her daughter, all except two were handmade. The two exceptions, both formal and black, were a fine "store-bought" silk taffeta cape, and a stole with jet beading.

Robertsons, Andersons, Butlers, Caldwells, and friends—all gathered at the Robertson home to bid goodbye to the matron they had known all their lives. A subdued Margarite orchestrated her mother's ceremony and then climbed into a buggy to lead the cortège to Lattaville and the cemetery at Concord Church.

Concord Church was becoming more and more familiar to Margarite, and after dealing with the lawyers and accountants—a process with which she was all too familiar—she returned alone in order to come to grips with her feelings.

She loved the church and its hillside burial site. It held the memories of Chautauqua and the tombs of her father, her mother, and her husband. What could she do for the lonely, remote setting?

Over the next few years Margarite hired an architect to design a pergola for the church entrance. Its covered walkway would welcome and protect the parishioners from the weather as they disembarked from their buggies or automobiles. Also needing help were the hillside grounds. The tombstones seemed neglected as they baked in the afternoon sun. Margarite brought a landscape designer from Dayton to offer suggestions, and Clara Edgington, a young lady from the congregation, met him at the train. Trees were the answer, he said. Margarite paid for a grove of seventeen spruce trees to be planted near the bell tower and around the perimeter of the cemetery, where today they tower above the burial ground, offering shade and shelter.

Reinventing a Life

While Margarite was immersed in the Concord Church improvements, back in town, Sadie and Delano were trying to come to terms with a recurring problem. It was Delano's hearing again. His world was slipping further and further away.

A great deal of Delano's time was spent speaking with clients and listening (or trying to listen) to court proceedings. Precision of the spoken word was vital to his profession. How could he go on being an attorney? It was no longer a question of being hard of hearing. Painful to admit, Delano was going deaf.

It turned out that the orphan from Adelphi had quite a few ideas for life without his law practice. He'd watched his adoptive father pitch hay, make loans, develop land and sell things. Delano Butler would attempt all of these vocations and more.

Farming might have been a natural occupation for anyone in Delano's straits, not because it suited him particularly, but because farmers could turn a profit. His wife's family had land, and it was good land. The Caldwells were currently under contract to manage the small Robertson farm; however, there was another problem—his mother-in-law.

Almost from the beginning, Margarite and Delano seemed to clash. Maybe it was a case of jealousy, having to share Sadie. In a letter written during the winter of 1902–3, Margarite had accused Delano of going around mad all the time. She seemed to blame her new son-in-law for "ruining everything." To be fair, in Margarite's eyes no man could ever measure up to her father, Robert Robertson. Eventually, the entire family agreed that the two would never see eye-to-eye, especially about farming. So Delano made the rounds, discussing farm issues with the neighbors, and looking at some potential ways to add acreage. But he kept his distance from the day-to-day running of the family farm, where Clyde and Henry were in charge. For this he would have to bide his time.

Margarite Goes to Washington

At the same time, Margarite was making plans of her own. Soon after she buried her mother, Margarite moved to Washington, D.C., where she began to devote her time and efforts to several causes. At first glance, for a single woman of her times to travel to a big city might seem to have been a daunting—not to mention expensive—undertaking. For the next eight years, each fall Margarite would make that trip. Somewhere in a boarding house she would arrange a desk and begin her writing. There she churned out patriotic lyrics while working as recording secretary for the Department of Songs, International. The Boy Scouts of America and Red Cross also claimed her attention, and she gave them large contributions. Closest to her heart, however, may have been the Old Soldiers' Home. This home stood next to the National Cemetery and its grounds were the site of President Lincoln's summer cottage during the Civil War. It was a place to which the beleaguered or depressed president could escape from the heat of the city to collect his thoughts. After the war it was this cottage that was converted into a retirement home for veterans.

Margarite may have visited with some of the men at the Old Soldiers's Home—some who might have fought alongside her husband Erskine in nearby Monocacy. It appears that she spent time with Mr. Robert Fleming, one of the home's architects and benefactors, because Margarite and Mr. Fleming later carried on a lengthy cor-respondence about plans for improvements to the home.[96]

While Margarite was in Washington, in Ohio Delano was casting around for other ways to make a living. First it was the business of selling furniture. At 37 Mulberry Street in Chillicothe, Delano Butler, along with a partner by the name of Ewing, opened a store dealing in furniture and heating stoves. Such heating devices were popular and became the standard means for warming rooms which lacked fireplaces. In the Mulberry Street store were also pianos, breakfronts, and, in some cases, fine antiques. Harkening back to his stepfather's banking experience, Delano decided to start a loan service. Soon Sadie stepped up to give her husband a hand; she would help him with his books.

Life in the Butler household took on a new rhythm. Marian started school in the fall of 1914. She wore a new plaid dress made by her mother over the summer and walked to the elementary school on the corner of Cherry and Mill Streets. Sadie's letters from this period are filled with details of the children's social lives. Marian attended a birthday party nearly every week, it seemed, and Philemon was proving to be a fine student. He became a leader in his class, and Wilgus, now three, needed lots of attention.

Sadie Butler's days must have been quite full. In addition to running the house-hold and helping her husband start a new business, she did volunteer work. The Ross County Garden Club was a big part of her life, as was her church, the Walnut Street United Methodist Church in Chillicothe. As a member of this church, Sadie did charity work. Energetic and popular, the gregarious young mother allowed her-self an occasional day with her beloved sewing circle where she could laugh and commiserate among friends.

Summers at Robertson Place, winters in the city—this was the rhythm of Sadie's life. In a year or two she planned to add wallpaper to her little house on Church Street. And a bathroom! "Won't it be grand?" she wrote to her mother. For the home place in Bourneville, she and Delano planned to add a "fine cement bridge and re-paint all our buildings." There would be budgets to keep and maybe she wouldn't spend so much on clothes; these were the topics of her letters to Margarite. Until, all of a sudden, things changed.

War Fever

*I*t is 1914. In the nation's capital, on July 26, Margarite wakes up to startling headlines in *The Washington Times*:

WAR DECLARED; ALL EUROPE IN TURMOIL

Europe's treaties are breaking. First it is Austria-Hungary and Germany, then Russia, France, and Belgium. In August, Britain declares war on Germany. In the heart of America, in Chillicothe, Ohio, the newspapers and the people next door talk of the menace abroad. They are relieved to learn that President Wilson vows our neutrality. Nevertheless, there is growing unease.

For the next two years, Sadie fought to keep the war at a distance. But when Margarite returns to Ohio, an exasperated Sadie writes to her mother on February 8, 1917:

> *Do not hear much else but WAR. Aren't you more thankful every day that we each have our quiet homes all safe and hid away? All our pleasure will be centered in the two homes, going back and forth. We can take Thurs. to rest and talk, and Fri. to plan and cut out; then in town Mon., and with the cutting out done, can start to sew Tues. Then by the time you go home I will start housecleaning, and expect you will too. Won't we enjoy it. To have both places clean, cool and restful, and all enjoy both. What more need we want?*

Margarite left the nation's capital to return to Robertson Place, but she did not leave behind the affairs of the world. Her writing cries out for peace. War fever affects her grandson Philemon differently. Now a junior in high school and editor of the school's newspaper, Philemon and his friends are talking of nothing but war. On August 6,

1917, the United States declares war on Germany and President Wilson announces a draft. Philemon and his friends suit themselves up as cadets, and Philemon becomes their captain. The entire town is abuzz about a training camp nearby. A whopping nine million dollars will be spent to establish this training center for soldiers, just north of the city, and it will be called Camp Sherman.

Just by a hair, Philemon Butler missed his only chance to serve in the war that would remain for most Americans "over there." On November 11, 1918, Germany signed the armistice, and in the following spring, Sadie and Delano's elder son donned his cap and gown and graduated at the top of his class as valedictorian.

Nearly coinciding with the war's end was the Great Influenza Pandemic. Although historians disagree about the origin of the disease, just weeks before the November armistice, it erupted at Camp Sherman. By the time it had run its course near the end of October, 11,000 of the camp's population had contracted the disease, and

1,177 were to perish.[97] According to Pat Medert, author of *Chillicothe, Ohio and the Great War, 1914–1918*, "The overwhelming number of dead (in just five days, October 5 to 9, 555 patients died) made it impossible for the quartermaster to keep up. He solved the problem by setting up a morgue in Chillicothe's Majestic Theatre, which had just reopened after undergoing renovations. Embalming was done on the stage, and seats were removed to make room for the coffins."[98] Many years later, Philemon told me he had seen a rivulet of blood running from the theater into the street.

Chillicothe was quarantined. Unlike most other diseases, this highly contagious flu took the hale and hearty. Presumably, Sadie took the younger children to the farm in Bourneville, but there was no escape. More than likely, it was the flu that in 1918 took the life of Sadie's beloved cousin, Ethel Caldwell, who had been flower girl for her wedding and who lived next door to Robertson Place.

War was indeed grim, and it took its toll on Delano. Perhaps during the conflict nobody was in the mood for buying furniture, but it is more likely that the opposite was true. Camp Sherman had became a conduit for money flowing into the region, and it may have brought in so much business to the Buckeye Furniture Company that Delano was overwhelmed. His future son-in-law would say that Delano didn't like to delegate work and was too perfectionistic to be an effective business man. Over the distance of time it is impossible to say what was the cause, but in 1919, Delano collapsed with a "nervous breakdown."[99]

Doctors advised the Butlers to leave the city and move back to the farm. It is unlikely that the family gave up their Chillicothe residence because at least Wilgus continued to attend school in the city. Their eldest, Philemon, moved to Columbus where he would enroll in civil engineering at Ohio State University, and there is some evidence that Marian might have gone with him to attend a junior high school nearby. Delano turned the day-to-day running of the furniture business over to his partners and retained a part ownership. Once again this man from Adelphi would prove his resilience. Despite his continuing conflict with his mother-in-law, Delano began to think about agriculture.

Meanwhile, Margarite was back in residence at Robertson Place, and at seventy-three, she was still a rather imposing character. Her granddaughter Marian was later to write about her grandmother, "I remember her as a handsome, rather formidable old lady, in complete command of every household and social situation. She lived with us toward the end of her life, and my most vivid image of her is sitting at her desk, writing interminably. We all loved her, though were always a little ill at ease in the presence of her great dignity and competence."[100]

Settling into the large front bedroom on the east side of the house, Margarite continued to carry on what Marian describes as "voluminous correspondence with relatives and friends throughout the entire country." But the war and its aftermath were never far from her thoughts. Margarite kept up a steady output of poems and songs, the theme of which was world peace and the League of Nations. Nevertheless, one hopes that the aging writer found time to pay attention to her eleven-year-old granddaughter because, nearly a century later, I was told by a contemporary of Marian's that she "idolized" her grandmother.[101]

Investing in Farmland

While Margarite wrote and Delano tended his interests, the center of gravity of the Butler household slowly shifted from Chillicothe to Bourneville. The family continued to straddle both worlds, but life during the 1920s would be centered at Robertson Place.

In 1920, Delano purchased the 240-acre Burgess farm just a mile north of the home farm, and in its large brick house he would install a tenant. Soon Delano is raising crops and animals—hogs, cattle, sheep, grains, wheat, soybeans, rye, dairy products, and nuts. In the first year alone, his sheep produced 850 pounds of wool. His arrangement with the tenant went this way: the tenant was to provide all the labor, machinery, and baling supplies. The owner, meanwhile, was to pay the taxes and provide—in addition to the land and house—the out buildings and fencing, plus the materials and labor for repairs to those fences and buildings, including the tenant house. Shared would be the expense of seed, fertilizer, feed, livestock, and the profit of crops and animals produced. As befitting a lawyer, everything is spelled out. For example, "milk from four cows to be separated, cream sold, skim fed to pigs, and no manure to be hauled away."[102]

A few years later, in 1923, Delano bought an additional sixty acres of bottom land in Bourneville. These fertile acres adjoined the twenty-eight that were to be part of Sadie's inheritance, and their fertility would become legendary. Bulletins in the *Gazette* claimed the corn stalks on Delano Butler's farm to be over fifteen-feet tall.[103] In time, along with his son Philemon as partner, Delano would purchase another ten acres above Bourneville which they intended to divide into residential lots. Farm records show that Delano Butler would eventually pay taxes on four-hundred acres.

Leaving her Mark

While Delano was beginning to hit his stride, Margarite was in decline. On February 9, 1921, due to an "unknown chronic disease," Mary Margarite Anderson, took her last breath. Favored by her father in childhood and loved by a young man cut down in his prime, she lived the bulk of her life as a widow. No further romance left its trace.

Although she may have been ill-prepared for her responsibilities, Margarite Anderson did not play the victim. Instead, she got an education, taught school, and published songs and poems. Although she took seriously her role as mother and manager of Robertson Place, she found the time to give to the world her best efforts. Perhaps the most fitting summary of her professional life appeared as a feature in the trade journal *Musical Progress*, dated October 1912. A panoramic photo of Robertson Place headed the story in which the author claimed the site was where Margarite Anderson had written her song "International Anthem of Peace." He went on to describe her as:

> . . . *a little woman with big ideals and high aims wrapped up in her song writing, and with one object ahead—to write songs true to life, that everyone, rich and poor alike, can enjoy—songs of Life, Love and Happiness, that really better mankind.*
>
> . . . *This broad-minded woman is making, in fact, has already made, a name for herself. Her works enjoy a good, healthy sale, which promises to be*

permanent, because whatever she has to say, she says in a clear, clean way that everyone can understand.[104]

Over the years Margarite Anderson left her mark in a number of ways. Aside from her book of quotations, titled *Cabinet of Blue and Purple and Gold*,[105] she wrote

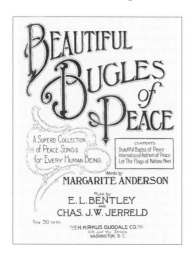

several newspaper articles and numerous poems. Perhaps she was proudest of her songs, especially her "Beautiful Bugles of Peace" and "The Temple Choir." She also used her pen to correspond with a number of government officials and, if agitated, could fire off a blistering letter, such as the one she wrote to the Secretary of the Navy imploring him to keep the Sabbath holy. She took pride in her work. She bound her poems in leather and procured copyrights from the Library of Congress. However, all of these efforts are today nearly forgotten. To her family, Margarite's legacy was the fierce love she felt for Robertson Place. In a letter to her daughter, she wrote:

> *I hope, my dear, that you will not let this land mold you as it has molded me. I love it too deeply to leave it now. But it absorbs all my affections, all my loyalty, all my substance. Away from it, I lose my identity, and must keep returning. I am married to it, and engulfed by it. I have not the strength nor the money to do with it what I would, yet it binds me to it forever.*[106]

In the lull that befell Robertson Place after the funeral, Sadie finished collecting the mementos of her mother's life. Into a cavernous trunk she packed away precious keepsakes, such as the tiny snippet of her father's hair which her mother had carried throughout her life in a tiny grey silk purse. And her father's shaving kit, from the days he served as a soldier in the War Between the States, went into that trunk. After tying up a collection of precious letters in satin ribbons, Sadie paused to fold up her mother's diaphanous wedding gown. Finally, she lowered the lid and dragged the heavy trunk into a spare room where it gathered dust. Years later, someone moved it to the attic of the wash house and the trunk was all but forgotten.

The Women of Robertson Place

Moving On

A kind of lethargy set in at Robertson Place following Margarite's death: she had so loved the place. In time, the Butler family regained its balance and started to make plans for the future, a future without the omnipresence of their strong-minded elder. Delano was the first to move on. With salvaged wood from Camp Sherman, he built a new barn in the pasture of Robertson Place. His was modest in size, and meant only to shelter livestock, a tractor, and hay. Sadie, for her part, began to dream about remodeling the farmhouse. When would it get an indoor bathroom?

Elsewhere, Americans were preoccupied with other things. It was an era of great social change. Conflict over alcohol and voting rights rocked the nation and captured the headlines. Twin Township had banned the sale of alcohol in 1910, but on January 16, 1919, prohibition became the law of the land. Women were making the news. So passionate were the suffragettes about their right to vote that some staged hunger strikes in Washington, and others were thrown into jail. Finally, after decades of struggle, on August 18, 1920, the 19th amendment was at last ratified and the women of America gained the right to vote.

No doubt the ladies of Robertson Place celebrated the news along with the suffragettes, although there is no solid evidence that they worked to advance this cause. The same is true for the temperance movement, which had a significant resurgence back in 1873 in Hillsboro. Nevertheless, in other regions of the country prohibition caused defiance, and alcohol became increasingly popular. Women began to imbibe in public.

Far reaching changes such as these helped loosen the constraints on Americans, and gave them an increasing sense of freedom during the 1920s. Young women began to bob their hair and shorten their skirts. After the long and repressive Victorian era, people were ready to relax—to the point that Emily Post found it necessary to remind Americans of their manners. So unpopular was Prohibition that "speak-easies" could be found in most of our cities where people were now shopping and buying on credit. It was a time of prosperity and optimism.

But in Bourneville, and indeed in most of rural America, a more modest lifestyle prevailed. Many in the Paint Valley region found their fun in a celebration of summer, the county fair. Over the years folks had gathered at the fairgrounds to compare their biggest ear of corn, their fastest horse, and their best apple pies. But in 1920, and for a few years thereafter, the fair in Ross County was suspended due to the lack of willing organizers and appropriate sites. To take its place, the Butlers and their friends organized an alternative entertainment, the Bourneville Fish Fries.[107]

The Bourneville Fish Fries

From 1920 through 1926, the Bourneville Fish Fries were held at Robertson Place in its lower pasture, which was a cool and shady expanse that ran along Lower Twin Creek. It was a place where the Butler family often spread a quilt for a picnic before wading in the shallow creek bed. It was a place where local children looked for mushrooms and chased fireflies. Shaded by towering cottonwoods and located within view of the church on the corner, it had been the scene of many a class picnic and ice cream social and had acquired a name of its own—Butler's Grove.

Here is what a newspaper clipping (of unknown source) had to say about the Bourneville Fish Fry of 1924:

> It was a success in every way and cleared $150. The Rainsboro band discoursed music, the Down East Minstrels gave a program, Hon. Harry Day, state treasurer, gave a talk about taxes. Hon. Edwin Ricketts of Logan, former member of Congress, gave a eulogy of the late President [Harding], which was very appropriate at this time. There were contests of different kinds, the prizes being donated by the merchants of Chillicothe. There was a ball game in the evening between the Methodist men and the woodmen. There were over 300 automobiles and no account was kept of the visitors. Almost every town in the county was represented. It is the plan now to make the homecoming an annual affair.

The following year's crowd was larger. "BOURNEVILLE MARKS UP RED LETTER DAY IN HER ANNALS," declared the headlines in the city's newspaper on August 5, 1925. The *Gazette* reported that Bourneville, the unincorporated hamlet in Twin Township and a community of less than 200, entertained and fed more than 6,000 visitors at the free, one-day "Fair and Fish Fry" in Butler's Grove. "That all this was brought about to so high a degree of perfection," claimed the reporter, "lies largely to the credit of Mr. D. W. Butler, who was the manager...".

Over seventy years later, there were some old-timers who still remembered either the event itself or the stories told about the fabled Fish Fries. Ed Steele, (1915–2003), recalled the running races which were divided into age groups or marital status. Prizes included a lady's union suit, bottles of auto polish, or a kettle and lid. Winner of the fat man's race won an inner tube, and the prize for the fat lady's race was a salad bowl. There were even more races: a three-legged race, a sack race, and an egg race. Fred Bowers stood on his head for thirty-one minutes. Women could test their mettle in a nail pounding contest, and men liked to see who could be the fastest to change a horseshoe. Mr. Steele remembered that Wilgus Butler had walked the tight-rope. Near the end of the fair, the boys always tried to climb a greased pole or to catch a greased pig. Such were the events which, in those days, caused great hilarity.[108]

"Our Little Boy is Gone"

Wearing an apron, Sadie helped flip the fish over the fire at the annual event in Butler's Grove. Under the shade of the towering cottonwoods, Delano, his poor hearing a handicap, kept a more reserved stance, but all three of the Butler children—even the collegiate Philemon—were in the hub of the Fish Fry festivities. Marian was beginning to flirt with the boys, and Wilgus could be found with a gang of boys in tow.

It was during these times, these warm halcyon days of summer, that an unthinkable tragedy struck. Marian was fourteen at the time. Her older brother was twenty-two, and Wilgus was eleven. Thirty years later, Marian would write:

> One late May afternoon in 1922, we all went swimming in a shallow
> part of Paint Creek just below the cornfields. What followed is burned indeli-

bly into my consciousness. We undressed quickly in the heavy hedge planted
as a protection against flood waters. The cool water felt good to our hot bod-
ies. The boys dived. I did not swim well, and was more cautious. Suddenly,
like a shadow cast by a momentary cloud, we knew something was wrong.
The water still eddied lazily, the hum of insects still filled the air—but we
were two where a moment before we had been three.[109]

On the bottom of Paint Creek, in the languid body of water whose flooding had
for a millennia replenished the bottom land, lay Sadie's and Delano's son.

Delano sat up all night, a pen rigid in his fingers.
At last, he found the words to spell out his grief.

Wilgus had a most lovable disposition—
all his playmates were his friends—always
ready to give more than he exacted, he en-
deared himself to them all.

He loved the outdoors; during our stay
in town he was not entirely happy, and was
continually talking of the farm. We came
to the farm April 1st, and here together we
spent two of the happiest months of our lives;
during which time while working together
we made our plans for future farm work and
betterments as two men might have done.

Our little boy is gone; no more on earth
shall I feel his eager arms clasp 'round my
neck, his eager lips pouring words into my
ears, patiently repeating when I did not hear.[110]

What parent can ever recover from the loss of a
child? Sadie never did. Her grief prevented her from
ever entering the child's bedroom, a room that was
never supposed to be empty. According to her son-
in-law, Sadie could never bring herself to remove Wilgus's clothing, the well-worn
baseball mitt, or his favorite game of jacks.

As the shock began to wear off, Sadie and Delano started the process of healing. Their long marriage became their solace. Sitting side by side, they shared a book. Visitors reported that Sadie read aloud to her nearly-deaf husband. It seemed to be a ritual for the mourning couple. They drew strength and comfort from the close proximity of their bodies, and Delano, if only faintly, may have been able to feel the resonance of the words he was sight reading along side her.

Although her *joie de vivre* was gone forever, Sadie would eventually re-enter the social fabric of the community. But from this time on, even though her friends considered her to be the central force in the Butler marriage, Sadie gained a reputation for being more quiet and reserved.[111]

Meanwhile, Philemon dropped out of school at Ohio State. He took a job teaching fifth-grade children in nearby Massieville. Marian, shocked to her core, needed to prepare to enter high school in Chillicothe.

In Bourneville, Delano turned his attentions to the Methodist church at the bottom of their drive, where Sadie's grandfather Robertson had been superintendent. Its congregation now drew the Butlers back into their fold by asking Delano to become its superintendent, a position he would fill for the next twenty-five years. Two years later he would persuade the church to build an annex.

A New School in Bourneville

Waiting in the wings was something else to distract the Butlers from their grief. In 1923 the township decided to build a new school for its growing population. Especially needed was a new high school. Where would they put it? Back in 1889 a one-room high school had been constructed across from the Twin Township cemetery on Virginia McCord's farm. Because of its location in the middle of a crop field, the townspeople nicknamed it Cornfield College. Sometime later, probably around 1910–12, the village fathers decided to move it closer to the village. According to Ed Steele, a team of men lifted it from its foundation and rolled it on logs down the dirt pike which is now U.S. Route 50. Around the corner on Upper Twin, the men set it down beside the church's new annex and across from Robertson Place. Subsequently, a four-room building was built two doors away. So a string of four buildings—these two plus two other older structures—comprised the township's entire school system. Still, they needed more room. In 1923, the school board picked a site to build a new school which could eventually house all the grades. That site was up the road a bit, smack in the middle of the Butler's crop field.

When the request to buy some acreage arrived in St. Cloud, Florida (where it became Sadie's and Delano's custom to vacation during the winter), there was immediate consternation. The thought of carving up the home farm was quite upsetting, especially to Sadie. They owned considerable acreage surrounding the village, but this particular site was only a stone's throw from their farmyard where they pastured the milk cow, housed their chickens and stored their corn. If built here, the school would be too near, too noisy, too everything. By this time Philemon had re-entered the university and was redirecting his focus. Law was to be his life's work. When the young law student learned of his parents' predicament, he offered assistance. Letters were fired back and forth among him, his parents, and the school board. The Butlers did not want to sell. An idea was floated to the board of education. Would they accept some property across the road at no cost—free for the taking?

No, came the reply. The board wanted to build on the east side of Upper Twin where it would be better located for disposal of the school's sewage into a new septic tank near the little Twin tributary. Unlike the property on the other side of the road, which was hemmed in by church-owned property, it held the possibility of future expansion.

It was a losing battle. Everyone was aware that the public, via the legal action of eminent domain, could obtain the property by demand. In the end, Sadie resigned herself to the inevitable. Rather than go to court, she would sell 2.9 acres of the farm she had inherited, a parcel just big enough to build the needed high school. In return for her token price of $3.00, Sadie asked that, if ever the property were no longer needed by the school board, it would be returned to the Butler estate. I was to learn this from friends and neighbors much later: at the time of the sale, apparently Sadie did not insist on a legal contract. It was a "gentleman's agreement."

Construction began immediately. When the Butlers returned home, they encountered chaos and noise which continued until a massive brick structure stood in their view. Life at Robertson Place took on a new reality. Fences were added, and farm machinery diverted. Trees were planted in strategic locations so as to obstruct its view. Over the years, as the farmhouse was expanded and remodeled, care was taken to avoid placing windows which might expose a glimpse of the school house. Such was the effect of the board of education's decision of 1923.

And yet, when fall approached and children were pulling on socks over their calloused feet, and, if they were lucky, lacing up a new pair of shoes, Sadie and Delano could no longer resist the community's excitement. It was a big deal for Bourneville. As people who had always championed the benefits of education, it was not long before the Butlers counted themselves among the school's biggest backers. Even though their own children would not be among its pupils, over the years Sadie and Delano Butler gave not only their property, they gave their time, their energy, and their ideas to after-school activities, such as 4-H and the popular Farmer's Institute.

Marian

During these years, the Butlers still had obligations in the city. They fell into a pattern of spending most weekends in the country, returning to the city during the week. It is now Marian's senior year in high school, and their daughter requires supervision. Marian is quite social; she has many friends in both places. Marian *dates* boys in both places. In her new red diary she recounts going to the movies, to high-school sporting events, to parties, and "out riding." She is somewhat of a flirt, teasing the boys with the promise of a kiss...or not.

In the family's formal portrait taken when Marian was just six years old, her wistful looks presage the thoughtful beauty she would eventually become. But in between those years, Marian was full of vim and vigor, and although the term had not yet been coined, she was the epitome of a teenager. In an essay written at age thirteen, she considers herself a martyr and lists all the outrageous things that parents enforce by their authority, *especially* housework. She does not pick up her mother's skill in sewing, nor does she learn to play the piano. She hates fourteen-year-old boys for taking the best candy, the most comfortable spots, and for their aloofness and air of superiority. Marian decides that marriage is as "unessential as measles." She considers altruism to be her goal; half of her efforts would be directed toward her fellow man, the other half for her animal friends.[112]

Then there was a sea change. When she reaches high school at age fifteen, Marian's letters to her older brother are filled with comments about boys, boys, boys. She becomes pensive, introspective. "You surely should be here to enjoy these nights. The moon is almost full now and it's warm and moonlit. I go out

every evening after supper and sit on the front lawn—and just think, and think, and think. There are so many things to think about any more."[113]

Marian is on the way to becoming an intellectual. She often goes to the theater with her brother, and they discuss the merits of the plays and actors. She reads and writes poetry. But it is the roaring 1920s, and Marian is catching the fever. She shortens her skirts, cuts her hair and learns to drive the family car. She plays tennis and goes to dances. Marian has girlfriends and boyfriends, but, hands down, it is the boys who capture her attention. What's next?

By the time she reaches high school, Marian has skipped a grade. In the senior yearbook, a classmate writes, "Marian Butler knows every word in Webster's dictionary and uses them every day."[114] Certainly college would be in Marian's future and plans are taking shape for her to join her brother in Columbus, and then to matriculate in the fall. But it is spring and her classmates are feeling their freedom. Love is in the air. Her girlfriends are talking about weddings and rings, and they are choosing their bridesmaids.

Close Call

*M*arian continues to play the field, but by the time she is ready to graduate from Chillicothe High School as its salutatorian, she wonders if she too may have found the one. Other boys continue to write notes to her and call on the telephone, and she continues to flirt. There are disagreements with her parents over the various boys she is seeing, and occasionally her brother Philemon is pressed into service to talk some caution into his sister. When Walter Chambers starts to call at the Butler house, there is a different reaction. Here is someone who might make Marian think about an exclusive romance, and here is someone who might win her parents' approval.

Walter Chambers is a very acceptable suitor in every way. He is smart in school and a leader in the various clubs to which he belongs: the Longfellow Literary Society, the Vacuum Science Club, and the school's historical society. Music, too, is one of his accomplishments; he plays a violin in the school orchestra. Walter's family owns a farm on the other side of Chillicothe, and the eager young man shows up in his car at Robertson Place on a regular basis. He exhibits an unusual interest in Sadie's garden and the trees on the Butler property and will later go on to study landscape gardening at Harvard. So Walter is indeed ambitious, and he is charming to boot! He is a bit moody, but this is not surprising because Walter Chambers is the class poet.

Over the summer the romance blossoms, and the young man becomes a fixture at Robertson Place. Little did Sadie and Delano realize just how intense this romance could become and how fast it could escalate. Little did they suspect that back in Columbus, on the eve of the first day of classes at OSU, Marian and Walter would secretly promise themselves to each other.

In Columbus, Marian and Walter take to campus life with enthusiasm. Each pledges into a fraternity or sorority, but, according to their agreement, each will be allowed an occasional "outside" date. Marian takes advantage of her little sliver of freedom, but as winter approaches the college freshman becomes increasingly reflective, while at the same time she is enjoying a more passionate relationship with her fiancé.

Walter begins to press Marian to set a wedding date. She puts him off. She confides to her diary that while on some days she is certain that she will love Walter forever and ever, on other days she realizes that something is not right. She analyzes herself and has wide swings of emotion. Walter's only faults, she concludes, are that he has a tendency to be self-centered and needs to be dominant. He is jealous of the time she spends with her sorority sisters and doesn't like it when she goes to parties. She wants to wear her new blue, cut-velvet dress, but Walter doesn't dance and prefers to go out alone on their dates.

Walter is winning. By spring Marian has dropped out of the sorority and agreed to a summer wedding. Will she give up her freedom and quit school to become a full-time wife? Her seventeen-year-old mind is spinning.

Back in Chillicothe Sadie and Delano are in a quandary. Last November, when they discovered the secret engagement, Delano had a talk with Walter. They think Marian is awfully young to be making such a big decision and wonder whether she can live without the stimulus of college life. But Marian is a strong-willed debater and makes her case. Realization sets in, and soon the family is planning parties and sending out invitations.

For young women of Marian's age, the idea of marriage had long been an honorable and sufficient goal. Walter Chambers is a likable young man who has her parents' blessing. The couple seems well suited, and their life might well be prosperous because Walter is talented, and his sights are high. As spring turns to summer, as well-wishers bring gifts to the door, Marian is plagued by increasing doubt. Is she ready to commit? There is a character trait in Walter that might be a problem. It could prevent her from becoming the person she dreams of being—whatever that is. Walter is *way* too possessive.

The knot in her stomach tightens. As gifts in the parlor await her opening, a stoic but teary-eyed Marian announces her decision. It's off!

Who knows how Walter reacted or how he took the news? In all likelihood he did not give up easily. Dismay and relief were the conflicting reactions of her parents. As for Marian? All she wanted to do was hide. By her own admission, Marian did not like to show her emotions. Her way of expressing them was to write and write and to write some more, but this was too much for any diary.

When the furor died down, it dawned on Marian that what she wanted to do was leave town. Everyone had been telling her that she should be a writer, and it was true that, since she was a little girl, she had written lots and written well. What she *really* wanted to do was to become an interior decorator. Where she got this idea is a mystery because in 1925 the profession did not exist. When she was a child, Marian would spread herself on the floor of her father's furniture store to cut and paste pictures of pianos and kitchen stoves from newspapers and magazines. Now that her life was once again her own, maybe she would strike out with a bold plan. Chi-

cago was where she wanted to go (maybe to the Art Institute of Chicago), and she proposed going there to get the necessary training to become a decorator.

Her parents shot the idea down. Instead, when the trauma of Marian's fiasco subsided, the family decided to move en masse to Columbus where, under the watchful eyes of her family, Marian could resume her studies. In past years the Butlers had frequently spent time during the winter months in the university town, so the protective maneuver did not appear awkward or contrived. Later, when it looked as though Marian was safely ensconced with her big brother in charge, Sadie and Delano retreated to Chillicothe.

Happy Coincidence

What followed was a happy coincidence and some well-needed relief from the the family's ordeal with Marian. Philemon found a private home where his sister could live and be safe from the advances of overzealous young men who might prey on single coeds. It was the residence of the jolly and endearing William North, the campus cop. In this home lived his wife, Minnie, and their two fun-loving daughters, Ethel and Gertrude. One was boisterous and had a head of fiery red hair; the other was pleasingly plump and could pack a pistol.

Philemon fell in love with Gertrude, and in the summer of 1928, he and his doe-eyed sweetie were wed. The bride quit her job as high-school teacher and moved with her husband to Chillicothe, where Philemon would start his law practice at 62 South Paint Street. The address was a sort of wedding present from his father Delano, who was able, somehow, to buy the property. This handsome Federal brick house was home to Woodrow Wilson's uncle, and Delano had purchased the three-story building as an investment because it would give his son a "good address." Situated on the edge of downtown, it was strategically located just one block from the county courthouse. What's more, its top floor could be rented out. The newlyweds could live in the middle floor, and the lower level could become—and did remain for the next forty-five years—Phil Butler's law office.

After graduating with highest honors from law school, he followed in his father's footsteps by getting his first professional experience with a law firm in

Toledo. Now back in his home town, he was ready to start his own practice. In a few years, Phil Butler would be running for county prosecutor and then city solicitor.

Marian was fond of her new sister-in-law—even considered her a best friend. Gertrude was welcomed at Robertson Place, and the young couple came to spend their weekends "tramping" and target shooting. They even brought their dogs. Happy times were here again.

On the Upswing

*M*arriage was not at all on Marian's mind. In the spring, about to earn her bachelor's degree in education, she decided to remain in school and to work on a master's degree in psychology. The future must have seemed bright for the enterprising Butler children.

In fact, the entire country was on the upswing in 1929. In rapid fire came news of inventions, new feats, and discoveries. Earlier in the century, brothers Orville and Wilber Wright had astonished the world with their invention of a flying machine. Dazzling the nation now was a new hero: Charles Lindberg was about to attempt his first-ever solo flight across the Atlantic. Amelia Earhart was close behind, capturing the nation's fascination by wanting to be the first woman, not just to cross the ocean, but to fly around the world.

Penicillin, the long-awaited all-purpose antibiotic, arrived in 1928 to stem the tide against all manner of infections. Men in Manhattan were lining up for jobs to work on what was touted to become the tallest building in the world, the Chrysler Building. Confidence in the future was at an all time high.

Flappers were kicking up their heels to the "Charleston." Radios were beaming advertisements of soap and toothpaste into the nation's living rooms, and folks were taking their money out from under their mattresses to invest in the ever-rising stock market. Even waitresses and school teachers were getting rich! Anything was possible.

It is now fall quarter at Ohio State. Just as Marian is purchasing her books and meeting her new professors, she gets wind of trouble. It's far away and of no import, she thinks. But on Tuesday, October 24, within the columned buildings of Wall Street, where gamblers and simple folks alike are joined together in the stock exchange's phenomenal climb to wealth and prosperity, the market starts its calamitous spiral downward. By lunchtime on Thursday, there are reports of suicides. In those few hours, billions of dollars of investment would evaporate, and very soon the life savings of many average Americans would be wiped out.

After the Crash

Although the Stock Market Crash of 1929 sent many of Marian's friends back to their hometowns, she remains in Columbus and is able to pay for tuition and her living expenses. Back in Chillicothe, the town's politics still percolate, and her brother is assured of work. While panic reigns in the lives of many, back on the farm the cattle continue to give milk, the chickens their eggs, and corn in the field stands tall.

But as depression settles over the land, farm commodities begin to lose their value. Then, farm land itself loses its worth. By 1930, the farmers of Ross County are beginning to lose hope. Their fields of corn—those beautiful, golden kernels of life which took not only investment, but timing and rain, toil and effort to bring to market—are selling for only ten cents a bushel. All around are signs of distress.

Delano's corn did not bring any more than his neighbor's. However, the Butlers are fortunate. They had not put money into the stock exchange. Just up the road their friends and farm tenants, Carl and Clara Edgington, are now in trouble. In 1924 Delano had agreed to sell them the 240-acre farm he had purchased as a tenant farm. Now it is back in Delano's hands. It turns out that even Midwestern farmers had bet their money on Wall Street. How were they to know there wouldn't be time to get their money out if the market reversed direction? How were they to know there would be no buyers for their stock certificates? Raising crops was a gamble they had been taking year after year, and to put money in a pot that only kept spiraling up, up, up didn't seem the least bit riskier. All the Edgingtons' savings were wiped out by the crash, and they had to default on their agreement to buy the farm they'd been toiling on for the past five years.

It is hard for the Butlers to watch their friends and relatives fall on hard times. In town, Delano is asked by the court system to act as receiver for the Buckeye Furniture store. His friend and former business partner, Mr. Ewing, is going bankrupt.

Sadness Speaks Loudly

*E*ventually, the long tentacles of the stock market crash reach Robertson Place. Delano and Philemon are summoned next door to the Caldwell farm. Sadness speaks loudly inside the walls of Aunt Sally's modest clapboard farmhouse because five years ago she became a widow, and in 1926, her son Clyde was forced to declare bankruptcy. She is now liable for his debt.

Clyde may have been replaced as head farmer at the Robertson Place, but he continues to manage his own family's farm after his father's death. However, no one seems to have been able to figure out how to curtail the young man's penchant for concocting reckless schemes. Not only did he run through his mother's money and go into debt, this well-intentioned grandson of Robert Robertson was unable to support his own family. Now they, too, are gone. According to his contemporary and friend Ed Steele, "There was not enough to eat, and his wife Wilhelmina, feeling desperate, packed up the four small boys and tried to take them away to her family's home up north. A neighbor had to be called to the Caldwell place to restrain Clyde." Mr. Steele claimed that everybody liked Clyde—that he was actually brilliant—but that he was ahead of his time. "Always thinking big, coming up with innovative and ambitious plans which always seemed to end in failure."[115]

Under a bankruptcy schedule that had been laid out four years ago in 1926 by Delano, Aunt Sally has slowly been paying back Clyde's debts. Now the Depression is making that impossible. The Caldwell farm still produces clover and alfalfa, soybeans, corn, wheat, straw and gravel. In addition, there is a pasture to rent, but all these things have lost their value, and Sally is no longer able to make ends meet. Her farm, the land she had inherited from father Robertson, is in jeopardy.

Philemon took over for his father and sat down with his mother's beloved aunt at her kitchen table. Patiently, they did the math. Hard choices would have to be made because Sally has already been living as frugally as possible. On $400 per year, the petite Robertson heir does not always draw her monthly allotment. She has even taken in ironing. Now, well into her seventies, if she is to continue to honor her agreement and retain her farm and home, it will be necessary for her to sell her furnishings. An auction, they decide, is the answer.

Seventeen years later, in 1947, Sally Caldwell was able to pay off all of her son's debts. With $4,000 in the bank, she celebrated by building a new corn-crib. Her neighbor, Helen Arrington, had this to say about Sally Caldwell. "She had a cow and an apple tree, and she practically *lived* on her homemade cottage cheese and apple sauce. She was determined to pay off Clyde's debt. Such a strong woman, she was. Such strong ethics!"[116]

Posing that same year for a photograph for the *Gazette*, the nonagenarian admitted she was proud to be able, after all these years, to fit into her wedding gown. Four years later, Sally Caldwell died at the age of ninety-five. She had buried three babies and lived long enough to bury her husband and two remaining children.

Clyde died at age fifty-one, "a broken man," according to Ed Steele. He had left the region to become a salesman and at the time of his death was earning a living by selling fire extinguishers. However, all four of Clyde's sons went on to live productive lives, the most illustrious being Philip Caldwell, who was the first person not a member of the Ford family to run the Ford Motor Company. Philip Caldwell went on to orchestrate one of the most dramatic and successful turnarounds in business history.

Many bleak years were yet ahead for the nation. What had started as a panic on Wall Street ended up lasting over a decade. Somewhere in America was a hobo lying down to sleep in an empty railroad car. Somewhere in Appalachia was a mother desperate to feed her children. Somewhere in the West was a farmer, aimlessly roaming the countryside.

Yet, through it all, somehow Delano Butler continued to do business and even to make money during the depression. His future son-in-law would later attribute this feat to Delano's close and careful management style. His interests were diverse, but he tended to each of them every single day. Sadie did her part, too. While the world seemed to be falling apart, the Butlers tucked themselves into Robertson Place to wait out the storm. There, Sadie would tend the vegetable garden and orchard, preserve the produce, raise chickens and sew nearly everything the family needed to wear—all in an effort to save a dollar—while Delano went out every day looking for one. The odds, however, were against them. Even if the economy were to recover, their crops would not. A severe drought was scorching the land. In southern Ohio it would last five long years, from 1931 to 1936. Year after year, while the Dust Bowl raged out West, the farmers of Ross County planted their seeds in the cool months of April and May, only to watch their seedlings wither and wilt in summer's unrelenting heat. Day after day, they watched the sky for a break in the weather and got only violent wind storms. By July there was a sickening feeling in the pits of their stomachs as they inspected their scorched and cracked fields. It was a desperate time to be a farmer.

Farmers' Institute

*I*n Washington, the Department of Agriculture was eager to ease the plight of the nation's farmers. The idea of paying farmers not to produce was yet to be introduced to the nation, but the government was already in the business of educating them. Through the popular 4-H programs, the USDA had found that the best way to change the habits of farmers was to encourage their children to experiment with new ideas. Sadie and Delano volunteered many hours to these after-school clubs, and became further involved with a new group called the Farmers' Institute. Information gleaned from two of its programs gives us a glimpse of their meetings, which were held in the auditorium of the new high school next to their farm.

The year is 1929, and Sadie is serving as corresponding secretary as Delano directs the election committees. The morning session begins with a singing of "America."

Speakers from Farm Bureau, Grange, 4-H, and the county agency address subjects of interest: Ross County as Adapted to Sheep Raising, What is a Flower Show?, Raising and Marketing our 4-H Club Pigs, and Raising Baby Chicks.

Members stage a style show, others participate in musical interludes (whistling solo and school orchestra), and one gentleman gives a talk entitled "My Trip Though Europe." Another demonstrates "How to Splice Rope." Charlotte Dresbach plays a piano solo, and Sadie Butler addresses the group on local 4-H work.

For thirty-five cents, a cafeteria dinner is served in the hall by girls of the Home Economics class. There are farm exhibits of grain and fruits, and juried contests for the best ten ears of white and yellow corn, the largest pumpkin, and the finest angel-food cake, plate of doughnuts, and can of beans.[117]

It was much like a county fair, and it was welcomed by an industry and a region under siege. At a time when farmers were struggling with an outbreak of hog cholera and their cattle were starving after four years of drought, the Farmers' Institute was a welcome note of confidence.

A Keen Eye for Business—The Butler Addition

During the lean years, Delano continued to think of new ways to bring in some income. By this time he was adept at reading lips; he also used an ear horn, but acquaintances claimed it was of little help. Antibiotics arrived too late for Delano, but since leaving the practice of law, Delano had acquired a keen eye for business. Across the road and behind Bourneville, Delano and his son Philemon owned several acres where the two of them envisioned a housing development. Surveying and putting in roads would take time, but at some point, when people again had money to spend, there would be thirty or forty building-lots to sell. The Butler Addition, as it came to be called, would expand Bourneville for the first time since its initial founding in 1832. Also available for development was some of the home farm's frontage property on the south side of U.S. Route 50. An idea came to the father and son team. Philemon, the half-trained civil engineer, began sketching out a design for a gasoline station. All of this would require either money or bank loans, but Delano knew that to build such a building and to develop the subdivision would provide the men of Bourneville with some badly needed jobs. In 1933 there were almost no jobs to be had. Many years later, the offspring of one of the DeLong boys told me that his family was facing starvation when Mr. Butler offered his father and uncle work. They were the lucky ones.[118]

The New Deal

When in 1933, Franklin Delano Roosevelt asked his fellow Americans to tune in their radios to hear his plan to rescue the economy, nearly everyone was listening. During his famous "Fireside Chat" on May 7, the nation's newly elected president began to spell out his bold steps to put people back to work. "First, we are giving opportunity of employment to one-quarter of a million of the unemployed, especially the young men who have dependents, to go into the forestry-and-flood prevention work." This proposal would become one of the most popular facets of FDR's New Deal. Fielding the Civilian Conservation Corps, better known as the CCC, was an enormous undertaking. FDR again: "This is a big task because it means feeding, clothing and caring for nearly twice as many men as we have in the regular army itself."

Not everyone liked what their president was proposing. Not everyone thought that the government should be trying to create work. But this isn't why Sadie and Delano were not listening to the radio on that first Sunday night in May, as the rest of the nation hushed their children and settled themselves around the radio. Had there been a radio at the farm, Delano might have pressed his ear to its speaker and been able to make out a few words of the president's speech, but there was no radio. There was no electricity yet at Robertson Place, nor was there any electricity in almost all the farmhouses across the nation. Private utility companies argued that it was too expensive to string electric lines to isolated rural farmsteads. Anyway, they said, most farmers were too poor to be able to afford the monthly bills. This is something the President was determined to change. With his Rural Electrification Act, the federal government would make low-cost loans to Farmers' cooperatives to bring electricity to much of rural America. When the time came to sign the papers in 1936, the Butlers readily agreed to pay for power. At last! The old farmhouse would get electricity.

Radical Changes

Despite the enormous pall cast on the nation by the Great Depression, these were exciting times at Robertson Place. After suffering the loss of their son in 1922, Sadie and Delano decided to give their home a whole new look. Away went the awnings. Down came the ivy. After the enormous clinging vines of dark green ivy had been ripped off the old brick house, they painted it white. Even though the eves and trim would be left a dark bottle green, this transformation was indeed drastic. For most of its three-quarters century existence the brick house had been painted grey and shrouded in vines. Now it looked fresh and clean and ready for a new start.

Inside there would be even more transformation. Now that power-line poles strode the fields of corn and brought electric lines to the house, Sadie could remodel the farm's kitchen. It is hard to imagine paying for a new kitchen during a decade so difficult as the 1930s, but in fact this is when the farmhouse became modernized. Perhaps Sadie and Delano had long been saving. Friends in the city had gotten indoor plumbing and modern appliances in the 1920s, when money and credit was loose. By the time electricity came to Robertson Place, and electricians had strung the house from top to bottom with knob-and-tube wiring, the nation was beginning to pull out of its doldrums. People started to buy building lots in the Butler Addition, and Delano was able to lease his cement-block filling station to the Pure Oil Company.

Lights throughout the house were the first order of business. After that, indoor plumbing! Forever the inhabitants of the house had pumped their water manually outside at the well or, more recently, from an iron hand pump mounted to the kitchen sink. With the help of a plumber, their son Philemon figured out a way to apply an electric pump to the well, and not only did that mean instant tap water in the kitchen, but also that Robertson Place could at last have a modern bathroom. However, as was often the case when a bathroom was added onto an existing house, this new luxury found its home right off the family's dining room. The Butlers may have thought it wonderful, but it would take another generation to correct the awkward arrangement.

Before the bathroom was added, there had been a back porch in its place. Its removal allowed the addition of a downstairs bedroom and a workshop. Philemon would claim this workspace and fill it with wrenches, hammers, saws and nails. It became his personal lair.

On to the kitchen. This is where the most dramatic changes would occur, and it was when the space would attain its modern configuration. Until now, according to Anne Mendelson, the author of *Stand Facing the Stove: The Story of the Women Who Gave America The Joy of Cooking*, women of Sadie's socio-economic group didn't know much about cooking. Instead, they had relied on others to do much of the real work in the kitchen. Although I doubt that Sadie ever had a professional cook in her kitchen, she probably hired young helpers whenever she could. However, by the 1930s, there was a shortage of young women who were willing to take these domestic jobs; they wanted to be secretaries or clerks. At the same time, the invention of modern appliances was making it possible—or at least more appealing—for women like Sadie to manage all the culinary tasks by themselves.

It was within this setting that Sadie threw herself into the challenge of designing a new kitchen for Robertson Place. She wanted cabinets to be built along one long wall of her galley style kitchen, and she chose linoleum for both the floor and the countertops. The artist in her would have enjoyed the process of picking out wallpaper for the walls, but it would take time to get accustomed to using an electric stove. To replace the old, black, wood-burning one, Sadie selected a white stove with a deep well for frying chicken. The wooden icebox would give way to a gleaming, all-metal refrigerator. When they could afford to do so, Sadie intended to buy a fan, a vacuum cleaner, and a light-weight iron to replace the heavy ones which had to be heated on the old range. All to be powered by electricity!

It was an exhilarating time at the home farm, and Delano also wanted improvements. He wanted a garage for his new Ford Deluxe two-door sedan. He would squeeze the garage between the new kitchen and the old wash house but make it large enough for another car, or perhaps a washing machine for Sadie. To shelter his Ford pick-up truck Delano asked carpenters to build a shed garage behind the old outhouse, which, with the arrival of indoor plumbing, was converted into a storage place for garden tools.

So much construction at Robertson Place in the late 1930s! But none of it met the standards of the work done in the last century. None of it compared to the craftsmanship and thought put into the Greek Revival facade of the house. It could not even be called architecture. This didn't seem to matter because all the changes were being made to the back of the house where only the family played and worked. And besides, Delano was in a hurry—catching up, you might say.

"Honey Dear"

Two years into the Great Depression, when the banks had run dry and the nation was begging for jobs, Marian burst onto the scene with a new beau. George Hammond was a colleague from work, she said, and this time it was serious.

Marian had started a career in social work, and it was at the Bureau of Juvenile Research that she met the Kenyon College graduate. Though not striking in appearance, her suitor was impeccably dressed when he came to Robertson Place for the first time. He greeted the Butlers with grace and ease, and it was obvious from the beginning that this man adored their daughter. He was a country boy from northern Ohio, he insisted, but it was clear that the well-mannered young man had not stayed on the farm. In fact, after his disastrous beginning at Asbury College (the religious school from which he pleaded to go home), he spent a disorienting year on the sprawling campus of Ohio State before finally settling at Kenyon College. The all-male college in Gambier, Ohio, was only a few miles from his home, and, on one of their first dates, George had taken Marian to see the historic school. The cluster of Gothic limestone buildings of Ohio's oldest private school was bound to have impressed her.

George ran track in college and acted in plays. Occasionally he was cast as a female due to his small stature and his fine singing voice. More important to Marian, however, was her suitor's mind and the fact that he had studied history and philosophy. Could he be her soul-mate?

No steamy diary was left behind to recount the romance that led to their engagement. Only one letter survives, the one written shortly before their wedding. In it Marian hints at the dynamics that fueled the courtship. George was experiencing cold feet. It sounds as though he was worried about finances, and Marian wrote a forceful last minute encouragement:

Honey dear,

I was glad to get your letter. You sounded a little low when you wrote it. Probably by the time you get this you'll be at the opposite end in mood, but if you aren't, listen to what I say.... We're not expecting a road completely smooth.... We're not asking that things be handed to us. Surely it will not hurt us to form some acquaintance with the word struggle.

And listen to another thing, my sweetheart. I like nice things—you know it.... However that does not mean that I am incapable of temporarily living below the standard I have set up, of living without complaint....

We both wanted to be married this fall. We are ready for marriage. It is a logical step for us to take. If we can't get through a few financially difficult months, we aren't the type of people who should get married—at least not to each other. But we'll prove that we're right.

And one more thing.... Tell Mr. Wright that we can't take the ring. We'll pick out a pretty $30 one at Mr. Henn's on Saturday, and I'll be very, very happy with it.[119]

Marian went further to add that their honeymoon need not be costly. They had planned a motor trip, but she vowed they would budget themselves strictly and no one would ever know the difference.

When the couple got engaged, they both had jobs in Columbus—a rare thing in 1933 while many were standing in bread lines. Marian worked as a social worker and George was selling insurance. Undoubtedly, this is what gave the couple the courage to launch into marriage. But Marian had stopped working to concentrate on her wedding plans, and, while George still had an official job, he later admitted he was just going through the motions because not many people were able to buy insurance when so many banks were closed. It is also understandable that, on the brink of a lifetime commitment, George would have been quite shaken by events back home. His father, a gambler by nature, had been one of the daring types

who had jumped into the stock market with both feet, borrowing money and using the family farm as collateral. His parents would eventually lose their farm, their house, and their own marriage as a result of this calamity. The fallout from all of this would play into George's and Marian's future. But on their wedding day, that sparkling fall day in 1933, it appeared that optimism would rule the hearts of this sunny-natured groom and his hazel-eyed beauty.

While a violin and piano played the familiar strains of Wagner's *Wedding March*, the groom's small niece and nephew, clad in colonial costumes, unfurled satin ribbons leading from the columned front doorway to the

trellised garden where the couple took their vows. The day had been picked in memory of Marian's grandmother, Margarite, and Marian wore her gown. Described as *mousse-line de soie* by the newspaper reporter, the organdy gown was made by Martha for Margarite to wear sixty-one years ago, on the very same date in September of 1872. Mellowed to a shade of ivory, the dress now framed Marian's figure and set off the waves in her hair.

For months leading up to the wedding, Sadie and Delano had been working to spruce up Robertson Place. It was two years into the long drought, but every week brought hope that the rain clouds would arrive in time to green up the yard. Marian had arrived from Columbus in time to add her energy to the frenzy, and in that last-minute letter to her fiancé, written on the eve of the wedding weekend, she recounted the day's activities:

> We got lots done today. Dad and Roy worked on the driveway. Will cut the grass. Edie washed the windows all over the house. Mother and I cleaned dresses in Naptha, made tomato-juice cocktail, and did various other jobs. Tomorrow will be a culmination of it all![120]

Marian would later recall that the time spent with her parents during the build-up to the wedding had been revelatory. They didn't always see eye-to-eye, but six months later on Mother's Day, Marian would write to her mother, "I am gaining an appreciation of the richness and breadth of your and Dad's life here which I have heretofore been too immature to see."[121]

On September 24, 1933, Marian began a phase of life that would shape and mature her. Wearing a wedding band costing thirty dollars and dressed in a "smart fall suit of olive green with brown accessories," the ebullient bride set out with her husband in a sporty coupe.[122] After a brief honeymoon at an undisclosed destination, the new Mr. and Mrs. George Hammond returned to Columbus, where they arranged their few things in a small rental house.

Rent Overdue

Giddiness prevailed for a few weeks—until the rent came due. The newlyweds were unable to pay it on time, and George lacked the cash to pay his parking tickets. Back home, Sadie and Delano were holding their breaths and wondering if their long talks with Marian had been in vain. From this day on, Marian and George kept a daily ledger in which they recorded every cent they spent. Marian set out to find work and was quickly hired as a case worker. George found work with the state, work which paid $110 each month. From this he would progress to another job before taking a position with a trade association. With the Ohio Council of Retail Merchants, George would build a career as a lobbyist and go on to be its director for the rest of his working days.

Not long after Marian went back to work, she was promoted. She was sent to Indianapolis and then to Pennsylvania, where she would direct the Johnstown Relief Agency. While in Johnstown, she was caught in its catastrophic flood of March 17, 1936. On the fourth day of rain, the two rivers surrounding Johnstown spilled over their banks and flooded the city, knocking down houses, bridges, and power lines. Before the river crested at fourteen feet, Marian saw the surging water carry away automobiles, light poles, and a grand piano. When the news hit the wires, the nation was aghast. Some could remember that in 1889, when the dam broke, Johnstown had lost over two thousand lives.

Telegrams flew between Marian and George. "SAFE DONT WORRY PLEASE NOTIFY FOLKS MARIAN," said the Western Union telegram. Authorities ordered the city evacuated and in came the guardsmen, militiamen, Red Cross nurses, Boy Scouts, and a whole slew of volunteers. Meanwhile, Philemon telegraphed his sister with an offer to go pick her up or to send funds for her return. She wrote back, "TRYING TO REACH YOU BY PHONE DONT COME HERE MARIAN."[123]

Climbing the incline to Westmont, Marian found shelter with friends. She stayed to help with the massive recovery that followed but was forced to return home five weeks later due to a foot infection. No doubt it was caused by the muddy and dangerous conditions in the streets of Johnstown during the flood's aftermath. After that, Marian quit working and did not return to the workforce for almost twenty years. She was ready to settle down to raise a family.

Children and War

Marian named her firstborn Phil, after her brother. She and her brother had long been close, and their lives would continue to be intertwined

both in life and after death. In 1936, it was discovered that Philemon had diabetes. For the rest of his life he would be dependent on daily injections of insulin and forced to follow a strict diet.

Little Phil, born in 1937, would soon fill the stage at Robertson Place. He was as cute and chubby as a cherub, and his pale blue eyes and blond curly hair brought a smile to everyone's face. At a moment's notice, Sadie would drop her current project—such as researching her roots for membership in DAR (Daughters of the American Revolution), or preparing a paper about women's history for the Century Club—in order to receive a visit from her first grandchild.

Having a grandson in her life helped distract Sadie from the fact that the school board in Twin Township was again talking about needing more land. It wanted, and would get in 1939, seven more acres of the Butler farm. The right to seize private property for public use was on the township's side, and by now Sadie and Delano were committed to the school in their midst. Sadie would sell her parcel of land for $1.00, and on the crop field would eventually be built a long wing of classrooms with a playground large enough for swings and slides and a big grassy ball diamond.

But meanwhile, the Butlers had things they wanted to accomplish in Bourneville. Their country home still depended on firewood and coal for heat in the winter. Coal fired the smaller of the five fireplaces, but the rest required a fair amount of firewood which had to be cut, split, stacked, aged, and lugged into the house. Because the drafty farmhouse was never quite warm enough in winter, Florida had been a great attraction to the Butlers over the years. Now there was a grandson, a small bundle of wiggling flesh and blood, who might come to visit them if they were to stay in Ohio over the winter. Maybe they would even celebrate Christmas at Robertson Place. In 1940, a furnace was installed.

In the cave-like cellar, the new furnace resembled a giant subterranean octopus, sending its aluminum ducts up, down, and around multiple corners to reach the second-floor bedrooms. When purchased in 1940, the new furnace was costly, and it required not only the skills of furnace specialists, but those of carpenters, plumbers, and electricians. Installing the monster in the basement was a long drawn-out process, taking several weeks. But oh, what a difference it made!

By the time Phil had reached his second year, the subject of President Roosevelt's "Fireside Chats" had changed from the state of the United States economy to war in Europe. Although his current policy was still one of neutrality, the president decided to order a build-up of American troops. His counterpart in Germany is unpredictable.

It is 1939. Hitler is moving fast. In September he invades Poland. The world is shocked and England declares

war. Hitler conquers France. He is sending his Luftwaffe over the channel to attack Britain.

Marian tries to stay focused on domestic concerns, balancing her care of a toddler with moving forward on their dream to own a home of their own. She hopes to be pregnant again. They walk and drive around Columbus neighborhoods looking for an empty lot on which to build. Wondering what their house should look like, they talk with an architect.

On a secluded little cul-de-sac in Clintonville, a leafy suburb just a few miles north of the OSU campus, the Hammonds find a small lot. It is just big enough to contain a modest three-bedroom house. Nestled in the woods, it borders a ravine, where trees are already in place to shade their future screened-in back porch.

Marian is in her element now. Motherhood becomes her, and she assumes a new sense of assurance. All the wild and confusing days of her youth pale in comparison to this satisfying phase of her life. She is busy sketching floor plans for the new house and making the myriad decisions needed for its completion. Still, she reserves time for a weekly hair appointment.

Little fellows have to be helped to see things. Phil Butler Hammond is only 2 and a lit-
the electric trains. So mama,
Mrs. George Hammond, 450 Fal-
lis-rd. held him while he looked

Meanwhile the world stage is about to explode. President Roosevelt has ordered up the draft, and Italy and Japan have aligned themselves with the confident German Führer, who is beginning to look unstoppable.

Marian is about to deliver her second baby. Phil will soon turn four, and she plans a little birthday party. Children are invited, the cake is baked, and George assembles a new tricycle. Phil is dancing with excitement. Marian's contractions start early. She picks up the telephone, calls her parents, and summons her husband and the doctor to the hospital. Phil's birthday party is canceled and he is crestfallen. Instead of birthday presents, he gets a baby sister.

Red-faced and crying, on that summer afternoon of August 9, 1941, it was I, the author of this book, who became Phil's new baby sister. The name chosen for me was Lynn.

"But Phil was such a cute baby," said one of my grandmothers, shaking her head. From Marian's diary, I would later learn that I was a "good" baby because I hardly ever cried. I was just learning to sleep through the night when, on the morning of December 7, 1941, the first wave of Japanese bomber pilots lowered themselves into the cockpits of their airplanes with orders to bomb Pearl Harbor. That the country could be attacked on its own shores defied the American imagination. We had no acquaintance with air-raid sirens or black-outs, but by April my parents had mastered the drill of rushing around to turn off lights. They covered the windows of my nursery with old army blankets left over from World War I, and Phil still remembers the scary sound of the air-raid sirens.

Nearly everybody became involved in the war effort. George, too old for the draft, was asked to be on a committee responsible for mobilization. He was charged with figuring out how to evacuate Columbus and to consider all the logistics necessary for handling a crisis. When he came home from the city, this good-natured father of mine pulled off his suit and tie, donned shorts and a T-shirt, and drove

The Women of Robertson Place

the family to our "victory garden." Gardening was considered a civic responsibility to reduce the need for food in time of war. Phil tried to help plant and water the vegetables, but was given the job of tending to me in a portable playpen.

Back in Bourneville the war effort took other forms. At the urging of our government, Delano bought extra seed to plant additional crops—as well as $600 worth of war bonds. Boys started dropping out of high school to enlist, and little kids came to the back door of Robertson Place asking Sadie for tinfoil and rubber bands for the war cause. Other children searched the farm's fence rows for milkweed pods so that its flossy seeds could fill the life preserver of an airman or a sailor. Some of their mothers took off their aprons and traveled to Chillicothe to work at National Fireworks, a munitions factory. Everyone was put on rations.

Rubber tires were one of the first commodities to be rationed. This rationing would affect George because his new job, representing the merchants of Ohio, required him to do a lot of driving. It wasn't too long before nearly everything a person could buy was under some sort of restriction. A trip to the grocery meant gathering up the ration booklets of stamps to offer the clerk at the check-out counter. Marian altered her recipes according to what she could buy that week. Even the style of her dresses would change during wartime because a scarcity of fabric caused the fashion designers to streamline their patterns by shortening the sleeves and eliminating cuffs. Marian was a bit of a clothes horse, and she was bound to have had an opinion about these changes.

Despite the rations, nearly every weekend our family would pile into the Buick to make the journey from Columbus to Robertson Place—which was always and only referred to simply as "the farm." Once we drove up the gravel driveway in Bourneville, I was free to run and climb outdoors or to play with the small collection of toys in the dining room cupboard. Upstairs in my bedroom, the small one between those of my parents and my Aunt Gertrude and Uncle Philemon, there was a calico quilt upon my bed. That quilt would become symbolic of the farmhouse itself, and would remain one of my earliest memories of Robertson Place. Every morning when I opened my sleepy eyes, surrounding me was a rainbow of bumpy, cutout shapes. The pattern of tumbling blocks—pink with yellow, blue with white—was made from the hand of my grandmother Sadie. Each block was different, each one sewn to the next with what seemed to be a million tiny stitches. I followed their maze with my eyes. Although sewing meant nothing to me at the time, the colors drew me in and carried me along. To my young eyes, they were candy.

Under this very quilt, I was awakened on May 8, 1945, by a blast of horns and firecrackers. Lights, careening at odd angles through the wavy panes of my bedroom window, splayed drunken patterns on the walls. It was what would be called V-E Day; Hitler was dead, and war in Europe over! Even though Bourneville was dry, the villagers broke out their bottles and cheered in the streets. Three months later, the allies would drop atomic bombs on Japan, and World War II would come to an end.

One-hundred-and-eighty young men from this farming community had fought in that war, and not all of them returned alive. The horror of war's death and destruction would haunt some Americans for decades, but for others, it was a different story. The military men and women who returned to American soil were embraced by their families with joy and relief.

These were jubilant times in America. Pop culture surged with the music of big bands and Broadway. Swing dancing was all the rage; weddings broke out all over. War brides set about learning the ways of their newly adopted country, and returning soldiers went back to school on the new G.I. Bill. A housing boom ensued, and the economy remained in high gear.

To join in the country's celebratory mood and to mark my brother's and my birthday, on August 9, 1945, Marian and George took their family to Cincinnati's Coney Island with its merry-go-round and Ferris wheel. Because of the novelty of our joint birthdays, Phil and I were invited to be guests on Ruth Lyon's folksy and popular radio show. When asked what we wanted to be when we grew up, Phil announced that he wanted to be a cowboy. And you, Lynn? "A movie star."

Loss of a Grandmother

While it seemed that everything was looking up in America's post-war euphoria, it was at this time that my grandmother began to fail. Five years ago, Sadie Butler had penned her will. Considering her age, it might have been a logical precaution, especially during wartime. Perhaps it was because Sadie knew that she had precious little time left.

Although now blind in one eye, Sadie taught me the rudiments of needle-work— the great tradition that was as important to women as carpentry was to men. On the front lawn of Robertson Place, just beyond the circle and on a small mound of grass, my grandmother gently gathered me onto her lap and began the lesson. Beside the mound was a stand of yucca plants, and, from the long razor edge of a spiky leaf, she carefully stripped a strand of fibrous thread. "This is the way the Indians did their sewing, Lynn," she explained.[124] With the point of the yucca leaf as a needle, she began to stitch together a few fleshy leaves from a nearby snowball bush. In a series of stitches, my grandmother poked the sharp tip of the yucca needle in and out, in and out. Before I knew it, there was a fairy hat upon my head.

Time was running out for Sadie Butler, and there were more things she wanted to do. Curling her granddaughter's silken hair was one of those things. By my fourth birthday, my white-gold head of hair was finally long enough to amount to something. Its thin quality made it almost like spun glass, causing strangers to smile and my parents to treat it as though it were a family treasure.

A barrel, placed outside the back door of Robertson Place, collected rain water. The ladies of the house preferred rain water to the hard, iron-tainted water which came from the farm's eighty-foot deep well. After Marian heated the precious water on the stove, my father stepped in and took over. Using naphtha soap and a lemon juice rinse for shine, he washed my hair twice before drying it vigorously with a Turkish towel.

Sadie then called me to an adjacent bedroom, where she sat on the edge of her bed. In my nightie, I stood between her knees as she took a length of limp wet hair and rolled it round and round a torn strip of white sheeting. She tied the ends in a knot and went on to the next one, repeating the process over and over as she worked her way around my head. At last Sadie proclaimed that tomorrow my hair would have curls. Indeed it did! After spending the night on a bunch of lumpy, bumpy damp knots, I had a ring of springy sausage curls just like Shirley Temple.

These two precious episodes are the only memories I have of my grandmother, Sadie. In November of 1945, when she was seventy-one years of age, Delano brought her from the farm to our home in Columbus. They went to a hospital where she was admitted, complaining of severe back pain. She never returned.

"It came unexpectedly, suddenly, unexplainably, and possibly, needlessly," Marian lamented when she wrote about her mother's death.[125] Others speculated that in 1945 it might have been due to the lack of doctors and penicillin after the war.

Marian's shock was made more painful by the realization that it was not until recently that she had come to know and admire her mother as a real person and friend. Marian was thirty-seven at the time of her mother's death. She would miss her. At least Marian could draw solace from the fact that she had told Sadie of her change of heart.

Delano was stricken; his world shaken to the core. He had retained his dignity despite his life's many challenges, but this loss would be the ultimate test. His daughter, Marian, could not fill the void, but she would try.

And Sadie's grandchildren? We were too young to understand death. How could we have known that, from the beginning of time, grandmothers have been treasure troves of learning and history? We did not learn from our mother the stories of our ancestors. Marian's antennae were tuned to the spirit of the times. She looked forward, not backward. Marian thought of herself as a modern woman—or so it appeared. But she was a private person, and only after her death would I learn of her deep reverence for the past.

A Sense of Duty

After Sadie's death, Marian's sense of duty was strong. She uprooted her family and moved us to Robertson Place for a year in order to help her father sort through Sadie's things and to try to get a hold on life without her. As was the case with many other men of his generation, Delano had little knowledge of how to take care of himself. He did not know how to cook, do his laundry or run a household. Above all else, he was deaf. How humbling for such a man to feel helpless. How would Delano manage alone?

Across the field, Marian marched her children to the school which sat on her parents' former farmland, and whose presence had caused the family so much anguish two decades ago. Phil could enter the fifth grade, and he soon had a best friend in the

superintendent's son. I was too young, the authorities insisted, because the school had no kindergarten. So while Marian sorted through Sadie's closets—her chests of sewing things, her boxes of newspaper clippings about the history Ross County—I was forced to amuse myself. When at last I ran out of ideas, at the top of the winding back stairs I stood pleading, "What can I do now, Mommy?"

In Delano's 1937 black Ford sedan, Marian took me with her on errands. One of those was to the meat locker. Located in town, this was where our family stored its beef, cut from the cattle raised on our farm. If I agreed to wear a big sheepskin coat and gloves, Marian would let me come inside the walk-in freezer to help her fill our basket with various cuts of meat wrapped in white paper, dated, and labeled as roast, steak, chuck, or tongue.

Playmates came in the form of two little girls with long sausage curls just like mine, Martha and Mary Ellen Arrington. Their father, Hugh Arrington, was our current farmer, and he and his wife had once resided in the apartment attached to Robertson Place, the apartment built for Clyde. Now the family lived just up the road in a big, old brick house—one just as big and old as Robertson Place. It was known as the "old Diggs place" and it stood next to the house the thrice-married Virginia Robertson had built after returning from Michigan. Mrs. Arrington played the piano, and she gave me my first music lessons. Later, as an English teacher in the school next to our farm, she would introduce the reluctant teenagers of Twin Township to Shakespeare by playing recordings of *Romeo and Juliet*.[126]

Not all was fun and games for me that year. In the 1940s nearly every child got a tonsillectomy. Off to the doctor's office we went, and when I awoke from the ether it felt as though there were razors in my throat. To mitigate my suffering, Marian set up a convalescence area for me in front of the bank of windows in the farmhouse's dining room. Here, where Martha Robertson had once slept, I lay on a maple, spool-spindled daybed. Next to the bed was a big roll-topped desk used by the menfolk, and the room smelled of pipe tobacco. Everything got better when my mother presented me with a special gift, a doll that Sadie had been planning to give to her first granddaughter when she could be trusted with such a delicate toy. The doll had eyelids that blinked and tiny realistic looking teeth. Having just returned from the "doll hospital," she wore a fresh head of curly brown hair and a bonnet and dress made of sheer pink organdy.

Paper dolls were another special treat. On Saturday, when my father returned from his long week of travel on the road, he might present me with a book of fashionably-dressed paper dolls. My parents were no strangers to separation, and the year at the farm did not seem to present a hardship for their marriage. It did, however, provide a time for everyone to pull together to figure out how in the world to take care of Delano and the farm itself.

Bad Omen

*B*efore the war, and for the first time, the farm business had suffered a loss. Crop income was especially low. In 1941, Delano's books showed that the sale of animals (ninety-six hogs, thirty-one sheep and six cows) had brought in more income than all the crops combined. The red ink set into motion a re-evaluation and subsequent changes, and it proved to be a bad omen.

But in 1946, Bourneville is beginning to thrive. Now that the war is over, lots in the Butler Addition are selling at a good clip; new houses are going up. Delano's foresight and business acumen is coming into play.

I am not allowed to go to the village alone, even though it holds attractions for a child. Bourneville's population is two hundred; there is now a variety store, a grocery, and two restaurants. Phil is curious about two new gas stations which have been added since the end of the war, and his grandfather and uncle Philemon are discussing whether this would be a good time to add an expansion to their own station.

Gertrude and Philemon arrive every Friday night from Chillicothe to join us for the weekend. On one of those Saturdays, our uncle announces that we may need to replace the roof. He climbs the ladder to inspect the old shingles. Gathering to discuss the pending expenditure, the family agrees to replace the wood shingles with metal. Changing the roof of the old farmhouse means that the family is beginning to simplify maintenance; by that very act, they begin to change its looks. When the roofers come to tear off the old shingles, they are given instructions to remove the dormers. Had the dormers been the cause of persistent leaks? Perhaps Marian wanted to restore the simple lines of the hip roof. A new roof with double-lock standing seams will be installed in 1948 at the cost of $1,169, and from that time forward the timpani of the raindrops will lull me to sleep.[127]

Sadie's Legacy:
"To the Unborn Children of My Grandchildren"

Inside the farmhouse, Marian held sway. She and her mother had chosen new wallpaper for the front hall, just months before Sadie died. Its lavish field of cabbage roses would forever brighten and characterize Robertson Place, and it would remind the family of Sadie's presence. In this most formal setting in the house, across from the graceful curve of the banister and above Sadie's carved library table, Marian hung a gilt-framed portrait of her mother.

Sadie Butler, the grandmother I knew fleetingly and would learn about much later through her letters and paintings, was many things for many people. To the neighbor children, she was a kind lady. They never forgot the summer when Clyde Caldwell's young sons were denied entrance to the 4-H camp. Having no money for the entrance fee, the boys picked several bags of corn and dragged them to town hoping to convince the ticket man of its value. Sadie discovered her cousin's boys crying their hearts out in a back alley where, according to Ed Steele (a contemporary of the boys), she dried their tears and quickly produced the needed $5.00. Mr. Steele would never forget "this great, kind act."[128]

To her mother, Sadie was the living reminder of Erskine. To her grandmother Martha, she was light, laughter and the future. And to Delano, who was now functioning in a silent world, Sadie was the "irreplaceable companion, and the ears he lacked."[129]

When her three children were young, Sadie was a vivacious mother who played the piano and knew how to have fun. She was resilient, too. After suffering the death of her son Wilgus, she was able to recover quickly enough to be a vigilant parent for a teen-aged Marian. And when her surviving children were grown, she proved to be a woman of poise who could listen with empathy, while standing by her own convictions.[130] Finally, Sadie Butler was to young Phil and me an attentive grandmother.

But this gentle woman left something other than memories. She left something that would inform and shape our futures for generations to come. In the second and last version of her will, written in May 1943, Sadie Anderson Butler bequeathed her greatest possession, Robertson Place, "to the unborn children of her grandchildren."

An entailment such as this is unheard of today. Smart lawyers look at it and shake their heads in amazement. Those unborn children of Sadie's grandchildren are now grown up and have children of their own, and they are on their way to fulfilling Sadie's dream that the property she so loved and cared for will not be broken up and scattered to the wind. Even today I look back to Sadie for inspiration because she taught us that the future should guide our thinking. Before planting a sapling, we calculate where its shadow will be cast on a hot afternoon some forty years hence.

Life After Sadie

With Sadie's death came a new era. Gone were the days when the three generations had their rightful places and duties. After her death, it was decided that Delano could not live on the farm alone, and Gertrude and Philemon took him into their home in Chillicothe. From there, he could continue to check on things in Bourneville. One by one the farm animals were sold off. The work horses, Topsy and Joe and Beauty, were replaced with a tractor. No longer would they work the garden, pivoting their turns in perfect unison. Chickens were the next to go; their clucking and pecking and crowing locked in my memory.

Also tucked away in my memory is the faint vision of a little old woman cresting the hill each morning and evening. Her calico dress brushed the tall grass, but as a child I never saw the wrinkled face under her floppy sun bonnet. Could this have been Edie or Fannie who first came to the house when Martha and Margarite were alive? Carrying a pail in one hand and a three-legged stool in the other, the old woman called out "Suu-cow! Suuuuuu-cow!" until across the pasture ambled Bossie to be milked.

Delano had discovered that renting the pastures to people with livestock could add $65 per year to the farm ledger. To the old woman and others in the village, $2.00 per cow per month seemed a fair deal in exchange for the lush grass of Butler's

Grove and the cool waters in its stream. It meant they could maintain a milk cow or fatten a few calves to sell at market in the fall. During his tenure as steward of the land, Delano maintained an exquisite balance. At a time when the farm economy was in such shambles that money itself was seldom used, he used everything from wind power to chicken droppings in order to keep the place going.

Intelligence alone was not enough to offset the rising costs of running a farm. In post-war America it was becoming harder and harder for small farmers to sustain their lifestyle. While the crop yields were going up, so were expenses. At a time when the price for farm products were going down, corn cribs and silos were filling up with surplus.

No ambivalence clouded the minds of Marian and George; they never expected to live off the land. Instead, their livelihood was earned in the city. They returned to the country only for sustenance and refreshment and to remember the old times.

Part 3
1946–1968

Life in the Suburbs

*D*uring the fifth year of my life when we were living at the farm after Sadie's death, I began to think that Robertson Place was going to be my home forever. But my parents were not weighing the pros and cons of living here; instead, they were house-hunting.

In the summer of 1946, George and Marian found a suitable house in the up-and-coming suburb of Upper Arlington. It was to improve their children's education that they decided to sell their house in Clintonville and to move across town. Here the family would settle into a planned community, where the lifestyle was different than any known by my ancestors. Streets were laid out in pleasing symmetry and tasteful homes sat close together, ensuring that Phil and I would be surrounded with other children.

Next door in a Dutch Colonial house were Carlotta, Catrina, and Colin Fink. Their mother spoke with a slight lisp and a Dutch accent, and her old-world sensibilities impressed my young mind. On their wall a cuckoo clock sang out the hours, and in the living room an Oriental rug covered a huge trunk. Carlotta's dolls had interesting names, and their handmade wardrobes came from Holland.

On the other side, in a traditional white frame house, was the Harmon family, an eccentric mix of five, whose adults had a passion for art and music. Here

was my introduction to the paintings of Manet and Monet and to the joy of making music. Their dining room was turned into a science lab where sweet potato vines twined around the window, and an ant colony sat on the table. Mimi, the eldest child of three, became my friend. Together we created paper-dolls, twin bears named Rosie and Posie. Hour after hour we lay on the floor, designing outfits for those circus bears.

Arlington was a world unto itself, one with sidewalks leading in all directions. One led to a little library which smelled of wood and books, another to a turquoise swimming pool. So unlike the farm creek in which we children had waded with tadpoles, its sparkling clear water smelled of chlorine and stung my eyes. But it was in this pool that my mother and I would learn to swim. Donning her bathing cap, Marian forced herself to overcome her fear of water, the water that had taken the life of her little brother, Wilgus.

Yet another sidewalk led to a stone schoolhouse where I would enter first grade. Birthday parties and the arrival of our first kitten marked the days of my childhood, but behind closed doors my parents spoke in hushed voices about an epidemic. Gone were worries of old about cholera and tuberculosis. Today it was polio. Throughout the 1940s and into the 1950s, until a vaccine was found in 1955, children were paralyzed—even killed in the thousands—by polio. Fear was so great that officials briefly closed our neighborhood swimming pool.

At the time of the polio scare, Marian and George were also coming to terms with what it meant to be in a Cold War. The Soviet Union, so recently our ally, was turning into an enemy. It would be only a matter of time before Russia would figure out how to make its own mega-bombs. America would once again feel unsafe and our teachers would put us through air-raid drills.

However, for the most part, post-war America refocused itself on domestic issues. Families got down to the business of making children, resulting in a baby boom. From a pediatrician named Benjamin Spock came *The Common Sense Book of Baby and Child Care*. "Trust yourself," he told new parents in the opening sentences of his book. "You know more than you think you do." His book was too late for Marian, but his ideas would replace the conflicting theories about child rearing, which—combined with a healthy dose of old-wives' tales—had been passed down over the generations.

More timely for my parents' generation were the startling *Kinsey Reports*. Published in 1948 and 1953 by a husband-and-wife team, these science-based treatises challenged conventional assumptions about human sexuality. The very fact that the subject would be discussed in the open was enough to shock most of the public, and it outraged many. Combined with Sigmund Freud's theories and Hugh Hefner's 1953 publication of *Playboy*, the Kinsey findings helped to set the stage for the sexual revolution that was to begin in the 1960s.

Farm Weekends

Throughout it all, my family continued the comforting tradition of returning to Robertson Place nearly every weekend. Caretakers in the attached apartment continued to watch over it while we were gone, and Gertrude and Philemon continued to arrive with their dogs. Mourning doves reassured us with their cooing, and cicadas gave us a sense of normality with their buzzing. But within the farmhouse walls, there would be gentle changes during the decade after the war. Along came a proliferation of appliances, so that even in the country Marian now had the use of a washing machine and dryer. Plastics were making their debut in the kitchen, and before long she made the switch from canning to freezing. Glass jars and metal lids still held their ground when the tomatoes were ripened to their climatic red, but the rest of the harvest went into her new chest-style freezer.

There was a lot to harvest from the garden because George had a green thumb. Throughout spring, in a progression of carefully strung rows, this week-end farmer planted his precious kernels of sweet corn, his potato eyes, and his minuscule dots of radish seeds. He caged his tomato plants and staked the Kentucky pole beans that would eventually climb so high they would threaten to fall over. My father looked forward to Fridays when he could leave the business world behind, drive the sixty miles to Bourneville, unpack the car, get out of his city clothes, and make for the garden to see whether his seeds had sprouted.

Over the years George planted untold numbers of trees and shrubs on the property of Robertson Place: locusts, maples, oaks and dogwood; forsythias, peonies, taxus bushes and lilacs. When snow covered the landscape outside, he sat by the fire, pencil in hand, to order his packets of seeds for the forty-by-sixty-foot vegetable garden plot. When the weather broke, he pulled on his boots to dig in the pungent-smelling earth.

On his Farmall Cub tractor, outfitted with a set of gang mowers, George spent many relaxing hours mowing the expansive lawns of Robertson Place. He was better than most with a shovel, but when the weather kept him indoors, he picked up a paint brush. All the woodwork in Robertson Place received his deft touch, and he refinished many an antique.

It was my Uncle Philemon, who was the fixer of things. After changing into his overalls, he would descend down the ladder into a pit in order to fiddle with the pressure tank for the well water. It was this would-be engineer who tinkered with the furnace and adjusted the grandfather clock in the living room. Philemon's shop by the back door held all manner of tools and smelled of oil and grease and wood chips. Alongside him on his round of chores padded one or two of his beloved dogs—Spot the Collie, Petty the mixed-breed from the pound, or Pammy, his blond Spaniel. When she was old and losing her sight, Pammy fell down into the deep maintenance hole beside the well, causing my brother and me to race to our parents with the news. Without a hint of panic, our unflappable uncle descended down the ladder to navigate the dog's rescue.

Meanwhile, Gertrude's buoyant presence at the farm was essential to our farm supper of hamburgers and French-fried potatoes, which were cooked in the kitchen's deep fryer. On Friday evenings, she come bustling through the kitchen door, her basket bulging with good things to eat. Despite my uncle's diabetes, Gertrude learned to turn out a memorable Wellesley Fudge Cake for the rest of us and to make the coveted treats of our holidays at Robertson Place—her chocolate-covered opera creams.

Delano always joined us at the farm, but there was no longer a sparkle in his eye. Living with his son in town was not going smoothly. Too many conflicts between father and son over their shared business ventures was making it difficult to cohabit. In a poignant letter to Marian he wrote, "If only [Sadie] were here. She could get us back together."[131]

Sign Language and Brownie Scouts

Eventually, Delano moved from Chillicothe into the spare bedroom of our home in Arlington. He brought along his four-door black 1937 Ford, which allowed Marian the use of a car when her husband was at work. However, we children almost never rode in that car. Our suburb was designed so that its residents could walk or ride bicycles everywhere: to the grocery, the drugstore, bakery, beauty and barber shops, dry cleaners and even to the offices of our doctor and dentist. A dance studio was also within walking distance from my home. Only when a folding chair collapsed on my baby finger did my mother back the Ford out of the garage to rush me to the hospital.

To do some of the heavier jobs around the house and yard, Marian hired a WWI veteran who had suffered from shell shock. And he was deaf, like Delano. This gave Phil and me the incentive to learn to spell out words by forming letters with our fingers. It was slow, but it worked.

After-school activities were plentiful in our upscale community, and Marian signed me up for classes in ballet, tap dancing, and acrobatics. I was not particularly good at dancing until Miss Kates, our pretty young teacher with heart-shaped lips, introduced us to a new type of movement called modern dance. To the surprise of my ballet-slippered peers, they saw their blonde-haired, blue-eyed classmate glee-fully slither around the floor with contorted fingers and grimaces, pretending to be a witch.

Brownies and Girl Scouts taught me more useful skills. As a second-grader, every Tuesday morning I buttoned up my brown cotton dress, pulled on matching socks, laced up my leather oxfords, and, with two bobby-pins, secured the little brown beanie on my head. After school, along with the other Brownies, we met in

a finished basement of one of our suburban houses, where a rotation of mothers acted as our troop leaders. One by one, those volunteering moms helped us chip away at a list of requirements needed to earn our badges. We learned how to make a bed with hospital corners, set a proper tea table, and wrap a present. We went camping and learned to pitch a tent, follow a trail, and roast a delicious concoction of graham crackers, Hersey's chocolate, and marsh-mallows—known to us as s'mores.

Designed to be fun, these scout activities helped us grow up and become independent. An important side effect was that we girls learned how to run a proper meeting and participate in the democratic way. It was perhaps the last chance for many of us to belong to a group that was not based on popularity, or looks, or brains, or athletic prowess. In fact these girls were of a rather diverse ethnic mix. Not a single African American family lived in Arlington at the time, but among my friends were children whose parents came to America from a variety of European countries including Greece, Macedonia, Germany, Holland, England and Italy.

Arlington was growing fast. Each year there were more children in my classes and more streets to learn. Once again, Marian and George were hunting for a lot on which to build. A larger lot with space for a bigger house was what they found on the corner of Waltham and Upper Chelsea, and it was just far enough away that I knew it signaled the end to my playtime with Carlotta and Mimi.

Mid-Century Modern

Not until I was a teenager would it fully sink in that, in 1950, we Hammonds had moved into a very modern house. It was unlike anything in the neighborhood and stood in sharp contrast to the Cape Cods and English Tudors, the French Provincials and New England Colonials. Not even remotely did it resemble Robertson Place.

The architecture of our house was inspired by the Prairie School style of architecture by Frank Lloyd Wright, and the key to it was low maintenance. With its exterior of stucco and stone, it was all about blending into the terrain, all about modern living with its interior of open spaces. Marian worked with the architect to design both a floor plan and the house's furniture—although there was very little of it. Our coffee and dining tables were made of birch doors on legs; instead of sofas, we sat on long wrap-around seating which was built into the walls and was covered with thick foam pads. Even at the dining table, some of us sat on this type of seating as we ate Sunday dinner or looked at the built-in television which was concealed in a wall of electronics. In the living room a massive stone fireplace rose to a cathedral ceiling, and there were built-in book-shelves in nearly every room. Black rubber tile was our flooring and striated birch wood our walls. Not a shred of wallpaper nor a ruffle was in sight.

Marian's up-to-the-minute modern kitchen, with all the latest appliances and wrap-around counters, connected to a screened-in back porch. Just outside, on a brick patio, George would master the skills of barbecuing; beyond it, he would plant a flower bed. In the mandatory backyard of perfect green turf, with Phil, he would practice swinging a golf club.

Everything about this move marked the beginning of a new era. Even the shape of the family changed. For Delano, Marian had designed a bedroom and bathroom into the first floor plan of our new Waltham Road house. However, during its construction, Delano began to fail. Hallucinations and night-wandering finally forced my parents to relinquish his care, and they took him to live in a private nursing home in George's hometown of Mt. Vernon, Ohio. Miraculously, it was here that Delano was finally able to shed all his worries; he seemed at peace after years of disorientation and grief. For the rest of his days, he spoke to visitors as if his Sadie were still alive.

Nammy

The death of my grandfather prompted the entry of another grandparent. George's mother, whose given name was Bonnie, was known to us as Nammy, and in 1950 my parents made accommodations for her in their new modern house.

Nammy came into our lives because she had no home. At the turn of the last century, my petite sixteen-year-old grandmother had married a man from northern Ohio's prominent Hammond family. They had three boys. In 1929 the stock market crash changed everything for this hard-working and capable woman. As a result of her husband's gambling in the stock exchange, the family eventually lost not only their farm but also their house. After her marriage fell apart, my grandmother became depressed and was put into a mental-health facility. Following treatment, Nammy tried living with the sons who had stayed in Knox County. It was in Columbus with George, her middle son, that she would finally settle.

This grandmother was rather short. She was compact and made even more so by her corset, which she laced and pulled tight around her midriff every single morning.

Nammy was not a particularly formal woman, but I never saw her in anything but a sensible dress and laced shoes. Her hair, by this time silver, circled round her face in ringlets; her light blue eyes, round nose, and rosy cheeks were soft and friendly. Jovial and young-at-heart, Nammy soon befriended our neighbors, and before we knew what was happening, she became their grandmother, too. In addition to sharing her vast supply of practical solutions, she was a good listener; the neighborhood children enjoyed her company and she gave wise council to their mothers.

In our new modern house, above the two-car attached garage, Nammy would have a complete apartment. At the top of a set of private stairs, her custom-designed quarters were an architectural wonder. Fitted into those six-hundred square feet were a living room (which could double as a guest room), a kitchenette, a bedroom and bath, and most importantly, a big closet which was divided into specially calibrated drawers and cubbies for the accouterments needed for her sewing business.

Never one to sit still, Nammy began to take in sewing. She had magic fingers and a head for numbers, and soon she was making draperies and slipcovers. Eventually, she moved on to couture clothing for Arlington's social set. Each weekday morning, beside one of her large picture windows, Nammy set up her sewing table. There I would find her when I arrived home from school, after taking the stairs two-at-a-time to her loft. "Namsky," I called her, worked as much as her accountant allowed, so as not to jeopardize her Social Security check. She broke only for lunch and her beloved soap operas, during which she did the hand sewing required by the complicated *Vogue* patterns.

On Friday afternoon, Nammy would fold up her sewing table and sweep up the scraps and pins in order to join us in the car headed south to the country. At Robertson Place, this likable lady formed a special bond with Gertrude. While Marian ran the kitchen and masterminded our weekends, the two of them ensconced themselves in the middle of the dining room, where they spread out their latest sewing projects on the formal table or turned the place into beauty parlor by giving one another permanent-wave hair treatments (which stank terribly). Ruffled curtains, bedspreads, slipcovers, and cushion covers spewed out of the old treadle sewing machine and into the many rooms of Robertson Place. Marian was the decider, the designer, and the recipient of these updates to her country home, but a slight frown on her face gave me the impression that the clutter and mess made by the seamstresses in the centrally located dining room got on her nerves.

Now that her city house was completed, Marian began to contemplate making changes to her country house. But we children were oblivious to any of its shortcomings. It was just fine, especially now that we were each allowed to bring along a friend. No more complaining about leaving the city. Carlotta, Mimi, Annette, or Mary Jill were my companions, and on summer evenings we played Kick the Can or a game called Statue, in which we spun one another around, letting go at the last minute and catapulting ourselves into sprawling shapes. "One, two, three, four,…all around my base is caught!" Hide and Seek was our favorite indoor game, and when still small enough, I could curl myself into a ball on a shelf in the big storage closet in my bedroom. It was prime hiding territory, smelling of olden times and grandmother's quilts.

More fun than those childhood games were the hours my girlfriends and I spent searching for clothing left behind from another era. We rummaged through the drawers and old trunks of Robertson Place and dressed up in long satin gowns and gloves, in jodhpurs and top hats. Aviator goggles and cameo jewelry were tried on, and one time we discovered a pocket watch made of gold. Costumed in period clothing, we wobbled down the hallway in high-heeled shoes to look at our images in the mirror. "Whose dress was this?" we asked my mother. Did it belong to one of the ladies in the pictures on the wall?

Maintenance and Beyond—The Rabbit Ranch

While we children played upstairs, lost in a world of make-believe, the adults were downstairs trying to figure out how they were going to pay for the property they had inherited. It was an extravagance, they were learning, to own a second home. It never occurred to my mother to sell Robertson Place, to try to overturn Sadie's will which was designed to extend its ownership over two more generations. Marian and her brother Philemon so loved the old homestead that they considered it not a burden, but a privilege. But its upkeep would cost a great deal of their time and effort, not to mention money.

Each of the adults had a role to play in assuring its future. Philemon, who served as a county farm agent from 1949 to 1960, assumed responsibility for managing all the farm business. Calves, hogs, lambs, wool, corn, wheat—he traded in them all. One of those years, he added to the ledger forty roots of canna flowers, no doubt my father's contribution.

My uncle began to think about growing trees to sell as timber. In 1952, he bought 250 jack-pine and 750 red-pine seedlings to reforest some land up the road on Upper Twin Road, land he had inherited from his father, Delano. Hilly and covered with trees, those 180 acres were well known to my uncle. When Philemon was a boy, he had camped all alone on the top of the hill and fed himself by shooting rabbits—and once a possum! At night, he slept on a bed of pine needles under a stand of pines, planted by the CCC during the depression. Those trees, having reached maturity, were harvested in 1948; it would take thirty or forty more years for his new seedlings to mature into timber.

As the years passed by, Philemon fell in love with those seedlings as they grew into trees. He visited them nearly every weekend, tramping up the winding path, through the briars and over fallen trunks of beech, maple, and hickory trees. He learned the identity of all the other trees in the forest, and in the end he could not bear the thought of allowing anyone near his trees with a saw. Pretty soon, he also couldn't bear the thought of shooting the rabbits! So he gave up logging *and* hunting. As a result, Delano's investment turned into a place to hike and camp—as well as a safe haven for rabbits. Hence, in jest, the family began to refer to the property as "The Rabbit Ranch." Every December, until it was sold in 1993, our family piled into the farm pick-up truck (kids in the back) for its annual trek to the Rabbit Ranch to harvest an offspring of Philemon's precious trees. After feasting on hot dogs and marshmallows and a thermos of hot chocolate, we chose and cut our annual Christmas tree and carried it back to Robertson Place.

So *where* would the money to support our weekends at the farm come from? A more certain way to make money was to sell off land. Not the Rabbit Ranch, we cried—-or would have cried, had we been eavesdropping. Delano had already sold the 240-acre tenant farm, thus explaining the improvements and the new roof at Robertson Place. Before his death in 1951, when both farms were in production, there could be as much as $5,000 yearly profit. Now, the only things remaining to be sold were some old horse-drawn farm equipment.

A check for fifty dollars came in every month from the mechanic who rented the newly-expanded filling station. From people who grazed their animals, there were a few dollars for rental of the pasture. Corn now commanded $1.66 per bushel, which was a lot more that its Depression Era value of ten cents, but with only 138 acres in production, the income from crops was not enough to balance the budget. In 1956, the United States government would set up its Soil Bank program, offering farmers the chance to rest some of their land in exchange for payments. This would help the bottom line, and it kept some farmers from going under.

The Soil Bank was only an idea being bounced around in Congress when Marian settled into her role as proprietor, and her visions for Robertson Place far outpaced those of the dwindling farm income and of her more conservative brother. Could changes to the farmhouse be accomplished on a shoestring?

Number one on her agenda was to refurbish the apartment, the one Martha and Margarite had attached to the side of the house in 1906 to accommodate Clyde and his new wife. Once remodeled, Marian hoped to find a middle-aged couple who would live there in exchange for work. The main advantage of this arrangement was that someone could watch over the property during the week when we were not in residence.

Mary and Tiny were the first tenants living in that apartment and they stayed for several years. Mary helped with house work, and when we were at the farm on Friday and Saturday nights, she washed the dinner dishes. With a little brass bell, Marian would signal Mary to come into the dining room to clear the table. Poor Mary, she had no teeth, and when we kids were behind closed doors, Mary became the subject of ridicule. Her husband chopped wood and fixed fences. However, Tiny had a drinking habit. It cost them their tenancy when he used a crowbar to pry open the prized antique chest in the living room where the adults hid their liquor.

During the year of 1955 alone, over ten-thousand dollars was spent sprucing up the house and apartment. Almost nine-thousand was spent on several new out buildings, including a corn crib. Pretty soon my parents were getting appraisals of the farmland in order to apply for a loan.

Growing Up—First Diary

It was while Marian and George were wrestling with the complications of owning and managing two properties that I began to take notice of the world beyond Arlington and Robertson Place. In fourth grade we studied the history of Ohio, and Marian arranged for our class to take a field trip to view the state's first capital in Chillicothe. Mound City and the Ross County Historical Society received our curious band of school children, and we ate sandwiches from our lunch boxes in my aunt's and uncle's backyard on South Paint Street. In 1950, our family took a trip to Washington, D.C. for a whirlwind tour of the nation's capital. That same summer Phil went to Valley Forge where he and fifty-thousand other boy scouts camped out for a blistering hot, week-long jamboree.

Much less was expected of Girl Scouts. When it came time for my troop to earn its badge in camping, we spent a Memorial Day weekend in the Rabbit Ranch. George and two other fathers organized and chaperoned the expedition, and in their caravan of station wagons we girls sang all the way to the hills of Ross County. But being young teenagers, we also liked to complain. In her diary, Carlotta described how difficult, how exhausting it was to trek our supplies *all the way* up the steep hill. However, on that overcast afternoon in May, we girl scouts did manage to pitch tents, gather wood, dig latrines, and cook dinners over a fire. "Rain!" someone yelled, just as we sat down to eat those meals. Carlotta: "We made a dash for our tents, food and all." The following morning, "We woke up early. Everything was damp. Bugs! Ugh!"

Child Care was another badge we earned for Girl Scouts. Learning to babysit was almost a requirement for girls our age, but I was not the least bit interested in little children. Boys were more of a curiosity to me now that I was about to start junior high school. In fact, I was positively crazy about boys.

Much like Marian's, my own first diary was filled with what I called my "secret love record." Did I, or did I not, see a certain boy that day? And did he call me on the telephone? On June 25, 1954, in capital letters, the heading reads "MAC or BILL?" Two weeks later, another name had been added.

"What a riot!" and "It was a panic!" peppered the pages. And here, on the last page of the 1954 diary, are my New Year's resolutions:

1. *Do not chew gum!*
2. *Do not gossip too much!*
3. *Put hand lotion on three times a day.*
4. *Always like Bill!*
5. *Always complement.*
6. *Keep good posture!*
7. *Be nice to everyone.*
8. *Try to make good grades*
9. *Don't talk so much when I am with boys.*
10. *Don't scream!*

Spin the bottle, dunking at the swimming pool, ballroom dancing at Cotillion, TV parties, kissing, Monopoly, card games, and ping-pong filled my after-school hours. "Creature from Black Lagoon" was the teenage blockbuster movie.

One day I slept until 12:30. I told my diary, "Mom blew up and told me I had to do more work around the house such as fix one course for dinner, change my bed, do my hand laundry." Mowing the lawn each week was the one chore I liked; it felt like a real job, not something required by my *mother*.

Coming-of-age was a head spinning and confusing time for me just as it had been for Marian, and probably for girls throughout history. Although a few things in my life were constant—such as piano lessons and choir practice, Girl Scouts, youth group, and weekends in the country—my life was joyfully turbulent. So smitten was I with my peers during these years, that I didn't spend much time alone with either of my parents.

On a rare and quiet Sunday afternoon—rare in that no girlfriends could be found—I settled across the dining room table from my mother. Between us were two pristine canvases and my very first set of oil paints. With timid fingers I began to squeeze the vibrant colors onto our palettes; with confidence, Marian arranged a blue-striped dish towel under a copper chafing dish.

Never had I seen Marian hold a brush. In silence we worked, mother and daughter. Imagine my surprise when at last we turned our canvases round to show one another. On the walls of Robertson Place were paintings created by my grand-mother, Sadie, but here was Marian's fully realized still-life painting, executed with skill and confidence.

Lipstick and Cinch Belts

As a rite of passage into seventh grade, we girls were allowed to wear our first lipstick. Whether we needed it or not, we all bought bras. A friend and I snuck off to buy ours at Woolworth's. Soon we were being advised to wear girdles and nylon hose with garter straps, but these I did not like. However, crin-oline underskirts were another thing. Stiffened with sugar rinses, they made our full cotton skirts stand out and allowed us to cut a wide swath as we sashayed down the school's crowded hallways. Cinch belts further accentuated our youth-ful waistlines, and we competed among one another for the fullest skirts and tiniest waists.

In the mid-1950s, high school girls could participate in team sports. Field hockey, basketball, volleyball, softball, and tennis were among those offered by my school. Lack of enthusiasm by some of us was due to a bias against physical exertion; it was viewed as unladylike because we might break out in a sweat.

Occasionally, I played tennis with a friend, but it was golf that piqued my inter-est. Golf was my brother's only sport in high school; he was on the golf team with Jack Nicklaus, who went on to become what many consider to be the greatest golfer of his generation. Phil was always practicing his swing in the backyard. My father tried his hand at it, and I too learned how to swing a club. Golf was in the air.

Social clubs were popular, too. When sororities were banned from our school, I acted as a ring-leader to form an all-inclusive girls' club. (Later I discovered that it was my own mother, Marian Hammond, who, as president of the school's par-ent-teacher organization, had secretly spearheaded the drive to end the sororities with their sometimes-hurtful exclusionary practices.) On most days when the last bell rang, I simply went straight home to be near my music and the telephone. The latest copy of *Seventeen* magazine was eagerly awaited while I worked on a sewing project. With matching funds from my parents, at the age of thirteen, I bought my first sewing machine. It was a Singer Featherweight, and the first thing I made was a red wool dress with princess seams.

Rock-'n-roll stormed the airwaves in the mid-1950s, and my peers invented the "bunny hop." At parties we slow-danced to the mellow voice of Johnny Mathis, and in a talent show I sang the soprano part in my trio's rendition of the McGuire sisters' "Sincerely." A boyfriend named Donnie got me interested in jazz and swing music; we played his father's old 78s on a turntable. Another boyfriend built me an amplifier from the Heath Kit he had ordered by mail. My parents were suspicious of my boyfriends because they were older and drove cars. Arguments broke out over whether or not I could ride with them, but soon I would be learning to drive myself.

In 1955 our family bought a car to go with our modern house. Compared to our dark-red Buick of the post-war years—or to Delano's black 1937 Ford!—here was a machine from another planet. Turquoise and white, our Chevy Nomad looked like a space ship. Phil had already begun his fascination with foreign cars, but I loved that sleek, pastel colored, American car. Glass-packs added to its exhaust system made the car sound like a hot rod. This fit right in with the neighborhood, where my next door neighbor, Annette, sported a black leather jacket, had her long hair cut short into a duck-tail, and played the records of a daring new singer named Elvis.

A Strange Sound

Between pep rallies and Friday night football games, and in between boyfriends and school musicals, all of a sudden something was terribly wrong. One day, coming home from school, I heard a strange sound. On the sofa, moaning softly, was my father. Marian was tending him, but I shall never forget his muffled sobbing. At the hospital, they said it was stomach ulcers, but it occurred to me later that this might have been his first descent into depression. After George was released from the hospital, my parents went to the country to the sheltered world of Robertson Place where my mother helped him convalesce by reading to him the entirety of Tolstoy's *War and Peace*.

During my parents' two- or three-weeks absence, Nammy and my brother acted as my supervisors. To express my temporary freedom from parental scrutiny, I cranked up the volume on my hi-fi until I blew out the speakers. Frank Sinatra and The Four Freshmen filled the neighborhood, a lot of Swanson's frozen chicken pot pies were eaten, and I fixed too many Brown Cows—a popular drink of the time which consisted of ice cream floating in root beer.

Was I a bit prudish in high school? Perhaps. I didn't seem to be drawn to typical teenage rebellious behavior, such as smoking and drinking; risky behavior did not tempt me. My attitude was shared with a new girlfriend, Barbara, who arrived in eighth grade. Quickly, we bonded. Although art and music appealed to me in high school, the two of us took challenging courses, such as physics and debate. We participated in student government and pushed ourselves to get top grades. Near the end of my junior year, at an all-school assembly, the school's principal came to the microphone: "Lynn Hammond is the teachers' choice to go to Girls' State." Girls's State was a week-long program designed for Ohio's young women to get a feel for government and politics. At the time, I wasn't aware of any females in politics, but it never occurred to me to question the premise. However, this was not how things worked out. Instead, Barbara, my alternate, went to Girls' State and I went off to Europe.

Lure of the Old World

American tourists began to hit Europe's shores after the end of World War II in waves. The first of these occurred during the 1950s, and among them were my parents. In their mid-forties, they crossed the ocean for their first time in the summer of 1954. But unlike most of their fellow passengers, when my parents disembarked from The Queen Elizabeth onto foreign soil, they did not board a tour bus. Instead, they rented a little Volkswagon car and traversed the countrysides of Europe with Kurt, their German exchange student, as guide. When they returned to America, Marian and George had a new zest for life and were was full of enthusiasm about the charms of the old world. The trip's effect would transform Marian's ideas about how to live and entertain and how to alter Robertson Place.

Next, it was my brother's turn. After bicycling across France with *The Experiment in International Living*, he too was smitten with Europe. Two years later, from his base at the University of Geneva, Switzerland, he hopped into an Isetta and hit the road with a girl in tow. At the age of twenty, Phil was fulfilling the young man's dream of touring the back roads of Europe. I would soon catch up with him.

It is June, 10, 1958, and I am sixteen years old. I am about to join my brother in Europe, and from the tiny window of a TWA jet-prop airplane, I wave goodbye to my family in Columbus, Ohio. My first time aboard an airplane gives my stomach butterflies. Wearing a navy blue checked suit, along with pumps and white gloves, I fiddle with the corsage on my lapel, a parting gift from my boyfriend.

Our plane's departure is delayed. At New York's La Guardia airport, a helicopter has been ordered to rush another passenger and me across the city to Idlewild, the city's international airport. Nevertheless, my connecting flight is missed. When I land in Zurich the next afternoon, Phil, who was to pick me up, is nowhere in sight. I wait and wait as the shadows grow longer. No Phil. In my purse is my only link to him— or, for that matter—to anyone in all of Europe! It is a long string of numbers. When a stewardess finally comes into view, my voice fails. Showing her the telephone number, she offers a few Swiss coins and goes on her way. After practicing the numbers in my high-school French, I manage to find a pay phone and enunciate those numbers to the operator. One-hundred kilometers away, in the small mountain village of Oberaegeri, Phil answers my call. "What happened to you?" he asks. He'd waited in vain for my original flight because TWA's telegram never arrived at the Swiss airport.

"You Have his Eyes"

Near Oberaegeri, Phil and I stayed for several days in a tiny log house called Chalet Escape. Our hostess was an elderly woman called Frau Dresbach. After serving us tea, she sat down to study my face. "You have his eyes," she said. I had no idea what she was talking about. I thought she was a family acquaintance from Chillicothe, but this eighty-year-old expatriate was none other than Sylvia Reedy, Delano's old flame. It turned out that over all these years, Syl-

via had never stopped loving our grandfather. After Delano's marriage to my grandmother Sadie, a disheartened Sylvia had accepted a marriage proposal from Melvin Dresbach, another Chillicothe native. However, this was a marriage of convenience. After her husband took a teaching position at Cornell University, Sylvia emigrated to Europe to pursue her career as concert pianist.

When World War II broke out, Sylvia found herself stranded in a suburb of Berlin, Germany. She feared she was being watched, and in order to get news she hid in her broom closet to listen to BBC on a shortwave radio. As soon as the war ended, Sylvia made her break; she was the first civilian permitted by the occupying forces to leave her region. Sylvia took a few precious items and headed for the neutral country of Switzerland where she built the little Swiss chalet and where we now sat drinking tea.

In 1946 the widowed Sylvia Dresbach returned to the states to settle her husband's estate. She came to visit the recently widowed Delano in Columbus. I was only five at the time and do not recall that evening around the dinner table. Was she trying to rekindle a relationship with my grandfather? Perhaps she was. But Sylvia, then in her sixties, returned to Europe alone.

Shortly thereafter, in letters to Marian and George, Sylvia confessed that she was running out of money. Could they help her? In exchange for financial help, Sylvia would deed to them her beloved chalet. This my parents agreed to, and for the rest of Sylvia's life, some twenty years, they sent a yearly check for $1,000 to Frau Sylvia Dresbach, Oberageri, Canton Zug, Switzerland.

Strange was the start of my summer in Europe, but for the next ten weeks, Phil took me to medieval palaces and dungeons, nightclubs and cathedrals. In a Borgward we buzzed along autobahns in Germany, snaked through the Alpine passes and sped around the race track at Nürburgring. Along the way we picked up a couple of travelers from Texas, named Stew and Fox; in Seefeld, Austria, Phil paid innkeepers $2.00 a day to care for me during my recovery from trench mouth. By the time we reached Spain I was well enough to drink my first champagne and cheer for the matador.

In my little green travel diary, I penciled a few sparse notes about the weather and sights. But to my friend back home, on a sheet of onion-skin, air-mail stationery, I confessed my enthusiasm for bullfighting:

July 27, 1958

Dear Connie,

The bullfights were really great—I thought I would just hate them because of the cruelty to the bull but I just told myself they're going to kill the

bull whether I watch or not—so I saw all. Once the matador was awarded
2 ears! Big deal. And really, I thought the crowd was more fascinating to
watch than the fighting. They would whistle (which means BOO) and hiss
and wave handkerchiefs and stamp their feet. Then if the matador does well,
they throw flowers, purses, jewelry, hats and shoes at him. And if they don't
like him they throw their seat cushion into the ring! [132]

When Phil and I ran out of funds, we canceled our plans to cross the channel to the British Isles and sailed for home on The *S.S. Groote Beer.* After WWII, this ship had been purchased by the Netherlands government from the U.S. for use as a transport ship for immigrants. They gave it a Dutch name, fitted it with dormitories, and now, a decade later, its cargo was students. By the time the ship arrived back on native soil, my young mind was spinning with questions about art, religion, and American culture.[133]

Readjustment—Affairs of the Heart

*I*t was now my senior year at Upper Arlington High School, and I felt a little detached. Pep rallies and slumber parties no longer seemed urgent. Throughout high school, clubs and social events were important; I had loved them all, but it was time to focus on other things.[134]

College was looming, and my friend Barbara and I began to discuss our options. It never occurred to either of us to consider the fine university in our midst, The Ohio State University. Instead, we developed a scheme to visit several elite women's colleges on the East Coast, known as the Seven Sisters. We requested interviews and mapped our route. Somehow—it seems hard to believe as I look back—we persuaded our parents to let us take one of the family cars, and off we went!

Wellesley College in Massachusetts was tops in our minds and hearts. Barbara was accepted; I was not. On the rebound, it was to another all-female school in the East that I applied.

Meanwhile, Phil helped me get a part-time job. Throughout my senior year, with my boyfriend Jim, I traveled downtown twice a week and on Saturdays to work as a clerk in the famous department store, Lazarus. Jewelry and children's clothing, men's shirts, and hula-hoops: these were my job to sell. But there was a downside to this job; it meant that I couldn't go to the country on weekends.

Affairs of the heart were never far from my teenage brain. When I did manage to get to Robertson Place, I often tried to bring along a boyfriend. Throughout junior high and high school, there were two boys who jock-  eyed for that position—Jim and Bill. Different from one another as day and night, they came in and out of my life in predictable succession. Jim was average looking, easy going, and solid. At times, he could be serious. On the other hand, Bill was high-strung, gorgeous, and flashy, but he was too possessive. He'd been sent to Culver Military Academy (for reasons unknown to me) for part of his high-school years. In contrast to Jim's father, an engineer who had died when Jim was in grade school, Bill's father was a real-estate tycoon. Two different worlds. However, in my heart of hearts, I knew neither of these boys would be my life's companion.

A Mind-Altering Year

In the spring of my senior year, the school's guidance counselor sent a note to me. "Would you like to attend a meeting about a traveling school?" The International School of America (ISA) was hatched at Harvard by a wealthy entrepreneur, a Columbus man named Karl Jaeger. Experimental in nature, the school's concept was idealistic and ambitious. Students and their teachers would travel around the world by airplane, hopping from one country to another, living with native families while studying the region's geography, history, religion, economy and culture. We were to travel not as tourists but as students. First-hand experience would inform us; the speed of air travel would condense and intensify our learning in a manner unlike that of any past generation.

On Harvard Square, under sunny skies on September 10, 1959, I met my fellow students and our five teachers. We came from all over the nation, and most of us were on scholarships. One student, Fathi Salama, came from Egypt. Among us was Andrew Weil, who would later start a revolution in alternative medicine.

In Boston we teenagers got to know one another and learn the protocol: classes two days each week, field trips on the others. Moving as a group, we were ready to travel. First on the itinerary was The United Nations in New York, then the Capitol in Washington D.C., followed by Chinatown in San Francisco.

Crossing the ocean, we made a stop in Hawaii, where we read from the works of anthropologist Margaret Mead and learned to eat poi. Next up, Japan, where a thousand clapping school girls lined our way to their school. It felt strange to be treated with such enthusiasm in a land so recently our mortal enemy. For my first meal in this exotic land, I sat cross-legged with my host family at a sunken dining table. Conversation was limited to gestures and smiles as we sipped clear soup from a bowl in which tiny fish, tied up in artful knots, were floating. After dinner, it was my honor as guest to be the first of the family to immerse myself into their hot—and I mean *hot!*—tub.

Challenges came daily. Next was the trick of fitting myself like a sardine into the crowded underground commuter train. "People fight their way on the train, and there is a man whose official job is to push people on the train from behind. Once on, you cannot budge, and people groan, etc. Really bad.," I wrote to my diary. [135]

A cultural shock lurked around every corner. In the marketplace, slithering eels repulsed me; on stage, kimono-clad Kabuki dancers enthralled me. This was total immersion. Yet to come were Hong Kong, Thailand, Cambodia, India, Egypt, Turkey, Greece, Italy, Germany, France and England. Through all of it, with cameras strapped around our necks, each of us lugged a full-sized suitcase, a duffle bag, and a cloth bag stuffed full of books.

Time magazine covered our trip in Japan where my blonde hair and blue eyes stood out in the sea of black that was post-war Japan. In Egypt, a photographer from *Life* magazine trailed us as we crept down the ladder into Tutankhamen's tomb. Of course, not everything we encountered was newsworthy or glamorous. In a rural Indian village, where Professor Taft lectured to us about the country's sanitation problems and over-population, he pointed to houses constructed of bricks made of cow dung. Starving beggars surrounded our bus in Calcutta. And in Thailand, where American military families hosted us, we read a sensational new book called *The Ugly American*. The book was a scathing critique of bad behavior by our diplomatic corps in Southeast Asia, and was to serve as inspiration to John F. Kennedy for his Peace Corps.

Christmas was spent in the Hindu country of India, and for the first time I experienced a little homesickness. A single package arrived from my family during the holiday, but only crumbs remained of Marian's tin of Christmas cookies. Letters from home arrived in each country, but in such an exotic environment it was futile, if not counter-productive, to try to conjure up the ambiance of home. Interestingly, it was not my house in Arlington that I missed, but the farm in southern Ohio. It was Robertson Place.

My host family in New Delhi was gracious and educated, and its daughter, Asha, and I corresponded for decades. On a Sunday afternoon in the spacious lawn of their ranch-style house, we were entertained by a man with a performing bear. When it came time for me to bathe, Asha signaled to a trio of white-turbaned Sikhs who lit a wood fire. After one of the men delivered a bucket of hot water to our cement-floored bathroom, I gave myself a sponge bath while standing over the drain.

Deep in the interior of Egypt, from the Valley of the Kings, our teachers attempted to arrange a long-distance call to Ohio where a group of the parents had gathered at our house in Columbus. It was to be our only phone conversation during the entire year, and it was disappointing. Conversation was stilted and rehearsed. So distant were their voices.

Wandering among the ancient ruins and theaters in Greece ignited in me a curiosity about Greek art and drama, and I vowed to take a peek at the volumes of Greek and Roman history in the bookcases at Robertson Place. Heading west from Greece, the countries of Europe felt more familiar to me. We slid into Italy with its wealth of Western art and architecture, and when visiting the Uffizi Gallery in Florence, in a room devoid of tourists, I paused to gaze at Botticelli's Venus.

Russia lay behind the Iron Curtain in 1960 and China's borders were still closed. East Germany, too, was sealed off with fortified barriers. Berlin was now divided, but when we touched down in the newly revitalized West Berlin, our teachers were able to persuade East German officials to allow our small group to cross the border from West to East Berlin.

On April 3, I made the following entry in my little white diary:

This is the closest we have ever been to a communist state (East Berlin) and I have observed many surprising things. When we got off the subway we were immediately confronted with huge propaganda posters depicting capitalists in black silk hats worshipping H-bombs, etc. I was really shocked. They played up the idea that the capitalist world wanted war, but that they were fighting desperately for peace. We came up from the underground and found ourselves in what sounded and looked like a 'dead city' almost void of people and automobiles (except for police and party cars and tanks.) The buildings were in shambles—never having been repaired after the war—and masses of stone lay strewn in the fields and on sidewalks. We walked into a church and found pigeons aimlessly wandering over the rubble. [136]

By the time we arrived in England, it was spring. Warm breezes and spring flowers greeted us, but we students were ready to get back to American soil. First, however, there would be exams. Nine months of study with the ISA was designed to equal an academic freshman year at Harvard. And so it did. The results of our exams were enough to give full credit to the few who went on to Harvard, Radcliffe, and Princeton. Ohio State was skeptical.

Mind-altering was how I would later describe my year of study and travel. After such a disorienting year, it felt as though I needed to stay home. My father had suffered another bout of depression during my absence, and that was reason enough for sticking around. Yet there was another reason that caused me to hesitate. Soon after we had begun our round-the-world journey, the founder and director of the school had singled me out. Twice my age and married with children, he had forced his unwanted attentions upon me. The other students and teachers helped to protect me, but his transgressions were kept a secret from our parents. If they had gotten wind of the situation, the ISA would certainly have ended quickly and in scandal. Now that we were all home, it was time to tell the truth. Should the director pay a price for his inappropriate behavior and the trauma it caused me? I turned the problem over to my parents.[137]

1960s: The College Years

College would not be the destination for many of America's graduating seniors in the fall of 1960. Across the nation, sixty percent of my female peers would end their schooling after graduation (as opposed to forty-six percent of males). Fewer than seven percent of all American women would have a college degree by 1964. In rural Southern Ohio, at the newly formed Paint Valley High School (a consolidation of Bourneville and Bainbridge), only a few of its class of fifty seniors would go on to pursue higher learning in a formal setting. For most of the students, graduating from high school had been their goal. Farm or factory jobs awaited the boys; marriage and children was expected of the girls. [138]

But college was not even a choice for me; it was an assumption. Upper Arlington's school system was designed to prepare its students for college, and ninety-eight percent fulfilled that promise. Getting formal education beyond high school had been a priority for my family for several generations—even when the cost meant sacrifice. Marian, Sadie, and Margarite had all gone on to earn certificates or diplomas. Indeed, the thrust of the entire family was to pursue learning. Where to go for that education was the only question posed to me.

The Ohio State University had never been anything to me but a sprawling local institution of higher learning where all comers were accepted. Unlike private schools, its tuition was relatively inexpensive. In 1960, $1,200 of tuition could buy an entire year of classes. Only vaguely was I aware of my family's history at OSU, and never did they apply pressure on me to attend their alma mater. But I am glad that I pursued the university in our midst because it gave me a first-rate education.

It was here that I settled on a career—although that was not due to any help from the college career counselor. "Sell art supplies?" she wondered aloud, after seeing my interest in art. Noting my frown, she reconsidered. Logical thinking was part of my profile so she suggested that I become a computer programmer. A what? I could not even picture a computer. By the 1960s, educated women were filling our nation's need for public school teachers, nurses, dental hygienists, and social workers. Other careers were beginning to open up, but we had few role models.

Over the summer, I wandered around campus, trying to get oriented. But OSU was huge. Gone now was Phil, having graduated from law school and headed out West. Instead, my mother would be my anchor. Once Marian's nest was empty, she had wasted no time picking up the threads of her life. Although she had a master's degree in psychology, Marian was needed in the Ohio State's English department to teach incoming freshman. All over the country, universities were gearing up for the first wave of baby boomers. With books and packed lunches, each morning the two of us drove to the massive parking lot beside the football stadium. From there, we hiked up to the campus.

Writing about my travel experiences was an urgent need, so I signed up for English composition. Solving life's big questions was my current challenge, so I tried courses in logic, philosophy and comparative religion. Once the fall quarter began, I joined the forty-thousand other students, rushing from class to class across the vast campus. Amidst the boisterous chaos of the student-union cafeteria, I often ate lunch alone.

Fitting into the social scene on campus proved to be difficult. Putting off college for just that one year made me feel as though I had skipped a beat. I was out of step. Coeds were wearing tight-fitting black dresses and dancing "the twist." It was going to be hard to catch up with my peers because, as a "townie," I wasn't permitted to live in the campus dorms. My isolation was somewhat alleviated by joining a sorority, just as Marian had done when she was a college student. Their exclusive nature and closed-door meetings were not appealing, but it was in the quiet setting of the

sorority house that I found friends. An added benefit of the sorority setting was a comfortable place to eat lunch, rest, and regroup before hitting the campus again. Waiters served our meals on white tablecloths while we conversed with one another and made small talk with the house mother. Beckoning me in the gracious living room was a grand piano or a game of bridge.

Choosing a major was confusing. Because of my recent experience with international travel, I had the vague notion that becoming a cultural attaché to a foreign ambassador might fit my aspirations. But sitting through several courses in the Department of International Relations cured me of that idea. Dominated by men from developing countries, I quickly realized what a misfit I would be. Instead, courses in world history, botany, zoology, English, Italian language, and art filled my liberal arts curriculum. Early work in fine arts brought praise; sculpture teachers singled me out and judges awarded me First Prize in a campus-wide painting competition. I loved the smell of turpentine in Hayes Hall. By graduation, I had the idea that I could become a real, working artist.

How I got this idea is a mystery. None of my art teachers were women. No female artists had I ever seen or met. In fact, no female artists had I learned about in my four years of art history courses. In all the pages of H. W. Janson's first edition of *History of Art*—considered by our teachers to be the bible of art history in 1962—Janson gave not one line to a person of my gender. When I asked my painting professor for advice about graduate school, he held up the fingers of one hand and said, "Lynn, I know only this many artists who can support themselves with their art. Why don't you just get married and have children?"

I was speechless. This was the sixties. Revolution was in the air. President Kennedy had been shot in Dallas, and my peers at OSU would soon take over the administration building and march on Selma. Although I never rioted and never marched, I was part of this generation. Don't tell me I can't become an artist!

Douglas

Affairs of the heart, however, would soon interfere with plans to further my art studies. Throughout my four years at Ohio State, dating had been a disappointment. Phil had found his future bride in college; by the time my sorority sisters were ready to graduate nearly all of them were engaged. Fraternity parties were fraught with pressure to drink and more, so I stayed around the fringe of campus life and threw myself into my books and my art. Occasionally, if a boy seemed promising, I would bring him to the country to Robertson Place. That was my test. But he never fit in; he always failed.

It so happened that I had met the man who would become my future husband in Southern Ohio at a camp retreat for college students. Camp Akita (in southern Ohio's Hocking Hills) was led by a charismatic youth minister and sponsored by The First Community Church, a very liberal, ecumenical church in Columbus. Parts of my summer had been spent at Camp Akita for many years, and I flat out loved the place. Maybe some of my old camping buddies would show up for the weekend retreat. Many did, but in the summer of 1961, there was a new face, a completely new and different boy.

He was tall and lean and nice-enough looking, but nothing to write home about. A little shy, a little reticent to speak, he had braces on his teeth. Yet there was a spark in his eyes. This Carden boy from the South wasn't what you would call cool. He wasn't smooth either, as he flung me around the square-dance floor. But smooth demeanor had always made me suspicious.

We began to talk. We talked and talked, and the more we talked, the more urgent it felt because the retreat would be over on Sunday, and then he would head back south to start his sophomore year at Vanderbilt University. We talked until dawn that Saturday night in his blue Chevrolet. When he told me of spending happy summers on his grandparents' farm and mentioned that he might become a country doctor, that was it. Suddenly I realized what Marian and Sadie and all the women before me who so loved Robertson Place were looking for in a husband. At last here was someone who might pass the farm test.

The following week, Doug came to our house to meet the parents. He astonished us by sitting down at our piano to play *Malaguena*—not very well, but by heart. I was walking on a cloud. And then he was gone. I wrote to him at Vanderbilt. I waited. I wrote a second letter. Still nothing. Classes were starting. Had I misunderstood his feelings? The shock and disappointment stung, but I would have to move on.

After Christmas, the missing boyfriend showed up on our doorstep. OH! So you think you can just push reset and pretend nothing happened? Not so quick. For the next year and a half, we played cat-and-mouse. Meanwhile, Doug transferred to Yale. Surely he would meet someone at one of the college mixers. But in the fall of our senior year I was invited to New Haven for a visit. Pretty soon he would be applying to Yale's medical school, so I took the opportunity to interview for the graduate program at the Yale School of Art. Things were heating up; we wanted to be together.

But our little scheme fell through. Doug's parents, who were expecting to pay his way, were strongly opposed to their son getting married either before or during medical school. They refused to support him if he decided to get married. Without a wedding band, no self-respecting girl from the Midwest could leave her parents' house to live with her fiancé. Or even live in the same city! What would folks back home think? Victorian morality was in my genes.

Cooling our heels, we put our plans on hold. Doug would be staying at Yale for medical school, but the momentum toward being together was too great to deny. Sunday night phone calls and passionate letters kept things warm while we finished out our senior years and wondered how and when we could be together.

"Come to the airport," he had said. It was at 5:00 a.m. on a Sunday morning in April when the telephone rang in the apartment where I was living with a classmate. "And bring your suitcase." My *suitcase*? He wanted to elope!

I pulled on some clothes in the dark, packed a small bag, and climbed into my Chevy Corvair. At the airport I offered to give up my plans for graduate school and to look for a job in New Haven. We could be married soon, I promised. But I could not, would not, upset my parents by running away.

Three generations of women had gotten married on the grounds of Robertson Place, and I wanted to be the fourth. After Doug was persuaded, we met with my parents and decided on a date. It would be August 22, 1964. Instead of drama and scandal, there would be a traditional wedding with flowers and a cake.

"All hands on deck!" George spent the summer moving sprinklers around while fretting about the drought; Marian worried about orchestrating a reception for one-hundred guests. Doug, too, had been feeling nervous. In a letter reminiscent of Marian's pep talk to George on the eve of their marriage, I sent reassurance:

> *Oh sweet, you were so low tonight and I ached to be with you... Douglas, the decision has changed me. Everyone sees it in my face, and I feel it with me all the while. Perhaps this inner glow is what is [keeping] me above the depressive thoughts of the remaining problems and details about next year. I know that they are not little, sweet-heart, but all that really matters is that we are in love with each other—we...are...in...love—and we are going to be allowed to live in it, to express it, nourish it and struggle for it.* [139]

Doug spent that final summer at home in New Jersey working a summer job and composing a set of contemporary wedding vows, which were destined to be brushed aside by the local, tradition-bound minister. When his family arrived at Robertson Place, they spent the day before our wedding shopping for proper attire for Allen, their hippie son. Carden relatives trickled in from the South, quietly worrying about the future of their beloved nephew. If she puts him through medical school, will she hold it up to him later to make him feel he owes her something?

Rain began to fall on Friday morning, and it didn't let up until the afternoon of our wedding day. In the spirit of the times, I canceled my long-standing hair appointment and rolled my unruly locks into a French twist. Gertrude and Philemon hosted a wedding breakfast at their home in Chillicothe. From Tennessee and Georgia, Doug's aunties arrived in their hats, and Doug charmed us with folk music on his guitar. Finally, back at the farmhouse, Nammy helped me step into the Jackie Kennedy-style wedding dress she had made for me, and I tugged and tugged to pull the tight kid gloves over my elbows. Nammy fussed with my veil. It was four o'clock. Everyone took their places on the front lawn of Robertson Place—except Doug's mother. She was in the bathroom crying.

It was not a blissful event for all: our mothers were stressed, and the in-laws were not on the best of terms. But of these undercurrents, we newlyweds were oblivious. Young and ecstatic, we greeted the guests and sipped our champagne. As we slipped away to our honeymoon, a rainbow arched over Robertson Place.

Early Married Life—Medical School

The 1960s were an exciting time to be living in America. It was full of promise—especially if you were young and starting out. The Soviet Union and the United States, the world's two superpowers, were in a race into space. The Peace Corps was sending its first wave of young people to Africa, and Pop Art was bursting on the scene. The Beatles arrived on our shore! Medicare was launched, and the first nuclear treaty was signed. By decade's end, America had landed an astronaut on the moon. Anything seemed possible.

Historians say that it was also a time of innocence. Jobs were plentiful, and we were expected to surpass our parents in both security and wealth. We had high hopes for the United Nations. Rock 'n' roll filled the airways and many of us had cars in which to cruise the drive-ins. Our boyfriends and young husbands wore khakis and Levi's, and they tucked in their shirts. We girls cinched our waists and rolled our hair on rollers the size of juice cans. Social etiquette still required that we wear skirts in the nation's schools, offices, and hospitals, but on the weekend we all wore Bermuda shorts.

However, the decade had its dark side. Crime and air pollution plagued our cities and social unrest erupted into violence. The assassination of our young president was the most shocking thing our generation had ever experienced. Before that, in the spring of 1963, Martin Luther King had organized a 200,000 person march on Washington where he delivered his "I Have a Dream" speech. Malcolm X was shot in New York, and riots broke out in the California neighborhood of Watts. Lyndon Johnson, our new president, engineered a raft of civil-rights bills to address the grievances of our African-American minority, but in the spring of Doug's last year in medical school, Martin Luther King was murdered. Soon after that, Bobby Kennedy was slain. Throughout it all was the Vietnam War. Near the end of the decade, on a barren expanse in Woodstock, New York, young people converged at a dairy farm for a musical festival that turned into a peaceful war protest and a days-long, drug-fueled love-in. It would be the symbol of our generation's cultural revolution.

This was the future into which Doug and I stepped as a young married couple in August of 1964. Just days after our wedding at Robertson Place, we packed all our earthly belongings into a small U-Haul trailer and set off for New Haven, Connecticut. Inside that trailer was an antique drop-leaf table from Robertson Place and a small Oriental rug—Gertrude's and Philemon's wedding gift to us. At our destination, a mattress and box springs on red building bricks would be our bed. A few boards on more bricks would be our bookshelves. On loan from Doug's parents was a chest of drawers, a mirror and a little folding table. That was it. Along with a church pew for seating, it was all we needed for our little third-floor, garret apartment.

Doug's parents' refusal to pay for medical school was meant to deter us, but women's liberation was around the corner. Women in my generation expected not only to earn an income outside the home, but to decide when and if to start a family. We had the pill.

Because of the intense cocoon of medical school, we were relatively insulated from the tumult of the times. Had it not been for my job with a Ford-Foundation grant organization called Higher Horizons, we might have missed the essence of the decade. As one of the earliest efforts in the War on Poverty, Higher Horizons was designed to raise the self-awareness and aspirations of minority children in New Haven. My new job was a far cry from the cushy public relations job I had left behind at the Columbus Gallery of Fine Arts. It paid well, and yet it was not enough.

My yearly salary of $5,280 would not quite cover our expenses and pay the $2,000 needed for Doug's tuition. To make ends meet, Doug took on some night work at a local hospital. These efforts, plus a monthly check of $100 from Ohio, kept us afloat during those four years. Never did we go into debt.

Down in the basement of an elementary school in a blue-collar neighbor-hood, I reported for work. Our task was to supply inner-city school teachers with material relevant to their African-American and Puerto-Rican pupils. At this time, virtually all the textbooks in America's public schools depicted only white children in white neighborhoods leading middle-class lives. If we could not find appropriate material, we created it. My first winter in New Haven was spent writing lesson plans for a fourth-grade unit on Africa. Small efforts like these were repeated throughout the city, and we felt as though we were on the cutting edge of a long-overdue effort to correct the inequities in our nation's schools.

Living in an apartment in a New Haven neighborhood left me feeling somewhat disconnected, and after a year, we moved into the hub of the Yale medical campus. Here, in a medical-student apartment complex (sandwiched between the medical school and the hospital), our subsidized rent was just $75, allowing us to purchase a bed frame and a good reading lamp. The entire place was no bigger than four-hundred square feet—little more than the size of a single front room at Robertson Place. But it was well designed and complete. In my tiny kitchenette I began to cook from scratch, making farm recipes of chili and pumpkin pies. How I wished I had learned some of Marian's cooking skills!

Social life picked up. We became fast friends with a few of the married couples in Doug's medical class of one hundred, (only four of whom were female.) On Saturday evenings we hosted each other for dinner and played cribbage or took in a movie. Going out for a pizza was a rare treat.

Tracking expenses came naturally after having watched my parents record every dime they spent. For the month of September, 1964, I entered the following: food $49.72, travel $12.50, entertainment $3.00, new shoes for Doug $27.16.

Studying day and night was Doug's routine. To match his stride, I signed up for some graduate courses in art history at the University of Southern Connecticut. Sewing projects absorbed and clothed me, tennis or squash gave us exercise. We even managed to budget a bare-bones ski trip to Vermont. Our lives were full, but in order to spend more time painting, I traded my full-time job with one that was part time. Working with disadvantaged children and their mothers as program director and story teller in one of its store-front branches was my new job. After a lot of badgering, the Yale house committee finally agreed to let me set up an easel in a storage room in the dormitory's basement.

Nostalgia for Robertson Place hit me hard from time to time. Standing at the window of our tiny apartment, tears streaming down my face, I looked out through the security bars of our iron fence. It was Easter Sunday, and I missed Ohio. I missed seeing the redbud and dogwood trees in bloom; I missed the farm.

In 1965, we arranged to spend our summer break at Robertson Place. While my parents vacationed, the two of us kept things watered and weeded, and Doug mowed the grounds and managed the farm sod business. This husband of mine fit right into the country scene: he had indeed passed the now famous farm test.

Our second summer's break was a family trip to Europe. Long anticipated, its purpose was for my parents to introduce Doug and my aunt and uncle to the European continent. In a rented Volkswagon van, the six of us drove through France, Italy, Germany, and Switzerland. When the older generation returned to the states, Doug and I, using Michelin Guides and Arthur Frommer's *Europe on $5 a Day*, continued the tour alone. We crossed the channel, switched to the left side of the road, and drove all the way up the British Isles to Balmoral Castle in Scotland. Picnicking by day, bedding down in bed-and-breakfast accommodations by night, we met the locals and soaked up their culture.

Graduation from medical school required that Doug do a thesis paper. History had been his college major, and he decided to study the practice of early western medicine in Clear Creek County, Colorado, 1865–1895. So, for this, our third and final free summer, we headed west with our station wagon loaded with my Singer and a year's worth of fresh paintings. At a trading post in Albuquerque, New Mexico, we bought our first piece of native American art, and I danced with a cowboy. In Phoenix, where my brother and his wife now lived, I staged a little show of my paintings by propping them against the living room furniture. People came and drank the wine, but only one of my thirty-five painting was purchased.

Internship, Pregnancy, and Hippies

Idyllic summers like this were soon to come to an end. Upon graduation in 1968, Doug would start a rotating internship in Cincinnati, a city neither of us knew, but which fit the requirement of being within driving distance of Robertson Place. We knew the year would be difficult because internships were notorious for their long hours and demanding schedule. Some of the rotations required Doug to be on duty in the hospital for thirty-six hours at a stretch.

Filing slides in the art history department at the University of Cincinnati was my day-time job. Designing and making clothing for the college hippie culture was my night job. Bell-bottomed jumpsuits, mini-skirts of red leather, dresses of metallic fringe made for disco dancing with strobe lights: these were the fashions that filled my sketchbooks and challenged my sewing skills.

"It's never convenient to be pregnant," my kindly gynecologist explained to me in October. Eyes wide open, I was speechless. Off the pill for only a month, I didn't expect to actually *get* pregnant—at least not so soon! We had decided to get going if we wanted children—maybe four—because doctors told us that after the age of thirty-five there would be greater risk for birth defects.

However, when the doctor announced my pregnancy, I was more concerned that when this baby was due in July, Doug would be finishing his internship and getting orders from the United States Army. All doctors were needed for the Vietnam war effort. Doug's applications for deferment had been denied, and now that the war was heating up, he might be sent overseas!

The war in Vietnam filled our nation's atmosphere and airwaves in 1968. On January 30, North Vietnam had launched its massive and deadly Tet offensive, and it turned out to be the turning point in the war. Young men fled to Canada; protestors took to the streets. Flags were burned. We had no television, but the radio droned on and on about the war on the other side of the world.

Day and night, during that year leading up to Doug's deployment, I kept myself busy cutting and sewing. Now a line of maternity clothing spun from my machine. Pregnancy was easy for me, but loneliness and uneasiness crept into my mind during that year in Cincinnati. What kept me focused was the fact that only an hour and a half away was Robertson Place. It was my refuge. After seeing the world, I had come to realize that my happiness depended upon being near a small dot on the map in southern Ohio.

Changes at Robertson Place—A New Kitchen for Marian

How the old farmhouse was changing! New sights greeted me every time I got a chance to spend a weekend at Robertson Place—not just different wallpaper and paint, but serious changes. Throughout the 1960s Marian and George had been very, very busy. After selling their contemporary house in Arlington, they had moved downtown where they remodeled side-by-side residences in the city's up-and-coming Columbus neighborhood called German Village. At Robertson Place, just in time for our August wedding in 1964, they had torn down the 1930s bedroom and bath to build an addition.

Modern and functional, the new two-story, clapboard addition nestled against the backside of the L-shaped brick house. For Philemon, there was a new workshop; for George, an office/den; and for Nammy, a sewing space. But for all the inhabitants of Robertson Place, the biggest improvement was on the second floor. Here was our first *upstairs* bathroom.

Finally, in 1968, there was to be a new kitchen for Marian. For years, she had been working on the plans for her kitchen, clipping ideas from House and Garden and learning the skill of drafting. After a twelve-year detour into teaching English at Ohio State—where she enjoyed the stimulating camaraderie but was stymied by the challenge to publish-or-perish—Marian returned to the work she most enjoyed. She was a born designer. Marian would go on to spend the next decade buying and rehabbing several houses in German Village, but during the summer of 1968, she lived at the farm and hired a local man to remodel the farm kitchen.

Homer was his name. He was a preacher/carpenter. For his first day on the job, Homer Swearingen arrived from Bainbridge with sledge hammers and crow bars. Down came the wall separating Sadie's old galley kitchen from the garage. In Marian's eye was a whole new space—an open kitchen. After so many years of being cooped up and out of earshot, women of the 60s wanted to be a part of the mix.

Homer built her a nine-foot desk under the west windows, and in the middle of the room, he created an immense center island. Above it, Marian positioned a large oval pot rack for her many pots and pans. Exposed brick became the backdrop for side-by-side ranges under a hammered-iron exhaust hood. A pair of refrigerators stood sentry. She chose birch for the flat-front cabinets, raw cedar for the walls, bead board for the ceiling, and a copper finish for the appliances. Even her laundry machines would be brought into this all-inclusive new space.

Every single inch was accounted for in Marian's carefully-drawn plans, but when we kids looked at her drawings, we cried, "Where's the fireplace?" And we also wanted more sunshine. In this room of low ceilings, Marian agreed to add a fireplace and a row of big windows along the wall where had been the garage doors. Rolls of brick-colored vinyl were unfurled to cover the floor and avocado-colored Formica was laid across the desk and countertops. It was a totally modern, eat-in kitchen. From this day forward, we would spend most of our time here in what functioned as our family room.

Christmas at the farm that year was different. I was three-months pregnant and the four of us sat on captain's chairs in the raw new space. It was exciting to smell the new wood and fresh paint, but it certainly didn't feel like the farm. Who was I to wax nostalgic? For the occasion, I wore fishnet stockings, a mini-skirt, false eyelashes, and a hairpiece.

Soon a shipload of Mexican furniture arrived. My brother's move to the Southwest had prompted our parents to visit Mexico, and after that, an enthusiasm for the Mexican aesthetic invaded Robertson Place. Decorated pottery, Spanish tiles, blown glassware, pierced tinware, leather and mesquite—Marian loved it all. She even managed to insert the Mexican theme into their new German Village home in Columbus. She was on a roll.

Part 4

---·---

1969–1990

Amy and the Army

*B*igger and bigger my tummy grew as Doug's internship drew to a close. Even though I didn't intend to undergo labor without anesthesia, just in case, I joined my hospital's Lamaze natural childbirth classes, which were all the rage in the late 1960s.

Much to our dismay, Doug got orders to go overseas. The Army needed doctors to give anesthesia, and Doug would be put through a crash training course and then sent to a MASH unit in Vietnam. His reporting date and my delivery date would nearly collide. We started to pack up our furniture. On July 1, Doug's internship ended, our lease was up, and we headed to Robertson Place.

It is now July 14, 1960, a sweltering hot day in the height of summer. Still no baby. I am a week late. No upright position is comfortable so we fashion a sling to go around my neck and under my belly to help support the awkward weight I must carry on my small frame. We have just returned from a mandatory trip to Cincinnati to see my obstetrician when Marian arrives from Columbus to help. She serves us dinner on the shady new brick terrace overlooking the lower lawn. Doug and I relax in the calm, letting the familiar night sounds of the tree frogs and cicadas wash over us. Then, early to bed.

Just as our heads hit the pillow, my water breaks. As we scurry to leave, Marian emerges from her bedroom to brew some coffee and pack Doug a sandwich. Ninety-five miles separate us from the delivery room in Cincinnati. Speeding into the night, Doug ignores red lights while I hold on to the dashboard. I practice my deep breathing and count the seconds between contractions. At Christ Hospital, we are rushed to the maternity ward where a barrage of personnel peppers me with questions. Our mothers were all put to sleep for childbirth, and many women of my generation still do not want to be conscious during delivery. But I choose a spinal block which will eliminate the pain while allowing me to remain awake and participate in the process. Doug suits up in scrubs, puts on a mask, and is allowed into the bright delivery room.

"A little girl!" announces the nurse. Tears flood my eyes and relief flows through my body.

The next few weeks were a blur. Sleep is all I wanted once we returned to Robertson Place. Never having babysat as a teenager, I had no preparation for a time

when I would be responsible for an infant. Please let others take care of the tiny stranger in our midst. When George and Nammy arrived, they could hardly contain their excitement. Teasing Doug for carrying our newborn around like a football, Nammy rescued our baby and made a beeline for the platform rocker in the living room of Robertson Place. Nestling Amy into the crook of her arm, Nammy then moistened her finger and began to make imaginary curls from the tiny wisps of hair on her great-granddaughter's head.

Being tethered to a newborn was something that didn't fit my picture of a modern woman. I never even considered breast feeding. No, it was Doug who stayed up to give the midnight bottle, and my parents who took the 4 a.m. feeding. I was left to sleep.

Recovering my strength, I slowly began to face my responsibilities. Doug was my teacher, and it wasn't long before we were in love with our firstborn.

Right about now is when Doug's military orders arrived: Report for boot camp

in San Antonio, Texas, on September 1. This gave us just enough time to show Amy to her grandparents in New Jersey. We traveled by plane, with a receiving blanket covering the two-week-old babe in our arms.

Now it was time to join the Army. Behind the driver's seat of our blue Chevy Impala, we lowered Amy into a collapsible baby bed alongside bottles, a case of formula, a few baby gowns, safety pins, and a stack of cloth diapers. Down the gravel driveway and out through the gates of Robertson Place, we headed west.

Traveling with a baby was an adventure. We took our newborn into restaurants and motels. Across the Mexican border, we ate tacos in Nuevo Laredo. Somewhere along Route 66, Amy gave us her first smile. When we arrived at Fort Sam Houston in San Antonio, we were sent to a local motel for the next five weeks.

Dressed in his newly-issued uniform, Doug learned how to salute and to use a gas mask. Amy and I, alone in our motel room, got to know one another. Taking take care of a tiny baby was turning out to be a difficult and full-time job. With scarcely enough time for a shower, I cut my hair short. Amy was starting to get colicky, and there seemed to be nothing that would ease her discomfort. We swaddled and rocked her, lit a candle for distraction, and read and reread our paperback copy of Dr. Spock.

Time to go again. San Francisco was our next destination. Traveling together was easy for us, and it was a good thing. During the first ten years of married life, we would move ten times. But once we left San Antonio, we would be on our own to find a place to live. Life for this young military family was going to be complicated; in San Francisco, almost every newspaper ad for temporary, furnished housing ended with the dispiriting barrier, "No children, no pets."

Captain Carden was posted at the Presidio near the Golden Gate for thirteen

weeks, just long enough for him to learn how to give anesthesia in a tent hospital in South East Asia. Much to his surprise, Doug found that he liked this field of medicine to which he'd been assigned. Meanwhile, back at Fort Sam Houston, an unmarried doctor in the program said he wanted to go to Vietnam. Army officials arranged a switch; instead of a wrenching separation, our little family returned to San Antonio where Doug would begin his anesthesia residency in the Army.

Where would we live in San Antonio? Military housing was now full to capacity everywhere in the United States. No officers' quarters for us. Was it time to purchase our first house? The realtor instinctively drove us to a new subdivision with streets

named after the characters in Camelot: Guinevere, Sir Lancelot, and King Arthur. No, thank you. A little cottage in a picturesque old neighborhood was more our style. We spent the next three years remodeling, redecorating, and working on its landscape while Amy watched us from her playpen. In the neighborhood was a shopping center with a fabric store, and I took up my sewing again. Even better, a couple blocks away was the Koogler McNay Art Museum.

In California, when stuck in a remote motel with a colicky baby, I had taken up my painting again. Little watercolor drawings of flowers were a far cry from the big abstract canvases I'd painted during the glory days at OSU, where I stood at an easel—dripping, brushing and slathering the luscious oil paint. But they were all I could manage. Brightening my day, they gave me reassurance that I was hanging on—if only by a thread—to my vision of becoming an artist.

In Texas, with the prospect of three years in one location, maybe I could make some progress. The San Antonio Institute of Fine Arts (which was on the grounds of the museum in our neighborhood), was the perfect environment in which to resume my life's work. Clay was a whole new experience for me, and it was a world away from changing diapers and shopping at the PX. Soon I grew to love the sensual feeling of kneading the raw clay and hearing the sound of the "thwack" as I slapped it down on the big table.

Then, once again I was pregnant. We paid for diaper service and were lucky to find Isidra, a wonderful Mexican grandmother, to help with cleaning and child care.

Jenny

On a hot July 4th weekend, as we sat around the dinner table with friends, the moment arrived. Our second baby was early, not late. Doug rushed me to Ft. Sam Houston to be admitted to the maternity ward of the massive army hospital.

Around midnight, a nurse snatched away my knitting, and announced that the doctor had arrived. One of Doug's colleagues gave me an epidural, and at just past midnight, on July 4th, 1972, Jennifer Lynn was born. Just like her sister, she had a high-pitched cry, but with Jenny, it was all about her eyes. Wide open and searching for clues, they captured everyone's attention.

In the spartan military ward, for the next two days I lay all but ignored, having hobbled there in pain from the recovery room to find a couple of green army-issue sheets folded neatly on my thin, bare, mattress. It was 1972 and the nation was a war. Nurses were too busy caring for wounded soldiers to pamper their healthy patients. Forty-eight hours later, they honored my request to go home early.

Such a little thing was she, lying in the crib that had only last week been home to her big sister. Doug made up a batch of formula before returning to his duties at the hospital, leaving me with the two of them. Now I was really on my own.

Hoping to deflect sibling rivalry, we showered Amy with attention. In the still of the night, Doug and I took turns springing out of bed at the first hint of Jenny's high-pitched squeal. Often her cloth diapers leaked beyond the plastic panties, and we would attempt the tricky maneuvers required to change her soaking nightgown without her fully wakening. Like ships passing in the night were we.

Two sleep-deprived weeks later, I broke down in tears. Help was needed. Only family would do, I thought. But that was not going to happen.

Death and Depression Back Home

In Ohio, things were not going well. Only months before Jenny was born, in the fall of 1972, my beloved Nammy had died. How I would miss that intelligent, fun-loving woman! My father's mother was not just my only living grandmother, but a friend. She had shared my enthusiasm for fashion and textiles and taught me how to read a pattern, put in zippers, and turn up a hem. With her passing came a flood of memories of homemade doughnuts and apple dumplings, of soap operas and her hearty laugh.

Another death brought tears and confusion to our family. My Uncle Philemon died from complications of diabetes in 1973 at the age of seventy-two. Known in Chillicothe as Phil Butler, the probate attorney, he had also served as its city solicitor and the U.S. Commissioner for Ross County. Conservative in demeanor and politics, my uncle had been an active member of Rotary and Sunset Club. He was a Mason, a protector of animals, and a dedicated church leader. Philemon's considerable efforts helped to support the Boy Scouts of America and the Ross County Historical Society.

While Philemon's death was expected, his will and testament was not. After Gertrude's death, a few years previous, Philemon's secretary had become his companion. Beside him now, on his deathbed, the secretary helped him alter his will. He would leave his estate not to Marian, but to her.

Marian later wrote that hearing her brother's will felt "like being kicked in the stomach." Throughout their lives, brother and sister had been unusually close. Together they had wept over Wilgus's drowning, cared for Delano, and sat talking around the dining room table until the wee hours of the night. They shared a logical approach and a reverence for education. Most of all, they shared a love for Robertson Place. Although Philemon had never contributed to the farm's coffers, he had assured Marian that the assets in his estate would help ensure its future. Now that estate was going to his secretary, who would soon sell at auction all the precious antiques that he and Gertrude had collected. Marian inherited only the Rabbit Ranch.

All of this traumatized my unsuspecting mother, and depressed my newly retired father. George's clinical depression seemed intractable this time, and my parents suffered for the next several years. Then one day he seemed to be getting better. George began buying up property in German Village and flirting with younger women. He rented downtown office space and formed a group to protest higher taxes. After so many years of silence and lethargy, Marian thought this was exciting—until she found him painting the house one night at 3:00 a.m. George was out of control, but where was the line between sanity and insanity? My brother returned to Ohio in the nick of time for us to put our father into the hospital. Then the hallucinations began: he was James Bond; he was going to bring about world peace. Doctors diagnosed George's condition as manic depression and put him on a drug called Lithium. After two weeks, the sleeplessness and crazy ideas were gone, and our father returned to normal. It seemed like a miracle.

With these family crises going on when I was struggling to care for a toddler and a newborn on my own, it was clear that there would be no one from home coming to my rescue in San Antonio. Instead, we hired a teenager to be a mother's helper. Slowly our little family regained its balance. By the time I was four-weeks postpartum, I was ready to get out of the house and resume my tennis lessons.

Colorado

*I*t felt so good to exercise my body again. In 1972, the idea of women in sports was gaining momentum. Less than six weeks ago, our sitting president, Richard Nixon, had signed into law Title IX. Here was a law requiring that women be given equal access to athletic programs in federally-funded institutions.

When I was in college, OSU had a brand new rule requiring coeds to take six quarters of physical education. Ice skating, bowling, modern dance, golf, archery, and camping skills were my choices. To pass camping, we girls had to demonstrate our fly casting technique and put up a tent in three minutes flat. But in the 1960s, our dress code dictated that we only wear skirts on campus. Now there would be an exception; to get to and from our gym classes we could wear pants.

Team sports were not for me, but as an adult I went on to embrace tennis, golf, and snow skiing. Even when five months into my second pregnancy, I felt emboldened enough to ski. More fool-hardy than that was my first attempt to ski during my year with the traveling school. In the Swiss Alps, we inexperienced teenagers strapped ourselves onto long, stiff boards, and after a few instructions we went careening down a mountain of ungroomed snow, our trench coats flapping behind us. It's a wonder I didn't break my neck!

Enthusiasm for skiing was something Doug and I shared, and for many years it was our goal to stay fit enough to take an annual trip to ski in the mountains. When he finished his three-year residency in Texas, his next and last army assignment would be at Colorado's Fitzsimons Army Medical Center in Denver. Ski country! However, more important things intervened. When Doug reported to work in Denver, the United States was pulling out of Vietnam in stunning defeat. Fitzsimons was in high gear treating our injured soldiers who were being evacuated from hospitals in Vietnam and Japan. In a grim little motel near the hospital, the girls and I camped out and got snowed in. Housing near the hospital was filled to capacity so I picked up the telephone to call a realtor. It took her six weeks to find a place for us to live—a tract house in nearby suburban Aurora which would have to be purchased. Scarletina struck both of the girls, and after several weeks of living out of boxes, I broke down and made my only SOS call: "Mother, can you come to help?" Although George's health was still precarious, Marian spared a week to fly to Denver to help while I got us unpacked and organized.

As transient residents, we were somewhat isolated in Denver. Sewing and painting saved my sanity, and the radio kept me informed. In May of 1973, the Watergate hearings riveted my attention. We adjusted our rabbit-ear antennas and turned on the television. The girls got a daily dose of *Sesame Street* and *Mr. Rogers*, and on Sunday evenings Doug and I luxuriated in the new British series, *Upstairs/Downstairs*.

Blizzards and waist-high snow were the norm during that first long winter. During our second and final winter in Colorado, we finally managed to get ourselves into the tantalizing mountains that had been beckoning in the distance. With chains on our tires and a portable crib in our trunk, we packed up the girls and drove to a ski lodge in Winter Park. Hot chocolate sustained the girls in a nursery, while their parents explored the mountains.

Friends were hard to make in snowy Denver. When winter finally broke, we ventured out to meet a few of the neighbors. Two came to our rescue when Doug was felled by a sudden illness, a strange and severe laryngitis that sent his temperature soaring and threatened his airways. He ended up in the hospital among the soldiers he was treating.

A teenage girl was our third friend. On the very last day of our brief eighteen-month stay in Colorado, the beloved babysitter arrived at our door with an offering—an armload of coveted Barbie dolls. Impossibly thin, too grown-up and sexy—in our house, they had been forbidden. But in the emotion of the moment, how could I turn away such a big-hearted gesture?

Return to Ohio

*W*atergate was behind us now and President Nixon was about to resign. It was August of 1974, and Doug's five-year obligation to his country was complete. Time to pack up again. I flew alone to Ohio to find a home where we could put down our roots. On a previous trip we had explored neighborhoods, and Doug had interviewed at hospitals in Dayton, Columbus and Cincinnati—all within easy driving distance of Robertson Place. Good Samaritan Hospital in Cincinnati was his pick, and mine was the Village of Terrace Park.

Homogeneous and tree-lined, this little community was something out of the past. Period homes lined its streets; each house was individual; each yard carefully tended. Children rode bikes or walked to school and to a tiny grocery store in its midst. As

The Women of Robertson Place

if by magic, milk arrived at back doors. In the heart of the village was a park in which young boys clamored over a World War I cannon when folks met for the annual Memorial Day parade.

During my house-purchasing weekend, I considered only three houses. The one I chose was a humdinger. It was the ultimate fixer-upper, built in 1880 as a country home, and in need of absolutely everything, inside and out. "Well, at least I can use my new ladder," Doug conceded, with his usual dry humor.

What an understatement! Nothing like Robertson Place with its pillars and symmetry, this Victorian house was dripping with turrets and whimsy.

For the next several years we stripped walls and floors, gutted kitchen and bathrooms, tore out overgrown bushes, and cleared out chicken coops and outhouses. Masterminding our renovation was the architect, John Grier. With good nature and patience, he guided us through several years of work. We chose a new roof, added a patio and screened-in porch, and refitted our

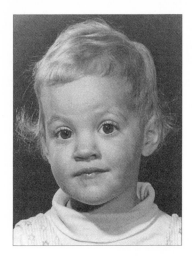

barn/garage with a greenhouse and an art studio. Like Marian, I threw myself into the design part of the work, making endless drawings, testing paint colors, and choosing hardware. Every last bit of my creative training came into play.

Friends came easily in Terrace Park. Before the moving van had pulled away, a cluster of barefooted children arrived on our front porch with a plate of cookies. Jenny found a playmate in Peanut; Amy found one in Julie. Dandelion, an orange tiger kitty, entered our lives. I found a best friend in Mary—

my first since high school. For our toddler Jenny, there was a preschool in the basement of the church across the street, and for Amy, kindergarten was just a few blocks away. Finally, an artist friend! During our second year in this idyllic neighborhood, a woman named Jerry Oberle came into my life. Bonding quickly, the two of us began to meet twice a week to paint.

Weekends at Robertson Place soon became a big part of our lives, and that first Christmas was a banner event. Phil and his wife Corky arrived from Arizona with their two little boys, Bud and Scott. Cousins made Robertson Place come alive with toys and laughter. Firing up the tractor, we filled a big thermos with hot chocolate. Time to make the annual trek to cut a tree in the Rabbit Ranch.

Marian's Final Burst of Energy

The new farm kitchen hummed with activity over the holidays. But Marian seemed tired. Perhaps it was understandable; she was sixty-six. Or was it was because she had just finished a year of massive redecoration? Already in place were new bathrooms, closets, and skylights. In what turned out to be her final burst of energy, Marian had finally allowed herself to indulge in the decoration of Robertson Place.

Stripping the wallpaper from every surface in the older part of the house was a messy ordeal. Never lacking for skilled workmen, Marian had taken on the challenge. So while George followed her from room to room, methodically painting all the woodwork and refinishing the floors, Marian tested her wallpaper samples. Down came the busy pheasant-themed paper in the dining room; up went a modern grass cloth. Down came the drab scenic papers in the upstairs bedrooms and up went lively paisleys of reds and greens. Swaths of aqua stripes went up in the guest bedroom, and the children's bedroom got little stylized flowers on a field of maroon.

Marian was influenced by America's popular interior designer, Dorothy Draper. Nammy had also left her mark on Robertson Place. Measuring and cutting, stitching and pressing, my grandmother had created drapes and slip-covers, bedspreads and cushions. Her colorful cushions were everywhere now, dozens of them.

Entertaining family and friends at the family homestead had always been a priority for Marian, and she did it with flair. Depending on the weather, she set her table in different locations. Breakfast was always in the kitchen around the Mexican leather-topped table; a summer lunch might be a picnic on the back patio under the arbor, where tendrils of wisteria and trumpet vines shaded us from summer's sun. Gone were the out buildings, the wood pile and the pump. Beyond the large vegetable garden and white board fences, layers of green now stretched all the way to a distant band of foothills. What looked like a herd of miniature cattle grazed in the near distance.

Marian's evening meals were the prize for our long days of mowing or painting, sewing or planting. Cocktails on the front lawn began our social time, and they were followed by gourmet offerings such as Salad Niçoise or Chicken Wings Bella. Conversation lasted long into the evening.

Candles glowed during the winter months when Marian served her meals in the dining or living room. Summer's heat often took us to the front terrace, our favorite location to dine. Sitting on the crest of the gentle hill, we could look down across the lower lawn to the row of small evergreens Doug and I had planted upon our return to Ohio. Majestic old trees of poplar and maple, cherry, elm and catalpa provided pools of shade. The occasional lilac bush or crabapple tree dotted the scene with color.

Food and cooking so dominated Marian's thoughts during these years that she began to write a cookbook. Based on a series of imaginary letters written to me as a young bride, the result was *Shall We Cook?* She summoned her nerves and took some early chapters to New York in search of a publisher.[140]

Although the publisher gently turned her down, from Marian's standpoint it must have seemed as though everything else was finally in place. Robertson Place was ready for many more years of enjoyment by the next generations, and her husband was whistling again. Lynn was settled into life nearby, and two granddaughters were growing up before her eyes.

Then one day, everything came to a halt. A telephone call from Columbus announced breast cancer. She would have surgery. Days turned into weeks, weeks turned into months, and months turned to six years of additional surgery, treatments, reconstruction, hope, disappointment, and, finally, a last ditch effort with offshore alternative medicine. Resigned to her fate, Marian returned to the farm to die in privacy. I brought her granddaughters for one last visit, and Marian was carried down to the front lawn to watch them play with a kitten. Conversation was minimal because cancer had invaded the brain of this articulate woman and denied her of speech. Lady that she was, her head wrapped in a scarf and the hint of a smile upon her face, Marian sat watching us in quiet dignity.

How she loved the land from which she was about to depart. Many years later, I would be struck by the poetry with which she described the ritual of watching the full moon rise above Spruce Hill.

> *"Nights without number we sat in front of the house,"* she had written as a young woman, *"our chairs arranged in a semi-circle facing the hill, with my brother fingering his guitar and a bat occasionally swooping from above as it came out cautiously to test the darkness of the evening."*[141]

Marian died on June 13, 1982, in the Ohio State University Hospital. She was seventy-four years old.

So devastated was George that he did not want a funeral. Theirs was a symbiotic relationship, and my father would never regain his balance. My own relationship with her was not overly close, not charged with emotion. Perhaps this is why we were spared the tug-of-war that characterized so many mother-daughter relationships of the era. As a mother, Marian was positive and supportive. As a private person, she respected *my* privacy and independence. And as an independent thinker, she was my role model. I already missed her terribly.

How different my life would be after her death. At forty-one, I inherited not only my father's care, but that of Robertson Place. From now on I would be responsible for the family's happiness and needs while we were in residence. Before, we had simply arrived.

Christmas, with its special menus and trappings, was especially challenging. "Mimi," the name Marian was called by her grandchildren, had spoiled us. When

Phil's family arrived from Arizona, everybody expected the old magic. We were now eleven. Cheese fondue on Christmas Eve, oyster stew (the first to go), and mince pie were beyond the likes of me. Lists of all kinds were essential for such a neophyte, and the day itself was a marathon. Required was a detailed timetable for producing Christmas dinner. When it was over, we had to dismantle everything—the tree, the wreaths, the lace tablecloth—and pack up the leftover food and dirty laundry. And then the cat had to be found and fitted into our station wagon for the trip back to the city, where we would pick up our lives again.

Terrace Park

Life in suburban Terrace Park was just getting started. It was rich and busy, and I didn't want to miss a minute of it—even though there would be less time for Robertson Place. It was a time of big hair and women's lib, dinner parties and volunteer work; I joined the garden club, the PTA, a book club, and a child-study group. We organized dances, round-robin tennis, and picnics at the swim club. After having worn a lot of prairie-style clothing in red, white and blue for the nation's bicentennial, by the 1980s we were ready for neon colors and big earrings. We let our children and pets run free. Our daughters signed up for classes in gymnastics and drama and joined a Brownie troop. Everyone played soccer.

Young mothers in Terrace Park were college-educated (many had been teachers or nurses), but very few now worked outside their homes. Virtually all of our husbands had white collar jobs. Monday through Friday, the men of Terrace Park left the village for their commute to work. Doctors, lawyers, teachers, ministers, and businessmen they were. Doug left the house before dawn during winter, and, in one or another of Good Samaritan Hospital's twelve operating rooms, he administered anesthesia until the last surgery was complete. In darkness, he commuted home to his family—unless it was his turn to stay overnight in the hospital.

Soaking up sunlight in our greenhouse brought Doug some relief. On weekends, in its steamy warmth, he rolled up his sleeves and got his hands dirty by planting flowers from seed. Digging  a vegetable garden was therapy, too, and Doug planted dozens of landscape bushes. Saturday mornings found him in the kitchen cooking eggs and bacon or kneading a ball of bread dough. In the basement he liked to mess around with his tools, which were growing in number and which he put to good use fixing things around the house or building cabinetry and a new storm cellar door. Music had always been an important part in our lives. Operatic arias now vied with country music; the Beatles gave way to jazz. Our record collection was as eclectic as the furnishings, which were a mixture of modern art and antiques from Robertson Place.

Working outdoors was a pleasure for us, not a chore. In good weather the entire family gravitated to the backyard, where Amy and Jenny played on the swing or rode their trikes as Doug and I weeded and pruned. Doug built fences and turned the soil in our flower beds, and one year he planted twelve dozen red tulip bulbs.

We poured our hearts and souls into our home in Terrace Park, and twice it was on the village house tour. But Robertson Place was still a magnet for our weekends. Holidays were almost always spent there, and much of the summer, too, when we kept my father company, and Doug arrived for weekends. During the summer of 1975, our kitchen in Terrace Park was gutted and rebuilt, and I packed up the girls to spend the entire month of August in the country.

The Women of Robertson Place

"Please, can we take the Barbie dolls?" they pleaded. I finally had to admit that those previously forbidden dolls kept my daughters engrossed for hours on end while I sewed their back-to-school clothing. Laura Ingalls Wilder's series of children's books about pioneer life was more to my taste. Or how about sorting a century's worth of buttons in the button basket? Always fun for the girls was to play dress-up in Marian's, Sadie's, and even Margarite's antique clothing.

For an outing, we shopped for Amy's first Brownie outfit in downtown Chillicothe. At Schachne's department store, the three of us stood transfixed by the novelty of watching our money disappear into copper tubes to travel their circuitous routes from the balcony to the cashier in the office below.

But Cincinnati was our home, and at last, Doug and I felt settled. We would keep up with it by subscribing to *The Cincinnati Enquirer*. Radio and television provided national and international news. By 1975, the war in Vietnam was finally over, and raw footage of soldiers slogging through the mud no longer invaded living rooms. The energy scare was on our minds, and we Americans began to pivot our focus to the Middle East. Space travel again fascinated us. In 1977 the runaway hit movie was *Star Wars*.

It was during the early 1980s when, after years of study and travel and service, our lives really began to take on their permanent shapes. Doug and I were in our forties; we were established in a neighborhood, and our children were thriving. Babysitters were plentiful, and for fifty cents an hour we employed the local teenagers nearly every weekend. For vacations, such as a ski trip or the backpacking trip we took to a wilderness area in northern Colorado, we employed an experienced adult sitter. Theater became an important part of our lives, just as it had been for our parents. We took up golf. And *finally*, I could resume painting.

Art Career—Kindred Spirits

High in a loft above our garage in Terrace Park, hay lay strewn about in dark corners. Cobwebs hung from the rafters. The building had once been a barn, but when house hunting, I knew this space would made a perfect art studio. At the Art Academy of Cincinnati, I began to take refresher courses. Then came the tricky business of extricating myself from all my volunteer organizations. It was slow going. Almost no one in this suburban neighborhood of ours thought of me as a serious artist; I certainly didn't fit their image. To them, an artist was a man who wore a beard and lived somewhere in Europe.

Kindred souls were what I needed. My artist friend, Jerry Oberle, introduced me to a group of eight professional artists from the metropolitan area. "We began by bringing our work to monthly meetings, and the electricity turned on," said founding member, Sara Wellington Dodge. [142] Here was a group of women for whom art was essential; they worked at it every single day. Sculptors, painters and printmakers, these women embraced me with open arms, and for the next thirty-five years they would nurture my art. We called ourselves The Crit Group. Others would later call us pioneers.

Slowly now, with the wind at my back, I made myself into the artist I intended to be. Luck had a big part to play. The Guerrilla Girls, an activist group of women artists, took to the streets of New York in 1985 to call attention to the fact that female artists were grossly under-represented in the city's commercial galleries. Dressing in gorilla costumes got the attention they sought; things slowly began to change. In the Midwest, galleries were never so biased against female artists, but for a woman to combine a professional career with her family life was still unusual—so much so that in 1991, a journalist headlined her article about me this way: "Career and family are successfully balanced by artist." [143]

Working in the studio every day, building a résumé of shows, becoming a businesswoman: all were required to reach such a goal. In 1983, a collection of my landscape paintings and still-life drawings was shown at a small gallery in the neighboring town of Milford. Because I was trained during the height of abstract expressionism, this first exposure was not what one might have expected. Painterly realism would be a better description. But solvents used in oil painting gave me headaches, so for this show, and for the next twenty years, there would be no paintings in oil. Instead, I worked in watercolor or pastel. However, this restriction did not slow me; my watercolor paintings got bigger and bolder, and soon I was selling them at Closson's, the city's upscale art gallery and furniture store.

"To Hell in a Handbasket"

Amy and Jenny were developing their own interests. What would they make of themselves? Where would their curiosity lead them? Here was the next generation to inherit Robertson Place. Here was the generation referred to by Sadie as "the unborn children of her grandchildren."

For them, it was also to be the arts. The School for Creative and Performing Arts, known as SCPA, was (and is today) a magnet school in the heart of downtown Cincinnati. Dynamic and exciting, the school held its students to the highest of standards. Children from all over the metropolitan area auditioned to get into the school, which by design, was fully integrated. Half of its students were black.

"To hell in a hand basket!" was how the Mariemont school superin-

Cincinnati desegregation: A midpoint review

Transfer Jenny Carden, who takes a 30-minute bus ride daily, works with clay at the School form Creative and Performing Arts

tendent reacted when I told him that we intended to transfer our daughters out of his acclaimed suburban system and into a school in the inner-city. But it was a great decision. Amy, our teenager, had become bored with the offerings of her traditional, sports-minded school; this was a worry. Jenny had been pleading since the fourth grade to be allowed to go to the arts school downtown. So the transfer was made, and soon the entire family caught SCPA's spirit. Over the next two years Amy played Ophelia in *Hamlet* and Maggie in *Cat on a Hot Tin Roof*. Jenny majored in both art and theater. She did gigs as a mime and played the star role in the Greek tragedy, *Medea*. Theater seemed to be in their genes.

Seldom during these years did the entire Carden family visit Robertson Place. While Doug was working hard, we ladies used the homestead for other purposes. Amy once took some girlfriends from Terrace Park to see the local outdoor theater production of *Tecumseh*. Much to my dismay, I discovered later that the girls had invited the actors back to Robert-

The 1991 Artists' Farm Retreat
June 23 - 28 and September 8 - 14

son Place for an unchaperoned party! I was sure to be present when Jenny staged a murder mystery weekend at Robertson Place.

In 1983, a tradition was begun at the farm when I hosted my first of many Artists' Farm Retreats. For the next ten years, professional women artists and writers came from Cincinnati to spend a week at Robertson Place for the purpose of sharing ideas and pursuing their own creative work. We worked independently by day, took turns preparing the meals, then met in the evenings for discussion over the dinner table.

The Sandwich Generation

Instead of pinafores and Halloween costumes, in our sewing room we were making prom dresses. As the girls were becoming more independent, their Grampa George was needing more assistance, and I began to understand the meaning of "sandwich generation."

College for our firstborn was our next obligation as parents. It fell on Doug's willing shoulders to take Amy on a road trip to visit schools. Up and down the East Coast they traveled, touring and interviewing at state universities, traditional female colleges, and elite Ivy Leagues. In the end, our daughter decided on Brown University in Providence, Rhode Island.

All summer long we prepared our firstborn for her departure. Then one afternoon, as we were sitting on our screened porch in Terrace Park, the telephone rang. George had suffered a stroke. His condition was so unstable that he could not feed himself. I rushed to the hospital in Chillicothe, and when I returned to spend the night at Robertson Place, there was a note taped to the back door. "We are leaving—key is on the kitchen counter." In a barely legible scrawl, it was signed by Sam and Faye, the longtime caretaker/tenants of Robertson Place. Tomorrow I would be touring nursing homes, looking for a new caretaker, and getting ready to put Amy on a plane alone to go off to college.

Nursing Home for Dad

Things would change fast after Amy left for college—most of all, for George. He needed assistance and nursing care. Although my father willingly gave up his checkbooks, he yearned to drive again. Flipping our roles was a strain on both of us. Phil interceded by phone when reinforcement was needed, but it was left to me to be the enforcer.

America had made a cultural shift in the way we thought about caring for our aging parents. By the 1970s, many retirement homes and care facilities dotted our communities, and there was a good one near our home. But I felt guilty not taking our father into our home, as my parents had done for theirs. It didn't seem fair. Sunday outings and visits were substituted for the effort and inconvenience of sheltering my father under our own roof. Occasionally, we took him to Robertson Place for a day.

But George's days were numbered. During the fall of 1990, as Jenny was settling into Northwestern University, he suffered another stroke. Lingering for weeks in a fragile state, George managed to hold on until she returned for a final visit. After that, he simply stopped eating. When the nurse called me on that November night in 1990, I felt the earth shake.

Why did my father's death affect me so? We were close over the years, this kind and loving man. I suppose I was the apple of his eye. Now there was no one alive who remembered my birth or my early childhood. So many memories were lost with his passing.

Part 5
1990–2010

Changing of the Guard—Breakthrough

$\mathcal{G}$one now was the older generation. It felt strange to be in charge of Robertson Place. But it wasn't just the house that felt different. Bourneville itself was changing.

Demolition of one of Bourneville's landmarks may have been my first clue. Soon after Marian's death in 1982, as I was slowing my speed in preparation for the turn off Route 50 onto Upper Twin Road, out of the corner of my eye, my attention was riveted by the sight of a wrecking ball. The Methodist church in Bourneville, having no current local members, had been sold. A local businessman had bought it for its corner property and was now tearing the building down. To offset the cost of demolition, he sold its pews and the steeple's brass bell. In this century-old church, my great-grandfather Robertson and grandfather Butler had been superintendents; from its podium, as a five-year-old, I had summoned the courage to recite a poem. High-school graduation had been held here for an earlier generation. My father, still alive at the time, joined my fight to stop the demolition. The owner offered to sell the corner property, but the price seemed high. In the end, on this corner lot was built a little dairy store where my grandchildren now buy ice cream cones. The loss of Bourneville's once vibrant church was the first indication that, in this rural township, something was amiss.

Demise of small farms across the country was one of the reasons that Bourneville's population was dwindling. By the end of the decade, almost all the produce and money in farming would be made by only three percent of America's farmers. George's old Farmall Cub tractor looked like a toy in comparison to today's huge bright-green harvesters. Our farmer, Dave Williams, boasted that a single man behind the wheel of one of these new implements could work sixteen rows at a time. Many of Bourneville's displaced farm workers had already left for factory work. Some had found work at the Mead Corporation, Chillicothe's paper mill. But in cities across the Midwest, factories such as this one were beginning to shut down. The jobs were going to Mexico or China.

Into such an abandoned factory in the inner city of Cincinnati, I now moved my art studio. Suburban life had lost its shine, and it was time to leave its comfort and safety. Pivoting from city to Bourneville, with a stop in the suburbs, became my life during these quiet years when Doug was busy with work, and Amy and Jenny were away at college.

Moving into an old factory space, where the tailoring jobs had been out-sourced to Mexico, turned out to be a good move for my career. Surrounded by other creative people, my work started to evolve and expand. My botanical still-life paintings grew so large that I could not contain them on double-elephant-sized sheets of watercolor paper. The Pump House Center for the Arts in Chillicothe offered me a show, and I filled its gallery spaces with more than fifty paintings. Why did I paint on such a large scale? asked the *Gazette* reporter. "It's more exciting, more physical, more athletic," I replied.[144] Four years later, a gallery owner from Louisville, Kentucky, asked me to join her stable of artists. B. Deemer Gallery was to host many one-person shows for me over the next two decades and would go on to sell hundreds of my paintings.

I had been putting flowers into my paintings for years, but discovering what was actually inside them—what made them *work*—was my next challenge. Cincinnati's Lloyd Library and Museum, the nationally known institution for botanical, medical and pharmaceutical research, was the place to find out. Would the library tolerate an artist working in its midst? I wondered. During the winters of 1996 and 1997, "…the staff cheerfully brought me book after book from its stacks, provided white gloves

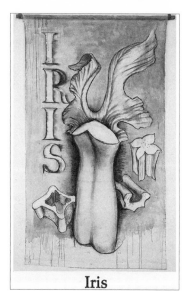

Iris

to use while handling their precious antiquities, and moved furniture so that I could work."[145] Rarest of the scientific books were those dating from the 1500s, and beside each of the flower illustrations was a tiny drawing depicting its reproductive parts. So fantastic were their sensual shapes that I knew immediately what I had to do.

With chalk and a magnifying glass, I made sketches; back in my studio, with the help of ladders, I blew up the inner parts of flowers until the eye of a pansy was six feet tall. Paint dripping, chalk breaking, fans whirring, a sense of urgency brought me back to the excitement of abstract expressionism. In June, 1998, a show of these floor-to-ceiling hangings filled the art gallery of the Cincinnati Art Academy. Art critic, Fran Watson, considered it a breakthrough.[146]

The Women of Robertson Place

My Muse

Now that my career was taking off, would being tethered to Robertson Place be a distraction? Others thought so. Instead, in the luxury of its quiet days, it had become my muse. "I can see more clearly here at the farm," I wrote in my journal.[147]

Its rugged crockery, its gleaming antique furniture, even Margarite's mandolin had became subjects for my still life series. A snow storm brought me to the window in awe. In spring I would be taking my easel outdoors to study the way the fence lines intersected the gardens. And how would I describe the blue mist rising from the distant ridges of the Appalachian foothills?

Delicate snowdrop flowers peek out from under the dormant lilac bushes in February. In March, great fountains of forsythia line the gravel driveway with a blast of yellow. There are redbuds in April and purple lilacs in May; then a long row of pink and red peonies unfold their voluptuous petals all the way to Memorial Day. The grounds of Robertson Place have always been a parade of

First Snow Storm

seasonal display just waiting for the artist's eye.

Over the years, as soon as the danger of frost has lifted, on hands and knees I planted new perennials and hundreds of bedding plants, much as did Sadie and Martha. Plucked in their prime and brought into the studio, these flowers became the subject of botanical paintings and a series which lasted more than twenty years. I was spending more and more time at Robertson Place during the last decade of the twentieth century, alone if need be, churning out hundreds of paintings. These were good years, focused and productive.

Helleborus (Christmas Rose)

A New Caretaker

Responsibility for Robertson Place after my father's death did pose new challenges. Never had the house been prey to vandals or thieves, but now that the apartment was empty, the property seemed vulnerable.

In the tiny one-room post office (that essential gathering place for Bourneville) was my answer. Phyllis Parks, the red-haired wife of a local lawyer and also our gentle-spoken postmistress, would become our new tenant and caretaker. As it turned out, Phyllis also became our contractor and friend. Capable in many ways, this woman took on the job of remodeling the apartment that my forebears had built for Clyde in 1906. I don't think either Martha or Margarite ever intended for this add-on structure to last for the ages, and its inferior construction was showing its age. In the 1950s my parents had squeezed another room onto the backside of the apartment, making the entire addition look jerry-built. Before any remodeling was to take place, I insisted that this room be removed. Not only was it blocking one of the large windows of the main house, it was an eyesore.

Reconfigured, re-plumbed, redecorated, and refitted with all new fixtures and appliances, the apartment was now habitable. Given a budget of $20,000, Phyllis made all the selections. We hoped that she and her husband would want to stay, and they did. However, just as my grandmothers did for Clyde, we would have to relinquish use of one of the front rooms of the main house in order for the couple to have a proper bedroom. This shrank our house and made for rather close quarters for both families. But these were days when we didn't need the extra space. With the girls away at college, we were using Robertson Place less and less.

The Cost of Ownership

While settling my father's estate, I became aware of the various needs of the 150-year-old homestead. Plying the once scenic U.S. Route 50 on my trips to and from the farm, I winced at the sight of abandoned houses, their roofs caving in, their windows broken, and their fine brick facades swallowed up in vines.

Mention of the farmhouse needing a new roof made Phil realize that his sister was not going to let Robertson Place go to rot. Money would have to be spent. But the Southwest had claimed Phil's heart; he would probably never leave Arizona for the Midwest. It made little sense for him to spend money, year after year, on a place that his own family would be using less and less and that my family would be using more and more. But his sons were inextricably tied to Robertson Place because they, along with my daughters, were the children of Sadie's grandchildren to whom she had willed the place forty-five years ago. I'm sure it was not an easy decision, but when Phil's sons reached adulthood, he and his family decided to sell me their stake in Robertson Place, and I was able to purchase it with my half of our father's estate.

Renovation Begins

Now began the renovation in earnest. Nostalgia would always bring me back to Robertson Place, but could I expect Doug or our guests to overlook the stained wallpaper, the drafty windows, or the lumpy mattresses? Shoring up the place was my first priority.

First came the roof. Asphalt singles would replace the old standing-seam metal roof. Roofers balanced themselves atop the pitched incline to peel great swaths of metal from the house and hurtle them to the ground. No more would I wake to the gentle patter of raindrops on the old tin roof. But neither would I moan upon discovery of yet another water stain on Sadie's cabbage-rose wallpaper.

Next came safety. Electricians combed through the labyrinth of wiring in the basement, replacing anything which might be a fire hazard. Climbing up into the

attic, they showed me the original knob-and-tube wiring from the 1930s and pointed to some old charred wood shingles, evidence that there had once been a fire.

Air-conditioning was another big expense. It caused no debate now— unlike when the last generation had argued its pros and cons. And that debate was nothing compared to the decade-long stalemate over whether or not to put up an antenna in order to receive television in the old farmhouse. In the 1960s, the standoff was finally broken when George got a black-and-white set in his paneled den.

Though air-conditioning was inevitable, the difference it would make in our lives was enormous. Closing the windows meant shutting out damaging dust, noise and humidity. It improved not only our own comfort, but the condition of the house's furnishings as well. No longer would we be kept awake by the incessant barking of a village dog or be wakened by the predawn racket of starlings. No longer would we be forced to listen to a neighbor's chainsaw or to the piercing whine of a teenager's go-cart. However, closing the windows had the effect of muting some of the sounds that made our experience in the country unique. It meant we did not hear the cicadas during a summer's night or the church bells on a Sunday morning. At Robertson Place there would be gains and losses with almost every "improvement."

Not so with the new lining for our chimney. A long, stainless steel tube was threaded down the flue into our living room fireplace. When the stone mason had to cut through the house's three-brick exterior wall in order to receive the lining, we winced. But from then on, there could be years of safe fires in the living room where a line of grandparents going back to Martha and Robert had warmed themselves.

Bats and Snakes

We were living a real-life version of television's long running *This Old House* series, but where were the episodes about bats? Yet bats must surely have invaded the old house when Martha and Margarite lived here as widows. Of course they did! Later, it occurred to me that what I had seen in the bedroom closet— Sadie's tennis racket—was probably used to fend off bats. But when the fluttering black jets zoomed over my own head, instead of running for the racket, I ran to the phone to call our neighbor. What a wimp was I! Why did the bats never show up when Doug was here?

Solitude had never appealed to me, but while staying alone in the farmhouse, it became my ally. Daydreaming, I allowed myself to imagine how my grandmothers might have lived here. What were their daily lives like? I wondered. Washstands and white porcelain pitchers in the bedrooms hinted at their bathing habits. No doubt the ladies filled vases with fragrant herbs, such as lavender and sage, to mask the odors of their chamberpots. Beaded purses and ivory fans made me wonder what kind of social life could have transpired here in the country. Then there were the daily issues that still plague us today, such as the creek bank caving in or the spring rains flooding the cottage. As I spent more time caring for the property, the lives of Sadie and Margarite became more vivid in my imagination. As my own challenges increased, I learned to channel their strength.

Bats were bad enough, but snakes were beyond the pale. I have *always* been afraid of snakes. One night while I was writing this book, working late at a make-shift, skirted table, out of the corner of my eye I caught a glimpse of something black and shiny and quick. Gingerly, I lifted the skirt, and there it was! Running from the room—screaming no doubt—I clamored up the stairs. Surely the little thing was harmless. But still! The thought of a snake in the house? It was unnerving. Snakes can't climb steps, can they? In fact, they can! In a flash I realized that not a wink of sleep would I get if I stayed in the house that night. After bedding down at a neigh-bor's house, I brought in a search party the following morning.

Local men are always willing to come to our rescue, regardless of the predic-ament. This is one thing I was learning about living in the country. Of course, as we hunted the house the next morning, the snake (or snakes, as it turned out) were nowhere to be seen. Only months later did we discover the source of their entry. As I was fixing my breakfast, our cat, Cowboy, sat transfixed beside the kitchen floor register. A baby snake popped out. And another. And another! After I recovered from the horror of those baby snakes pouring into the house, a light went off in my brain. Electricians had been crawling under the floor in the front part of the house. Did one of them accidentally disconnect furnace ducts?

Discovery of an innocent baby black snake led to a chain of efforts to seal up the house's every last point of entry. A parade of inspectors with flashlights and tubes of caulking wound around the perimeter of the house, inside and out, searching not just for cracks in the foundation where a reptile might slither in, but for crevices small enough for a bat to make its entry.

A chink in the brick chimney above Margarite's bedroom may have been the en-try point of the bats, who were probably spending their daytime hours in our attic. Telltale black smudges around a tiny opening in the ceiling of that same bedroom closet led us to suspect we had discovered another of their entry points. Crevices got filled and gaps around doors got weather-stripping against bugs and cold drafts.

It was two years of detective work, plus the addition of storm windows, before we could rest assured that the house was finally tight.

Traveling Daughters

It is now 1991. While I am painting and doing battle with bats and snakes at Robertson Place, our daughters are exploring the world. The Berlin wall is down and the Soviet Union is collapsing. Jenny jumps at the chance to get behind the Iron Curtain. She travels to Moscow to study Russian theater. But in the United States, on the morning of August 19, the news on our little black and white television in the kitchen is interrupted with pictures of Red Square. There has been a coup! Gorbachev is out; the hardliners are back in power. Doug and I stare slack-jawed as tanks roll into Moscow. A fax arrives the following day. It is from a Russian post office where Jenny has crammed onto a single page the story of how she ventured outside, pressing herself against the building walls, as Russian tanks ground by her on their way to Red Square. All the while, both her classmates and Gorbachev's sympathizers remained inside, their doors barricaded. Three days later, we watch soldiers and citizens mix, as Russia's President Yeltsin addresses the crowds.

It is graduation time for Amy. After spending her junior year in Bologna, Italy, she had returned to Brown to continue her work in Renaissance Studies. Jobs in *any* field are scarce in the current economic downturn, and interviews lead nowhere. At her graduation ceremonies, we meet her boyfriend, a student from India. Amy visits him in Bombay (now Mumbai), but is treated with suspicion by all but his cosmopolitan family. The romance fizzles, and our daughter returns home to regroup. Volunteer work with the Cincinnati Opera helps to fill the void, but in the end Amy decides to return to the East Coast. It is in New York City where she will find the tempo and energy she so craves.

"A roommate, a place to live, or a job." These were the stipulations we laid out for our daughter before we would support her move to New York City. She did it in steps, and the staging area was her grandparents' house in Summit, New Jersey.

Amy was particularly close to Doug's parents, Agnes and Wade, and the arrangement worked well. Before his recent retirement, Wade had boarded a train to Wall Street where he worked for American Express. Republican politics were his passion, and, with Clinton in the White House, Amy's grandfather was always ready with a torrent of doomsday predictions.

Agnes preferred the domestic life, although in college she had won several starring roles in theater productions. Church now played the central role in her life, and she did her best to instill her Southern Baptist fundamentalism in our daughter. When Agnes had first learned about my agnostic leanings, in a fit of anger she had pronounced me unfit to raise her grandchildren. Her zealous ways did not mellow over the years, and this intrusion into our personal lives tainted our relationship.[148]

Where did Doug come from? This thoughtful, middle child, so mild-tempered and book-smart. He turned out nothing like his siblings. His brother had dodged the draft, changed his name, and become a rock singer. Carole, both gregarious and emotional, could be found in the front row of her church every Sunday. Not Doug. He was too rational. Yale was to blame, his parents suspected. For Doug, the college years were meant for broadening one's mind. It was the place to question doctrine and to acquire the foundation for a life of learning and critical thinking.

Telling Time

1850-1950
a century of stories

THURSDAY JUNE 16
8pm
UNIVERSITY HALL RM. 102

A DOCUMENTARY BY JENNY CARDEN

Attitudes about the purpose of a college education underwent a subtle change in America during the later part of the twentieth century and by the time our daughters were ready to go, the emphasis was not on the classics, but on job training. Jenny started out with an emphasis on theater, but she gravitated to the more technical field of film making. "It's what all the artsy people want to do," she explained. When in 1993 she arrived at Robertson Place for a summer break before her senior year, Jenny burst onto the scene with her usual enthusiasm. "Mom, I want to do a documentary!" By the time she had edited her footage and put it up on the screen,[150] Amy was in New York City writing about summers in Ohio, and I was back in my studio painting again.

"Grab the Wheel, Mom!"

One afternoon in late August of 1994, the telephone rang in my studio. "Mom, will you go west with me?" I lay down my brushes. In the euphoria of college graduation, Jenny and a few of her friends had concocted a plan to take a road trip across the country. By traveling the old roads, the blue highways, her friends hoped to discover an America unknown to them. Jenny claimed she wanted to see how ordinary people lived in the legendary country of cowboys, Indians, miners and trailblazers. Four had started planning the trip, then three, then two, and then... the phone call. Here was a chance to reconnect with a daughter who had spent very little time at home since high school; perhaps it would be my last chance. "Grab the wheel, Mom!" and I did.

Into our Volkswagon station wagon, we packed sleeping bags, cameras, paint brushes, canvases, and a pistol—which Doug made us take along. His revolver and the sleeping bags never saw action because we stayed in locked and lighted AAA motels. Travel no more than 250 miles per day, spend no more than $35 on each of those days, always be settled by nightfall: these were our self-imposed rules.

Picnicking, painting, and photographing our way across the Great Plains and the Rocky Mountains, Jenny and I spent the next three weeks alone together. Pronghorn antelopes ambled across a deserted highway in Nevada and a blazing sunset inspired us to set up our easels in Big Sky Montana. It was ludicrous to think we could capture its glory—or any landscape—on the fly. However, I did make some landscape notes from these attempts.

"We saw pink and red earth, gorges of blue, purple, coral, yellow. Mountains ranges of pink, blue, white, and chocolate brown. The sky itself turned from white to brown to black, or from yellow to green to purple. We saw clouds in New Mexico lined with neon red. Truly, I should never worry about being literal. Anything is possible."[149]

With maps unfolded across our laps, and a AAA TripTik as guide, we charted each day's travel. On one stretch of road we were a hundred miles from the nearest gas station. It was thrilling, our trip into the interior.

Amy was on the West Coast to receive us. She had left New York to study anthropology at the University of California, Berkeley. Pivoting south, we gambled our nickels in Las Vegas and danced with the locals on a Saturday night in a remote road house in Oklahoma.

Turning into the familiar driveway at 111 Terrace Place, our mother-daughter adventure was over. While we were gone those three weeks, Doug, too, had been kicking up his heels. There sat a yellow Mustang! Little boys in the neighborhood gave him a thumbs up as he revved the motor into second gear. Upstairs was another purchase—an Apple computer. Finally, he had come up with a justification to buy his first computer: it was to process our family's historic photographs. After that, Doug spent a year editing and publishing Marian's cookbook. Access to the internet was a novelty. Emails could keep our family connected no matter how far our daughters were to roam.

Empty Nest

*E*mpty was our nest in Cincinnati. More and more, I spent time alone at Robertson Place, painting and thinking. Jenny's documentary had lit a fire in me. Groundbreaking in nature, it got the ball rolling. But there was so much about the history of Robertson Place that could not be fit into those thirty-six minutes. Much of it would be lost if someone did not capture it soon. It began to dawn on me that I was the only one for the job.

With legal-sized writing pads, I began to write. Early in the morning and late at night, I wrote. Seated in my grandmother's rocking chair in the living room, with those yellow-lined papers spread out on the floor around me, I wrote about how it felt to live in a house so evocative and mysterious. I wrote about waking up to the soft cooing of the mourning doves, of wondering about the urn on the mantle said to contain the ashes of my mother's little brother. In that rocking chair, I just let my mind go while I wrote and wrote. So little did I actually know about my ancestors that most of what I wrote came from my imagination or scant oral history. Search for the missing facts would come later.

A computer? Jenny encouraged me to take advantage of modern technology. But I wasn't ready. Instead, I bought an electric typewriter. It soon became clear, however, that a better writing machine was needed. With my right-brain rebelling, I forced myself to learn how to use a computer. It was slow going. Doug got frustrated. Jenny cracked the code when she coached me to "think like a computer, Mom."

Phyllis left her job as caretaker and manager of the farm property during that summer of 1995. When I was not in residence, Robertson Place would again be empty and vulnerable. Like a rubber ball, I bounced back and forth between our two houses, keeping up with payroll and supervising employees at both ends. Weeds began to overtake the massive old vegetable garden at the farm. A small herd of cattle needed management, and Delano's old gas station had to be rented and maintained. It was all too much.

Responsibility for two complicated and high-maintenance old properties finally forced my hand. Might a condominium be the answer? At the end of the twentieth century, many Americans our age were asking the same question.

In the 1950s, Marian had asked her architect to design a modern house which would be the antithesis of Robertson Place. Now I found myself looking for a similar contrast, after living in our four-story Victorian house for twenty-four years. In 1998, we left our secure nest in Terrace Park and moved into a brand new, one-floor, three-unit, urban condominium. Perched on one of Cincinnati's seven hills in the neighborhood of East Walnut Hills, our new home overlooked the Ohio River and was a rare example of post-modern architecture. Luxuriating in the clean and airy space of the modern condo, I suddenly felt free. "Living in a cloud" was how our

future son-in-law would describe it.

Great spans of glass opened up spectacular views of the river below; in nearby Eden Park we strolled to Mirror Lake and the Krohn Conservatory. Lunch in Mt. Adams and plays at the Marx Theater filled our weekends. The Cincinnati Art Museum was within walking distance. The location of our condominium was perfect, but its group-living lifestyle and construction were not.

Three years of searching had it taken to find our condo; ten years would it take to stop its leaks. Meetings were convened. Phone calls were left unanswered. Faulty installation of the large windows was ultimately discovered to be the cause of the elusive and maddening leaks. What better way to reconsider the virtues of the solid, old-school construction of Robertson Place?

Still, our urban life was refreshing and stimulating. My studio was only five minutes away, allowing me to work there every day. At the same time, Doug was thinking about retiring from medicine. Across the nation, during the 1990s medical practice was under pressure from insurance companies, lawyers, hospital administrations, and even the nurses. Hurry, hurry, they seemed to say. Fit in as many cases as possible; take twenty-four-hour, in-house call once or twice a week. At one point, as head of the anesthesia group which served Good Samaritan Hospital, Doug oversaw a practice of twenty-four doctors and nurses. By the time we moved to the condo, he had cut back his hours; in 1999, he made the decision to retire.

Internet Romance

*F*ast forward. It is the year 2000, a new century. Things are happening quickly now. Doug is retiring and Amy is in love. We have only four months to get ready for a wedding, and she wants to be married at the farm.

Amy's fiancé is a young Italian doctor, and we have never laid eyes on him. Arrangements are made for us to meet him at Robertson Place when he and Amy pass through Ohio on a road trip across the country. (Amy has returned to the East Coast). Enrico Suardi is well-mannered, but we rarely hear his baritone voice. He is probably hesitant to speak English, we think. No, his English is perfect. He must be in shock.

Email had been the conduit for Amy's and Enrico's meeting. He had wanted to meet an American poetess, so Stefania, a mutual Italian friend in New York, had introduced the two online in January of 2000. A trickle of polite missives began to drift back and forth across the Atlantic without much excitement until our family took a ski trip to Italy a few weeks later. Enrico was in London at the time, but Stefania suggested that Amy look up their mutual friends while in Milan. On our last night Amy got a phone call. Would she and her sister like to see the town? Of course they would! Our daughters were taken to a hip new nightclub and the next day Enrico got a report about this American poetess. "She's a fox!"

Back in New York, Amy noticed an uptick in Enrico's mood. His interest was palpable. The pace quickened. Amy invited her Italian suitor to come to America for a visit. Unbeknownst to his parents, Enrico drained his bank account, bought a ticket to New York, and arrived with instructions for finding the girl he'd fallen in love with by email. Photograph in hand, he circled the fountain at Lincoln Center until

their eyes locked. At the end of a whirlwind week, the two were convinced they had found their soul mates. All it took to finalize their plans was a trip to Milan for Amy to meet his family.

Suddenly, I was planning a wedding. It was nearly summer, and they wanted to be married soon. Could it be done? Amy was a traditionalist at heart, and nowhere but Robertson Place would do for her marriage ceremony. She would be the fifth generation. But Robertson Place was torn up. We were in the middle of a massive, multi-year renovation. At the same time, I was working on the Cincinnati condo, fitting out closets, designing bookcases and furniture, and sewing drapes for all those windows. The condo would have to wait. I moved to the farm to speed things up, and Doug came to help on weekends.

Luckily, two years ago we had begun to update Robertson Place. Redoing the upstairs bathroom had led us to a local remodeler, Bill Scherer. His work was top-notch, and after finishing the upstairs we had put him to work on the first floor. With aplomb, he had peeled the old stained wallpaper from the living room walls; with precision he had cut strips of crown molding. This local craftsman could do anything, and he worked for months on end tearing up carpet, repairing plaster, building new bookshelves in the library, and painting all the woodwork. It was hard to keep ahead of him.

My job of picking new paint colors, bathroom fixtures, carpeting, and wallpaper might have been easy, but it was all-consuming and difficult. To update things at Robertson Place meant to destroy something familiar and beloved, and to replace it with something new and untested.

Wallpaper hangers were in the midst of applying rolls of new paper to the master bedroom in May of 2000 when Amy announced her intentions to get married. Workmen, on hands and knees, were laying boards of cherry on the dining room floor. Joining them, with brushes and rags, I began to test stains.

Outside, there were flowers to plant; cock's comb and zinnias, snapdragons and baby's breath—flowers which would reach their peak for the wedding in September. Studs for the new garage were in place, but plans for a new kitchen would be put on hold. Everything else could be ready for the autumn wedding.

The Women of Robertson Place

Twenty-First Century Wedding at Robertson Place

Thunder and lightning shook the house on September 23, 2000. It was one week until Amy's wedding. Reinforcements had just arrived from the west coast; Jenny, the family's mover and shaker and "can do" girl was here. The next morning broke clear, and the two of us bundled up in parkas and gloves to string lights in the arbor and lay out stakes for the wedding tent. Contingency plans for foul weather were drawn up and posted on the walls of the unfinished garage. In the old kitchen, Jenny got out the family recipes and rolled up her sleeves. A mountain of Marian's four-bean salad soon filled earthen bowls. Tablecloths and napkins, dishes and glasses, and every piece of silver was brought from the cupboards of Robertson Place to be washed, counted, pressed or polished.

Two days before the wedding, Enrico and his family arrived from Italy. Months of Italian language study and practice flew out the window, and Doug and I resorted to clumsy sign language with his parents. Help arrived in numbers now. Clyde's old apartment, vacant at present, became a work station, and in Grandfather Robertson's old carriage barn, florists filled giant urns with fresh flowers picked from a local grower's garden. The weather improved. On Friday evening our Mennonite friends, the Martin family, arrived in their traditional dress to help us stage a hoedown for the growing number of friends and family from Honolulu, Los Angeles, Houston, San Antonio, Phoenix, New Orleans, Atlanta, Manhattan, and Milan.

It is four o'clock, on the final Saturday in September, in the year 2000. Robertson Place is ready at last for the ceremony to begin. One hundred guests have been streaming onto the property all afternoon, parking their cars in rows across the pasture. As part of the planned scenario, Doug—looking so handsome in his new black suit—now steps out onto the balcony, ready to scan the horizon for the groom's arrival. Below, our guests sit patiently, soaking up the warm autumn sunshine while musicians tune up their Renaissance instruments.

Up the gravel driveway comes a sleek black horse-and-buggy. Enrico and his younger brother, Giacomo, step down onto the grassy front lawn, while Amy, dressed in a stylish sheath wedding gown, is about to join her father in the front hall of Robertson Place. Amy breaks into a radiant smile as she hears the first chords of "Here Comes the Bride." Father and daughter, matching their steps as they begin the processional, walk in unison out the front door, between the Doric columns, and toward the altar on the front lawn.

All eyes are on the groom now. A man we already trust but barely know begins to repeat his vows, first in English, then in Italian. Amy had burst into nervous giggles during the rehearsal, and now she struggles to maintain her decorum. When the ceremony comes to an end, bride and groom turn in jubilation to the rows of seated guests. Among them, sitting in the front row, are Agnes and Wade, Doug's ninety-year-old parents.

Champagne corks pop and guests mingle on the front terrace. Slowly making their way through the house to the big white wedding tent in the back yard, the guests stop to peer into one of the front rooms of Robertson Place where they discover my "history room." Running around the perimeter of this front parlor is the giant time line I have filled in with pen and pencil notes to indicate names and events, marriages and deaths. Its twenty-six foot length is divided into decades, and within those time periods are posted events that occurred in Bourneville, Ross County, the state of Ohio, USA, and the world. Our guests linger to decipher some of my notes. On a table nearby are Delano's white gloves and displayed on a dress form is Margarite's wedding dress.

Visitors then turn to the left to stroll through the living room with its corner cupboard and Sadie's hand-carved mantelpiece. They pass through the pocket doors into the library, then on through the dining room into the mid-century kitchen with its vinyl-flooring and Mexican accents. Finally, they exit to the back yard, where, under the tent, candlelight and pink tablecloths set the mood.

"We did it!" exclaims Jenny, as the two of us approach the tent. A buffet awaits the guests; a band strikes up a dance tempo and invites them to dance. This evening is the culmination of four months of planning, list making, and work which included the creation of invitations, dresses, favors, flower beds, and the painting of thirty-four pieces of outdoor furniture. Amy was involved the whole way, and her special request was for fireworks at the end of the evening. Around midnight, a spray of fireworks explodes from the ridge over Butler's Grove. A deputy sheriff, parked at the entrance, watches from his car.

Sunday brunch on the front lawn of Robertson Place allows our guests to gather for final farewells. One of our Italian guests asks to be taught the game of croquet. Ever so carefully, Graziella lines up her wooden ball. When she whiffs it, the beautiful young woman convulses in laughter and collapses to the ground. In the pasture, young men play a pick-up game of soccer. Giacomo is invited by our farmer to take a ride in his big combine. Enrico's friend from Milan drapes the American flag around his shoulders and asks to take it home to Italy. And then, they are gone.

Tomorrow our firstborn will pack up to leave for Europe, where she will begin married life on the other side of the ocean. During the night, I break down in tears. Robertson Place will once again stand empty. When the last crystal goblet is washed, the last string of lights rolled up and stored in the attic, we pause to savor the memories.

Light, Height, and Symmetry

On the first day of December, Doug and I, dressed in work clothes, began to dismantle the old farm kitchen. "Why remodel? It's functional, isn't it?" he asked. But it was Marian's kitchen, filled with outdated appliances and Mexican decor. Low-ceilinged and dark, it was out of the past. I wanted the hub of the house to express my generation's aesthetic.

More light, height, and symmetry for the new kitchen: those were my goals. Removal of the Mexican element achieved the added benefit of authenticity. After a week of demolition in January of 2001, the crew got the space down to its bare bones. Our contractor, John Parks, remarked, "If I had known you were going to change *everything*, I'd have told you to tear it down and start all over."

Tear it down? That wouldn't have felt right. It would have meant obliterating what had once been Sadie's kitchen, Delano's garage, and Philemon's workshop. Already gone was the old summer kitchen, and the decision to remove that historic building had been wrenching. It was where my great grandmothers had washed their clothes, cooked applesauce, hung herbs, and stored their keepsakes. Moving this historic building to a new location might have been possible, had the structure been solid. Eventually the overarching desire for an attached garage had trumped our nostalgia.

Instead of demolishing Marian's kitchen, we decided to relocate its back door and poked a doorway into Philemon's old workshop to make a laundry room. But how could the ceiling be raised? Standing in the old kitchen, hand on hip, I dialed our architect in Cincinnati. John explained how we could punch a hole in the ceiling and raise it by four feet. When we met later, he took a pencil and sketched on the proverbial back of a paper napkin how the facade would look with its new roof line. That was the extent of our guidance for this job. Surprising to me was that neither of us could improve on my mother's layout. At kitchen design, Marian was a master.

Fresh drywall went up first. What a dramatic change from its former walls of exposed brick, rough cedar, and yes, Spanish-tile wallpaper! Refreshing though it was, it meant change, and change is always difficult at Robertson Place. I had learned this the hard way during the process of replacing the gold-patterned wallpaper which had lined the living room walls during Marian's days. When my new choice was proposed, (one which had taken countless hours of searching through wallpaper books and then countless trips back and forth from Cincinnati), our daughter Jenny, home for a Christmas break, welled up in tears. So in the new kitchen, I tried to moderate the transition from old to new.

Marian's old vinyl flooring would be replaced with cherry flooring. The warm color of the wood was similar enough in color that I hoped our sentimental souls would not be too jarred. When Phil and his wife came breezing into the wide-open new space, they stopped in their tracks and gasped at the beauty of it.

Up in the attic of the old summer kitchen where my grandmothers had stored their trunks, I had found two small stained-glass windows. Were they from Margarite's and Martha's 1880's kitchen? Fitted into our new pantry wall, they would be a reminder of the past. An old hall tree from the front hall of Robertson Place was brought into service for hats and umbrellas in the hallway leading to the garage. Into the main room we brought a leather couch, Sadie's oak table and chairs, and a pie safe we found in the barn. By the time we had hung on the walls a ticking wall clock and Sadie's still-life painting with its dark, carved frame, our new kitchen—despite all the changes—finally felt as though it belonged in Robertson Place.

Weeds were winning the battle in the massive, generations-old vegetable garden, and now that the drapes were down and big windows spanned the back of the house, the view from the new kitchen was disappointing. And cars, arriving in our driveway, looked as though they might plow into the house if their brakes were to fail.

Time to call in a landscaper designer. Marian and George had already begun the process of transforming the old farmyard into a contemporary backyard. Tearing down the old tractor shed, the tool room, and the outhouse cleared the way; by the 1950s and 60s, our outdoor space had become a place for barbecuing, picnicking, playing, and hobby gardening. Now, in 2001, my generation would replace the forty-by-sixty-foot garden which had fed my family for generations with green turf. In the era of supermarkets, two long strips of freshly-tilled earth was going to be plenty of space to grow our tomatoes and vegetables.

George's long row of high-maintenance roses was the next to go. To create new flower beds, our landscaper, Mike McGinnis, suggested we tear down Marian's beloved shady arbor. I knew he was right, but I had to cover my eyes when the wisteria-covered trellis came toppling to the ground. I couldn't even be at the property when workers pulled up the old hand-pump and began to rip out my father's hand-laid patio—it was too painful. But two weeks later, guiding our car past a new patio and gardens via the graceful curve of a freshly-cut driveway, a broad smile broke over my face.

9/11

Things were going along swimmingly now; construction was nearly complete. Roger and Delbert, our hard-working duo, returned to finish Doug's new woodworking shop. Bill Scherer stopped by to do some finish painting. They were all here on that crisp September morning in 2001. I was dressed in a plaid flannel shirt and focused on pruning some shrubbery. My mother-in-law's instructions were clear as a bell: "Pick a tall stem and follow it way down into the bush until you reach its origin; Now *that's* where to make your cut."

If only I could turn back the years to this moment and start all over again. Because, after that, the world would never be the same.

Around the corner came Roger. "A plane just hit the World Trade Center in New York!", he exclaimed. I continued my work on the taxus bushes that were the formal foundation plantings for Robertson Place. On a farm in the heart of the Midwest, this announcement over the local country-music station was too bizarre for belief. Minutes passed while I tried to wrap my mind around the unwanted words. Defeated, and a little annoyed to be interrupted from my task, I wiped the grass off my shoes and went into George's paneled den where I turned on the television set. There I sat, motionless, clippers still in my gloved hand.

When the phone rang an hour later, I was still in that chair. It was Doug calling from Cincinnati.

"Have you heard from Amy?"

"No."

On this eleventh day of September, our daughter, five-months pregnant, was here in the United States, visiting her former roommates in New York City. Hearing the news, she had run outside their apartment on Jane Street in Greenwich Village to watch the twin towers fill with smoke. Before her eyes, both towers collapsed.

Forty-two years ago, when I was traveling with the International School of America, as students we read about New York's skyline creating such perfect targets.

Now, in the surreal moment of the present, the telephone lines were jammed. We would not hear from our daughter in New York for twenty-four hours. Meanwhile, in California, Jenny was safe. But the following afternoon, from a phone booth somewhere along a Los Angeles freeway, we got a call. She was sobbing. Our twenty-nine-year-old daughter had just learned that her brilliant boss, Danny Lewin, had gone down in the plane from Boston that hit the second tower. Unknown to us, the head of a high-flying technology company was also the object of her affection.

When at last the planes started flying again over North America, Amy was at the airport, heading to Ohio for a visit; Enrico soon followed from Italy, and Jenny was heading for Washington to start a new life.

Grandchildren and Kitty Cats

At Christmas time, Amy and Erico returned to Ohio. We spruced up a bassinet from Marian's babyhood and filled it with gifts of knitted sweaters and baby clothes for their first baby and our first grandchild. In her seventh month of pregnancy, Amy was radiant with health and happiness. It was a joyous time at Robertson Place.

On Valentine's Day, Amy went into labor in Milan. Sofia Stefania Maria Suardi was the name chosen for their tiny girl baby—the extra name Maria having been added because Enrico's mother had made a promise to God on 9/11. Baby Sofia would come home from the hospital to an apartment whose windows looked out over a street buzzing with motor scooters and buses. Our family was growing, but how could the legacy of Robertson Place survive if our grandchildren grew up on the other side of the world?

The following year, it was just too sad to celebrate Christmas alone at the farm. Jenny flew home to be with us in our modern condo, and we got new decorations for a tree bought at the grocery store. Doug lit the gas logs in our fireplace, and I played seasonal music on our baby-grand piano, but the holiday felt strange and hollow and way too modern. To help fill the void we adopted a kitty. Coco followed a long line of felines, dating back a century to Bluebell, the house cat of my great-great-grandmother, Martha. In between were Juliet, Chessie, Princess the orange Persian, Tuffy her flat-faced son, Dandelion, Pepper, Thomas, and Amy's Cowboy.

We found Coco at an animal shelter, and she became our beloved pet for the next seventeen years.

Thomas, the long-haired tuxedo cat, had come to us at the farm. He was good company, staying up late at night with me in the history room, while the soft clicking of my computer churned out the eighth and ninth drafts of the early Robertson Place history project. Spreading himself out amongst the artifacts on the dining room table where I was preparing to start illustrations, he fell asleep on my pristine paper. Would he upset Delano's top hat? Knock over the glass oil lamp? I worried about my open bottles of sepia colored ink.

Across the ocean in Italy, Amy was expecting her second child. When Virginia Emilia Lynn Suardi was born on December 21, 2003, Doug and I flew across the Atlantic to spend Christmas in Milan. We helped as best we could, but things were a little crowded in their one-bedroom apartment, where the newborn was wheeled from room to room in a rolling crib. Still, Amy had managed to prop up a little American-style Christmas tree, and we celebrated the holiday with her little family.

Eric and the Old Cottage

While our daughters were living far away, Doug and I began to focus again on ourselves. How did we want to spend the rest of our own lives?

Time spent at Robertson Place was essential to my soul. And yet, like Marian, it seemed important for me to keep one foot in the city. Decades later, I discovered a snippet of paper in an old purse from around 2005–7, when we were pondering the question of whether to move to the country. Down the center was a line: on either side was a list of pros or cons. Under the heading CITY, I had scribbled the words *museums, restaurants, shopping, architecture, studio, friends, doctors, hospitals, ease of appointments, airports, theater, art profession.* Under COUNTRY I wrote *space, views, gardens, history, love, holidays, animals/nature, soul, much cheaper, country club, golf, simple lifestyle, travel, winters south.*

Security in the country continued to be an issue. A string of renters moved in and out of Clyde's old apartment, but each occupant seemed harder to come by and less and less reliable. Then along came Eric Bissey. He was jovial and young and had a big personality. Eric took to the job of caretaker with ease. Master of all trades, this man could divide perennials, cook a pork roast, fire up a chain saw, and then stop to help me choose a new wall paint color. Eric came to the farm as a renter, but soon morphed into the best caretaker Robertson Place would ever know. Trading his work for rent, he stayed for eight years.

Eric's sense of humor and repartee made life easier for me in the country, but Doug was still spending most of his retirement days in the city. He wasn't well-suited to the idea of living in two places. What else, I wondered, would entice him to join me at Robertson Place?

My man liked new equipment; he was not amused by historic tools and rusticity. There would have to be better buildings in which to store any new machines. Soon the two of us were thinking about replacing the old fallen-down barn that housed George's little tractor. Rough-hewn beams still held the structure together, but the roof was caving in and the floor boards in the inner room were unsafe.

Great-great-grandfather Robertson had used the building in the 1800s, not only as a barn for his horse and buggy, but as his office. That was when Robert I. Robertson served as justice of the peace. Here was where Clyde had started his chicken business. Later it became known as the old "cottage," which may have been a reference to its use as temporary space for overnight visitors or even for domestic servants during earlier times. Now it was dark and dank, and its neglected interior chamber served as a graveyard for old washstands, iron bed frames, wicker furniture, and bookcases full of moldy old ledgers and law books. Its pink, water-stained wallpaper flopped off the wall, and the room reeked of rat droppings and mildew.

As a child I knew to avoid this out-building. Later, as a nesting homemaker in hopes of finding a treasure, I would unlock the door of the old cottage, flashlight gripped firmly in one hand, to pick my way through the furniture piled from floor to ceiling in lopsided disarray. Not all of my scavenger hunts were successful. One time my head brushed against a dangling snake skin, causing me to run away shrieking.

Eric was the person to help us untangle the puzzle in the barn. He was a big, strong guy, capable of pulling every last night stand and wooden sled out of the dark interior and into the bright sunshine. Eric was the one willing to line up the contents on the grass for inspection.

I went to the house for my camera and called the local antique dealer. When I returned, there was more to discover. A ladder was propped against the barn's loft and Eric was peering over the ledge. There was our black-and-white tuxedo cat hiding in the shadows, and beside Thomas was a plaster cast bust. It was Virgil, the ancient Roman poet; I immediately thought of Margarite and reclaimed it for the farmhouse.

"Not interested, not interested," Rosemary Keaton pronounced as she walked among our collections of antiques and vintage furniture. How could this be? I wondered. Antiques were still hot in the market place, or so I thought. But the dealer knew differently. "Do you have any mid-century stuff?" Ouch. In the end, she took only Delano's old roll-top desk (which she doubted she could sell now that everyone was buying computers) and a couple of old gilt mirrors. She shook her head at Margarite's fainting couch which could be opened into a bed. I rescued two high chairs, but dozens of rocking chairs sat beckoning. More phone calls were made. Phyllis stopped by with her pickup truck to cart off a chest of drawers plus Marian's kitchen table and chairs of Mexican leather and mesquite. We piled a few nostalgic pieces onto a flatbed wagon and sent them to the corncrib for storage. Finally, our former renters took the rest away to use or to burn in a bonfire. I did not want to know which.

Modernization was painful. If necessary for the continuation of Robertson Place—not as a museum but as a living, breathing home—then my thinking would have to be adjusted, my emotions suppressed. Until now, the homestead had been all about my family roots. From now on, if it were to become our only home, it would also embrace those of my husband.

In the footprint of the old barn, in 2004 we built a brand new one. Along one wall, Doug created a workbench and storage shelves for his ample supply of wood, some of which had been retrieved from the barn of Delano's era. Parked on the other side of the new barn was Doug's newly-acquired 1998 Ford pickup truck. Was my sports-car driver turning into a country boy?

Parked in the center of this new barn, which would from then on be called the "truck barn," was the main attraction: a bright red machine. It was a Snapper zero-turn mower, and it was Robertson Place's first professional lawn mower. With five acres of grass to groom every week, it proved itself essential, and it was fun to see it turn on a dime. Beside the Snapper, on the barn's broad and smooth cement floor, sat the tiller, the fertilizer spreader, and the air compressor. The place was already beginning to fill up!

Upstairs? Yes, there had to be an attic in which to preserve the most historic items. I was well into my history writing and knew that some of the contents of the former barn were simply too important or too curious to let go. Among other treasures, into that new attic space we now arranged a row of painted blue chairs from Sadie's farm kitchen, the most graceful of the cane-seated rocking chairs (which were now out of favor), a small marble-topped Arts and Crafts chest, Sadie's sewing machine table with foot pedals, and a little maple table and chair set from my childhood.

Downstairs, in a corner of the building, we saved space for a garden room, where we could finally store and keep track of the myriad garden tools needed for lopping, pruning, snipping, digging, staking, and spraying the landscape and gardens of Robertson Place.

Guilt Sets In

Next to go was the old milk house. Adjacent to the apartment, this quaint structure was listing badly under the weight of its overhang. In my childhood, a row of tall metal milk cans stood in a line on a bench under the shade of the overhang. More clearly etched on my brain is the memory of a little cartoon-shaped cat hole that Philemon had thoughtfully cut into the milk house door for whatever resident cat needed to escape his dogs. Of all the old out-buildings, it would hurt most to tear this one down. Its small size made it seem vulnerable, but it turned out that I was its only champion. Like dominoes, the old familiar landmarks of a small Ohio farm were falling down.

Guilt set in as I lay awake contemplating all the changes we were making to Robertson Place, a homestead that had served so many generations. Yet why stop now? We had a team of trusted builders who could accomplish almost anything. Liz Tuttle Miller, our dear friend and house historian, put it this way: "Throughout time, when families move into a home, they almost always change it— put their stamp on it. So here's the choice. You can be a purist and restore everything to a certain time period, or you can make the changes your generation sees fit, and history will label the periods accordingly. Either approach is valid."

I chose the later. Form had to follow function if Robertson Place were to continue to be our family's gathering place. Surely, that is what Marian and Sadie—and, stretching back even further to Margarite or Martha—had imagined. Overall, the big picture of Robertson Place as a spacious and welcoming country home was beginning to emerge from that of a working farm.

Taking Turns

Weeks of remodeling turned into months, months turned into years. By the time this thirteen-year period of renovation finally drew to a close in 2004, we had transformed Robertson Place. Not only had we remodeled the house itself, we had replaced out-buildings. However, in the midst of wrapping things up, we began to detect mumblings from abroad. Amy and Enrico wanted to move back to the states. We put all our projects on hold and returned to Cincinnati where we made room for the young family in our condo. Sofia was almost three, Virginia still crawling. Doug and I enjoyed the youthful company, but we kept to our routines. I spent mornings writing at home and afternoons painting in the studio where my easels now shared space with boxes from Italy. Occasionally the two of us escaped to the country.

By spring of 2005, Enrico had landed a residency in psychiatry at a hospital in Washington D.C. We packed them up and traveled together by caravan, with Doug driving a U-Haul rental truck all 425 miles over the Appalachian Mountains to a townhouse in the suburbs of the nation's capital.

No sooner had Amy returned to the United States, than Jenny was off to South America. Were our daughters explorers at heart? Had tales of my early travel experiences influenced them? Mongolia or Bangladesh was where Jenny really wanted to go, so it was with relief that she finally settled on South America. In 2005, in Cordoba, Argentina, Jenny was to meet Lucas, a young man who was working on his degree in computer engineering.

American Gothic

At Robertson Place, our caretaker Eric had become outright indispensable. Something had to do be done about his quarters. Remodel Clyde's old tacked-on apartment again? Ugh! It seemed foolish to pour more money into a poorly built structure which was downright ugly. Attached to the main house, its location was also a problem; we wanted more privacy.

But where to place a new dwelling for a caretaker? To our rescue again came Liz Miller, the historian who had first researched Robertson Place. She suggested a

Carpenter Gothic cottage set among the pine trees. Soon we discovered that even a cottage needed the sure hand of an architect, and our architect answered with a drawing inspired by the wooden farmhouse depicted in Grant Wood's painting, *American Gothic*. We loved it instantly.

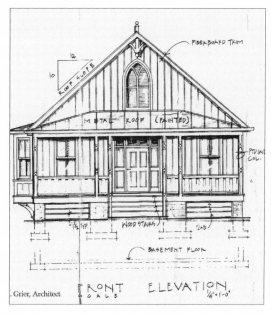

On top of the hill opposite the main house, in 2007 we built a simple caretaker cottage. Its exterior is board and batten, painted the color of old lace. Doug replicated the architectural details and built the curved arch windows in his new shop. Knotty-pine flooring and a bay window gave the modern interior its character and charm. A screened back porch offered views in three directions: corn crops and tree-covered foothills to the north, a giant white sycamore silhouetted against the sky to the east, and, in the southern foreground, a slope covered with Queen Anne's Lace. I covet that porch.

We left the lower level unfinished, but John gave wise council: "You never know who will live in that house." And he was right.

Turning Point

*S*hould we pull up stakes and move to the country full-time? The idea began to enter our minds. Our lives were beginning to feel harried and contrived; running two households, commuting back and forth, continuing to write and paint, keeping up with friends in both places—it made us dizzy..

None of my recent ancestors had lived on the family homestead year-round. You had to go back to Martha and Robert to find a family who was so firmly planted at Robertson Place that they would know no other house to call home. Margarite had a deep and abiding love for her family's home, but she went south every winter and lived for several years in Washington D.C., only returning to her birthplace for the last years of her life. Sadie and Delano lived in Chillicothe, and only summered at the farm.[151] Marian and George held on to their home in the city through thick and thin. Although they loved their time at the farm, never did my mother spend weekdays there unless a remodeling project was in full swing. So it was a bit radical for Doug and me to think of giving up our urban roost to live out the rest of our days in the country. But once the decision was fully embraced, we plunged into the farmhouse's final transformation with gusto.

A New Wing for Robertson Place

A studio. I would need a real studio if we were to live at the farm. For years I had wondered if Clyde's old apartment could be turned into a studio, but it was dark and low-ceilinged and smelled of stale cooking odors. Delano's old cement-block filling station across the highway might have served as a studio, but that was before we decided to tear it down after a string of renters nearly drove us crazy. My "history room," the big front room across the hall, was the only remaining option for a studio. Far from the household hustle and bustle, the eighteen-by-eighteen-foot space would be adequate, if not ideal. However, that idea was shot down by Doug when he realized that it would make a perfect man cave.

So where would I paint? Kitchen, laundry room, and now the dining room were scenes of my makeshift studios. But after twenty-five years of painting in watercolor, I was once again using the messy, demanding medium of oil. A new and safer solvent had made it possible for me to return to the classic medium, and it was like being in love again. Oil paint is so luscious, rich, and sensual.

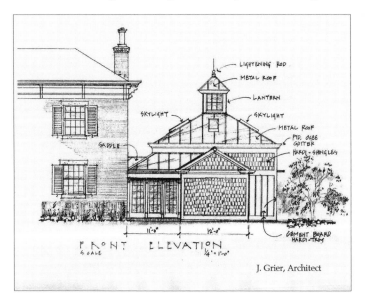

J. Grier, Architect

Down came Clyde's old apartment. Into the ground went stakes marking out the perimeter of a new studio. Once again, we were working with our architect, and

Doug put in a bid for space to put exercise equipment and a hot tub. John obliged, but it was becoming a wing. How could that wing be connected to the main house? It had us stumped. Then I remembered the portico that my great-grandmother Margarite had added to Concord Church in 1917. We would add a portico to connect old to new. How, though, could we make a structure of the twenty-first century harmonize with the historic Robertson Place? Could the new structure be made to look like a previous generation's outbuilding, maybe even a barn? Here was the architect's concept.

"Finally, the house has flow!" John declared when he came on site to view the actualization of his drawings. Starting in the back of the main house, we strode across the portico into the studio, then passed through Doug's spa, and returned to the main house through the "history" room. One could go full circle.

Flipping the light switch in the studio brought a chorus of swoons. Under exposed rafters, halogen track lights glowed bright on an expanse of bare, white walls. What a contrast to my cave-like cubicle in the basement of the Yale student dorm! Soaring and light-filled, this was a space capable of inspiring new work. And the prediction proved to be true; my best work was yet to come.

Meanwhile, in his new workshop, Doug happily organized his tools and the intricate world of his bolts and screws, hammers and saws. He devised a shooting range in the lower pasture where Philemon had practiced his aim. Then he explored the back roads of Ross County and reconnected with our friends in the Mennonite community.

Golf in America was winding down by the early part of the twenty-first century; country clubs were going under and public links were reverting to weeds. But a little historic country club in Chillicothe was hanging on, and a single round on its scenic course persuaded us to become members. It was here on Friday nights that we began to meet friends for dinner. Among them was Jane Hilty, whose father owned the pharmacy where I'd eaten an ice cream sundae after my tonsillectomy. Others were Roscoe Swartz, an oral surgeon, and his wife Beth, an artist, who lived down the road from us in another historic farmhouse. It turned out there were many people living in Ross County with whom we had similar interests and backgrounds.

Optimism was running high now. We were making the turn toward residency when, all of a sudden, we felt the earth move.

School for Sale

Clad in jeans and flannel work shirts, Doug and I were raking leaves on that windy October day in 2007 when a truck mounted the hill and caught our attention. Our old friend and helper, Dale Skaggs, nursing his gimpy leg, slowly climbed out of his pick-up truck. He was (and still is) a talker, and in turn, he gathers a wealth of information before it hits the newspapers. In his gravelly voice he asked "Have you heard?"

"Heard what?" we asked.

"They're putting the old school up for auction." My jaw dropped.

"December 8," he added. Dale was referring to the enormous brick schoolhouse which sat next to Robertson Place, built on land requisitioned by the local government from Sadie and Delano back in 1923. In 2001, the school had been abandoned; consolidation of Bourneville and Bainbridge school systems was the cause. The sheriff's department had used the vacant building for a while, but eventually vandals managed to break a few windows and scribble their graffiti. Defaced, but defiant, for seven years the massive brick hulk had stood its ground in eerie silence.

Who would want the outdated building? What could they do with it? Speculation about the property's future had surfaced over the years, but no buyer could be found. All of a sudden Robertson Place was vulnerable. We had no choice. On December 8, we would have to go to that auction and try to wrest the property back into our possession. Local lore had it that when Sadie and Delano gave up the strip of their farmland, they were promised return of the property should the school no longer need the 9.7 acres; many villagers took the trouble to tell us of their mutual understanding with the Butler family. Alas, with the current administration, that gentleman's agreement now held no weight. In an attempt to preempt the sale, I made an offer. "Could we buy it outright?"

"No," came the answer. "The board wants it to be sold at a public sale." Doug and I had a lot to think about. No zoning laws were in place to protect homeowners in this area. If the property were to change hands, we would have no say about its use. Soon we would be getting an inheritance from Doug's father's estate. Should we spend it to secure the peace and serenity of Robertson Place? We tried to remain steady as we headed into the final phase of the renovation.

It is now December 7. Looming in our hearts and minds for the past two months has been tomorrow's auction. Phone calls erupt; well-wishers offer advice and contractors offer to bid on the tear-down.

December 8 breaks cold and gray, and we bundle ourselves to walk across the field to the old Twin Township School. Eric accompanies us for moral support, but my stomach feels queasy. Cars are already lining the parking lot and folks are streaming into the chilly, dark building. Its electricity and heat had long been turned off. Still in our coats, we join others to wander through its echoing halls and peer into the barren rooms where chalkboards hang askew. Does toxic asbestos lurk in the construction? As the hour draws near, in the crowded gymnasium we settle onto frigid metal chairs.

Nostalgia is palpable in this room. For more than seventy-five years, the building has housed the township's children; spirited basketball games have been won and lost in this gym; symphonies have been played; and minutes of Future Farmers of America read at meetings. Locals hoped that a business would want to convert the 22,000 square-foot brick building into a factory. Some had even suggested a nursing home. In the six years since the school was vacated, no buyer had come forth. Nobody seemed interested.

Starting the bid at $30,000, the auctioneer quickly assumes the fast patter of his profession. Doug and I are novices at this, and we hold on tight. A few others join the fray. Our neighbor drops out at $40,000, then another group at $70,000. But there is someone off to the side who continues to raise his hand. Who is he? Why is he intent on getting this obsolete building so far from town? Folks understand why we want it, and they glance our way. Doug and I crane our necks to locate our competitor, but we don't recognize the man in the back of the room. How high will he go? Up and up go the numbers. $80,000, $90,000; at $100,000 we pause. This is crazy! It will have to be torn down! $110,000? Our shoulders slump and the bidding stops.

"Sold!"

His name is Brad Johnson. A maintenance worker for the township, he lives about a mile up the road on Upper Twin. Rumors fly around the village. At the village post office, Mr. Johnson lets it be known that he intends to convert the dilapidated school into low-cost housing. He adds, however, that he might let it go for $150,000.

When I came out of shock, I realized that we must do whatever was necessary to get the property back. We reluctantly met his price. Mr. Johnson was pleased, and the sale would go down in local history as the most expensive ten acres ever purchased for the purpose of growing crops.

I began to breathe again, although more drama was around the corner when we brought in the bulldozers. Former students of the Twin Township school—many now grandparents—climbed over the rubble to select bricks as mementos. They started telling stories about how the boys always got into trouble for shooting paper wads, how one of them put a fake snake in the top drawer of Mr. Schenault's desk, and how, in the 1950s, their English teacher, Mrs. Arrington, had driven them to Canada for a Shakespeare festival.

Stories such as these needed to be recorded, and it occurred to me that Doug and I might create a memorial booklet. Although the old vacant school had become a menace, it was going to be hard for the community to erase the image of dump trucks carting away 350 loads of bricks—and with them a building that held so many memories. A young man who had attended the school later told me that when he drove by the corn field where his school had stood, it felt almost surreal.

SCHOOL STORIES

Recollections of school days; 1889–2001
Bourneville Twin School, Ross County, Ohio

In Bourneville's fire house, where the community gathers for its annual Fish Fry each Memorial Day to raise funds for its volunteer fire department, I introduced myself as the descendant of Sadie and Delano Butler. Would any former students be willing to share with us some tales from their school days? On June 30, 2008, a front-page story in *The Chillicothe Gazette* helped us get the word out. Ever so slowly, we were able to extract and edit a number of stories and photographs, and on the following Memorial Day in 2009, we gave back to community a booklet, entitled *School Stories*.[152]

Race to the Finish

The school drama was over in mid-December of 2007, only weeks before our children were to arrive at Robertson Place for the holidays. Jenny was planning to bring her boyfriend from Argentina (it must be serious), and we expected Amy (pregnant again) to bring her family.

During the architect's walk through in September, Doug and I had laid out our goals and made decisions for the final phase of our renovation. Destroying what had been my father's office in the fall was painful. I shielded my eyes as workers peeled off his strips of faux cherry paneling and sent them sailing out the open doorway. George's era was gone. Emptied, the space would now become his daughter's study. Sadie's chaise and a big pine computer armoire were brought into the room, and Doug promised to fill the walls with matching knotty-pine bookshelves.

Doug's personal space would be made from my "history room." In past generations, this big front room had served as a store room, a sick room, an extra bedroom, and home to various tenants-caretakers. Once again, this "room across the hall," as we called it when I was growing up, would be transformed. Down came the time line, out went the carpet. Tradesmen arrived from Bainbridge to re-plaster the ceiling. On stilts strapped to their legs, they worked gracefully around the room while I tested wall paint in various shades of deep red. Doug would build a wall of cherry cabinetry for the high-tech equipment needed to bring the homestead into the 21st century.

We hurried to the family-owned Globe Furniture Store in downtown Chillicothe to order new furniture. I had always followed the policy of refinishing and recovering the furniture of Robertson Place so as not to confuse future generations. However, never before had there been a man-cave in Robertson Place.

All at once, the kids were upon us. Virginia and Sofia were three and five years old, and we were looking forward to immersing our granddaughters in the first Christmas they might remember. Christmas was always a little magical at Robertson Place, in part because for this one week we left behind our fast-paced city lives and entered a world of its own, one defined by tradition. Here we partook of a ritual that would be repeated over many generations: the building of fires in the fireplaces, singing of carols around the piano, and decorating the big tree in the living room. Cookies would be iced at the kitchen table, cheese fondue served in the living room on Christmas Eve, and, for the day itself, we would dress the dining room table with china and crystal and construct a lavish centerpiece. Turkey with Doug's stuffing, snowy white mashed potatoes, cranberry sauce and pecan pie were essential ingredients for our holiday dinner. Outside on the doors would be wreaths with red ribbons; inside at their stations would be poinsettias on ped-

estals. And at the back door, announcing the coming and going of friends and family, would always be an old leather strap of sleigh bells.

Into this quintessential American scene came Jenny with her young man from Argentina. Until she met Lucas Caro, our independent daughter had told us that she didn't think she was cut out for marriage or family life. Lucas, classic in South American good looks with jet black hair and dark eyes, was a technology whiz. I fretted that the poor guy might be overwhelmed by our high-spirited American banter and our famously extravagant holiday—not to mention the fact that he was traveling out of his native country for the first time and meeting THE PARENTS. Both steady and good-natured, Lucas took in our Christmas with ease. We longed to hear his voice (he was fluent in English), but he spoke barely a word.

After the carefully-wrapped presents were all unwrapped and we had made soup of the left-over turkey, the family began to pack up. Doug and I dried the last silver fork, stripped multiple beds, then packed up our tired selves to head back to the city.

Hard work awaited us in Cincinnati. After ten years of unexplained leaks, the verdict was delivered: every last one of the windows in the condo's three-storied building would have to be replaced. Gnashing our teeth, we paid the price and withstood the punishment. By the following autumn, the condo was ready to be put up for sale; by week's end we were signing a contract. The next day, we headed for Argentina to meet our future in-laws.

When our plane landed back in Ohio, in mid-November of 2008, there was no time to spare. A household had to be dismantled, its contents packed up, sold, or given away. It was finally time to pull up stakes and move permanently to Robertson Place.

Home

A giant yellow moving van, emblazoned with its blue insignia of the Mayflower, rumbled through the village of Bourneville at dusk, on December 10, 2008. Turning off Route 50, it squeezed through the block pillars and slowly ground its way up the gravel driveway to Robertson Place.

"What could this mean?" the villagers may have wondered, parting their curtains. For as long as any of them could remember, there had been only weekend visitors. "Maybe it's the artist lady from Cincinnati—the one with two daughters? Do you suppose she's the heir?"

Today, few of the neighbors know the history of what they call the "big house" sitting at the end of their village. Few know that some 150 years ago, during the Civil War, from their midst in the community, the artist's great-great-grandmother, Martha Robertson, had moved her family up the gravel driveway and into that house.

Do they know that next door, on the other side of the creek, there is no trace of the house where Sally Caldwell once lived? After the Caldwell heirs headed north to Michigan and elsewhere, the house was torn down, its backyard filled with crops. Clyde's huge barn stood empty and useless until the turn of this century, when at last it fell in upon itself.

Over on the next hill, Virginia's house still stands, but her heirs departed long ago, some of them to Florida; today a farmer owns and tills the land. Further up the road, at the corner of U.S. Route 50 and Lower Twin Road, is a fallen down shell of the once-fine brick home built by the Diggs family in the 1860s and where lived the two little girls with sausage curls. Its roof is caved in, the walls are covered in vines. A farm worker lives in a trailer behind the house, a house almost forgotten by its current owner, a Diggs descendant, who now lives in a nursing home somewhere in California.[153]

West of Bourneville is Oakland farm, Enos and Zero Prather's eighteen-room dream home which was lost to bankruptcy in 1857. It is still standing, but in the year 2010, pigeons were taking over an upstairs bedroom and cattle roamed the front yard. Virtually all the descendants of the early settlers who built this row of houses in the 1800s have left Ohio and scattered in all directions. But for some reason, the daughters of Robertson Place have always come back. As the generations advanced through the decades, each of these women was faced with decisions: whether to leave and forget, or return to carry on. Would we try to maintain it, improve it, or allow the vines to claim it?

I am reminded of the words of my great-grandmother, the poet Margarite, who cautioned her daughter, Sadie:

> I hope, my dear, that you will not let this land mold you as it has molded me. I love it too deeply to leave it now. But it absorbs all my affections, all my loyalty, all my substance. Away from it, I lose my identity, and must keep returning. I am married to it, and engulfed by it. I have not the strength nor the money to do with it what I would, yet it binds me to it forever.[154]

I am just the most recent in a long line of daughters to come under the spell of this property. When the decisions were mine to make, I chose to embrace my history. I chose to embrace Robertson Place and to let it embrace me.

It is now clear to me what drew my mother, her mother, and hers to this place of towering trees. All my years of research and writing earned me an affinity for my female forebears and a deep respect for the men who supported them and helped make their dreams for Robertson Place a reality.

But I am left to wonder. Who will climb the fences of Robertson Place when our grandchildren have all grown up? Who will harvest the rhubarb and prune the snowball bushes? And will there still be someone to put out the wreaths at Christmas time? Perhaps it is not for me to know.

For now, my husband and I will continue to love and care for Robertson Place. In winter we will stack the firewood, sit by its light, and welcome the grandchildren over the holidays. When the snows of winter are melted, we will venture out to smell the wet earth and search for the tiny pips of spring's first crocuses. In summer, we will stake up the tomatoes and gather beans to the familiar rise and fall of a cicada chorus. When autumn's chill touches the valley, we will bundle up in woolens to tuck a few more crocuses bulbs into the earth and put the garden to bed. And come evening, as we seek the warmth of the house, the moon will once again crest Spruce Hill to begin its timeless, unhurried journey across the sky above Robertson Place.

Acknowledgments

Several individuals had a major impact on the realization of this book. First and foremost was my husband Doug, who, from the very beginning, encouraged my lofty efforts. As a history major himself, he urged me forward and offered expert technical support. He brought all the faded photographs to life; he coached me when I faltered, and was my first reader and editor. Most of all, he allowed me time and space to actually *do* the work, which spread itself out over two decades.

Early on, I had asked independent historian Liz Tuttle Miller to do some legal and architectural research on Robertson Place. Her work provided the foundation for my narrative about the house.

Once I begin to write, both daughters cheered me on. Jenny helped me focus on the drama of our ancestors' stories. Amy (in her eighth month of pregnancy) read my very first version; twelve years later, she paused her even busier life to edit a final revision.

Readers of my early manuscript include my brother Phil, his wife, Corky, and friends, Elizabeth Swartz and Annette Zelkoff Trembly. Their enthusiasm, along with that of my beloved book club members, propelled me to the finish line.

Finally, I owe a huge debt of gratitude to Patricia Medert. As historian and archivist at the Ross County Historical Society in Chillicothe, Ohio, she shared her knowledge of the region's local history. At the end, she generously offered to read and edit my manuscript.

When it was ready, I took the results to Ohio's largest and most experienced independent publisher of Ohio history. Orange Frazer Press saw the book's potential, appreciated my vision, and gave it life. Their expertise in formatting and design turned my work into the elegant book that it is. My sincere thanks go to the entire staff at Orange Frazer Press.

Notes

1. Over the years the Vinsonhaller name changes to Vinsonhaler, Vinson Haller, Vincent Haller, and later, simply Haller.

2. Later retelling of this venture by Vinsonhaller's granddaughter, Asenath Kellough, makes it unclear whether the trip began in 1793 or 1794.

3. The exact route taken by the Vinsonhaller party is not known, but historian and archivist Pat Medert of the Ross County Historical Society thinks they would have gone through the Cumberland Gap.

4. Massie, David. Life of Nathaniel Massie; p. 502 and Howe, Henry. *Historical Collections of Ohio, vol. I*, p. 513.

5. References to Vinsonhaller's participation in some of these surveys comes from: *History of Ross and Highland Counties, Ohio; Scioto Gazette*; family letters; and from both his and his daughter Mary Poole's obituaries. See Bibliography.

6. Information about the Massie surveys was taken from the following sources: *Finley's Pioneer Record*; McDonald's *Biographical Sketches; History of Ross and Highland Counties, Ohio, 1880* and from Eckert's *Frontiersmen*.

7. Descriptions of the native land are primarily from *History of Ross and Highland Counties, Ohio, 1880*, pp. 56 and 292.

8. Today, this is where Blain Highway meets US Route 50 and a portion of it has become a private campground.

9. This information comes from family letters.

10. *The History of Ross and Highland County*, p.293.

11. Ibid, p. 292. This story is also found in Finley and Putnam, *Pioneer Record of Ross . County, Ohio; Twin Township*; p.44.

12. As of this writing, the original clapboard schoolhouse still stands off Blain highway amidst a field of corn. Edward Steele verified this in 1992.

13. From a letter written to Margarite from Aunt Asenath, dated Feb. 21, 1908, and labeled "Grandma's birthday letter." Aunt Asenath Kellough is the daughter of Henry and Mary Poole and granddaughter of George and Mary Vinsonhaller.

14. Adams County Book of Records, p. 431.

15. Letter written to Margarite from Asenath, Feb. 21, 1908. Information about the departing Vinsonhaller children came from this letter.

16. Richter, *The Town*, p. 191. Reprint by Chicago Review Press Incorporated, 2018, p. 274.

17. General description of the land during the settlement years was taken from Conrad Richter's three books: *Trees; The Fields; The Towns.*

18. Letter written to Margarite from Aunt Asenath, Feb. 21, 1908.

19. Green, Harvey. *Light of the Home*; Pantheon Books, New York, 1983, p. 21.

20. Ibid., pp. 30-32.

21. Description of Captain Molly and her work is from *History of Ross and Highland Counties, Ohio*; p. 299.

22. Finley and Putnam, *Pioneer Record of Ross County, Ohio; 1880; Twin Township*; p. 57. Mrs. McKenzie [b. 1796] states that she and her mother were one of the first white women in Paint Creek region and that her playmates were the young squaws. "Many a romp have I had with them, and as fearless of danger as though they had been white children."

23. *History of Ross and Highland Counties, Ohio; 1880*; p. 41.

24. The early history of Bourneville comes from *The History of Ross and Highland County*, p. 299 and from Gragg's *The Story of Bourneville (Ohio)*, p. 1.

25. Letter to Margarite from Aunt Asenath, Feb. 21, 1908.

26. Story taken from *Pioneer Record, Ross County, Ohio; 1880; Twin Township*; pp. 59-60.

27. *Scioto Gazette*, Sept. 12, 1839.

28. Robert I. Robertson's legal journal; 1848-1857, p. 75.

29. Ibid., p. 96.

30. Tuttle, Elizabeth."*Robertson Place, Twin Township, Ross County, Ohio*," privately published in Cincinnati, 1987. Information regarding the legal history of Robertson Place and the property on which it stands comes from this treatise. Historian Tuttle writes that in 1802, Nathaniel Massie sold this land for 500 pounds to Samuel Henderson, et al, who in turn sold it to Henry Porter, et al. John and Priscilla Mick were the settlers who then bought the property and built a cabin on it. In turn, they sold 41 acres to Jeptha Perrill for $2000 in 1834 and 11 years later Perrill sold it to the Prather brothers.

31. Ibid., p. 4, 6.

32. Howard Newman may have been the brick mason; in 1850 he married Americas Robertson, the first cousin to Robert Robertson. This speculation comes from Orloff Miller, archaeologist.

33. Green, op. cit., p. 81.

34. Store ledger for S.&P. and Co. 1834-56; p. 7.

35. Ibid., pp. 39, 54, 55.

36. Tuttle, op. cit., pps. 5,6.

37. Ibid., p. 6. See Mechanics Lien Book 1:29, Ross County.

38. Ibid., p. 6.

39. Letter from Aunt Asenath to Maggie, "My darling niece," dated Nov. 24, 1911.

40. These items were all listed in Robert I. Robertson's store ledgers for 1856-8.

41. Tuttle, op. cit. p. 7

42. The actual fate of the house during the Civil War is not known. However, local oral histories place the Robertsons in residence during the war. Beverly Gray, the keeper of the region's black history, is one historian who believes that the Robertsons were living on the property and that the house served as a station along the Underground Railroad. If this were the case, it means the Robertson family moved into the house several years before they were able to purchase it in 1868—perhaps as renters or caretakers.

43. Salem Academy literature from the period

44. Listed in Squire Robertson's estate is "One Piano Brake, NY."

45. Beverly Gray believes that at this time RIR owned the house and 100 acres to the creek and that he served as superintendent of the Underground Railroad. Additional oral history about the cabin and sitings is from George Hammond, who enacted the bell ringing on the crest of the bank. He is father of the author and husband to Marian, Margarite's granddaughter.

46. Information about Chillicothe's reaction to the raids is from Pat Medert's *Stories from Chillicothe's Past*, pp. 41-2. References to my ancestor's memory comes from a *Chillicothe Gazette* clipping dated 1947 and from "The Land," an essay by her great-niece, Marian Hammond.

47. Perkins, George. *A Summer in Maryland and Virginia, or Campaigning with the 149th O.V.I.* Chillicothe, Ohio. The names of officers and privates in the 149th Regiment come from the Field and Staff registries recorded in this book.

48. *History of Ross and Highland Counties, Ohio; 1800*; p. 123.

49. Evans, Lyle S., ed. *A Standard History of Ross County, Ohio*: Volume 2, , 1917, pp. 907-8.

50. Tuttle, op. cit.,p. 8.

51. Technical note to the reader:

County records establish that Robert I. Robertson bought his estate in 1868, and I have conjectured that the Robertson family lived here for several years *before* the purchase. But exactly who lived in the house during the decade leading up to 1868 is unknowable. Its ownership changed hands five times during the period; four of those times buyers signed up in pairs, in what seemed to be an attempt to spread the risk. During the war years occupancy of the house remains especially elusive.

Interpretation of the 1860 census is of little help because during this period census takers did not attempt to attach an address to each household. Upon arriving in town, they simply walked up one side of the street and down the other knocking on doors and taking information. To further complicate matters, the Prather house was not even considered part of Bourneville until two decades later.

In the 1860 census the Robertson family showed up in their usual position in the Bourneville cottage; Poage, the "boss farmer," appeared in the Ross County area, but not in the particular house in question. Evidence of his residency comes from a Ross County directory, family letters and a newspaper reference, (see below). To make matters even more murky, McMillan did not show up as head of household anywhere in the township. But the name Alexander McMillan almost certainly belongs to Martha's uncle, the husband of her beloved great-aunt Ada, who for years lived just a few doors away from them in Bourneville. Letters between Ada and Margarite point to a very close relationship. This opens the door for any number of possibilities which could have put the Robertson family into the house before their actual purchase of it in 1868.

We do know that the Poages sold the house to the Steeles in 1865, but in 1887 Margarite told a newspaper reporter that her family bought the house from Mr. Poage. This is technically incorrect, but further points to the probability that the Steeles never lived in the house, and that the Robertsons moved in soon after the Poages left. Within this scenario, the Robertsons might have moved into and possibly become renters of the house as early as 1861. Martha's elderly relatives might have invited their niece's family to move into the spacious house either to live with them (possibly to care for them) or simply to inhabit the building rather than to leave it vacant.

Both recorded and oral history (see Ed Steele) deny that the Steeles ever lived in the house. Their ownership, however, is important because the Steeles knew Robert Robertson well and were ardent abolitionists (father and five sons all operators on the Underground Railroad), who played a role in the house's lore.

Beverly Gray insists that Robert I. Robertson played a role in the Underground Railroad and that the house on the hill was the site for his work. Local people con-firm this notion. Together with my family's lore this opinion leads me to conclude that sometime during the Civil War the Robertson family moved up the hill into the brick house, and then, when conditions were right, forged the deal which enabled them to buy it for $8,000 in 1868.

52. Hammond, Marian. "The Land," April, 1953. An essay by great-granddaughter, Marian.

53. Although the events are factual, the story of Henry's schoolboy love for Rebecca is the author's conjecture, as noted.

54. Description of conditions at Libby Prison from *Military History of Ohio Illustrated (Soldiers Edition)*, H.H.Hardesty, Publisher; N.Y.; 1887, p. 289.

55. *History of Ross and Highland Counties, Ohio; 1880.*

56. Green, op. cit., p 22.

57. Medert, *Memoirs of a Pioneer Family*, p. 71.

58. *Scioto Gazette*. Obituary, undated.

59. Reverend R. C. Galbraith; funeral speech for Erskine Anderson.

60. Henry Caldwell is referred to as Frank in family letters.

61. Newspaper clippings are from unknown source and dates.

62. *History of Ross and Highland Counties, Ohio; 1880*; p. 297

63. Richter, *The Town*, (need page number)

64. Gragg, J. Rodney. *The Story of Bourneville (Ohio); Paint Creek Valley Folk Research Project; Chillicothe, Ohio: 1963*. I am indebted to Mr. Gragg for mapping and describing his hometown as it was when he was a boy. With the exception of the description of the Methodist church—which is from my own recollection—Mr. Gragg's work formed the basis for this imagined tour of Bourneville in the late 1800s.

65. This information came from local historian June Gregg, (1911-2017), who was the niece of J. Rodney Gragg, the author of The Story of Bourneville. (The different name spelling is intentional)

66. Tuttle, op. cit., p. 12.

67. Social expectations of young women in Victorian America come from Green's *Light of the Home*.

68. Mathews, Nancy Mowll. *Mary Cassatt; A Life*. Villard Books, New York, 1994. (p.26)

69. Green, op. cit., p. 117.

70. Ibid., p. 118.

71. Help visualizing Hillsboro during the 1880s was provided by Jean Wallis, historian, Hillsboro, OH.

72. *Press-Gazette*; Hillsboro, Ohio; June 10, 1958; p. 11.

73. Ibid, p.11.

74. Information about Virginia's divorce comes from Ross County Common Pleas, Summons in Action for Divorce, received on April 23, 1891. No. 5357, (Doc. and page not legible.)

75. *The Leader*, undated newspaper clipping.

76. Squier and Davis; *Ancient Monuments of the Mississippi Valley; 1821-1888*, face page 85. According to an 1847 archaeological survey, the Caldwell farm sits on an ancient Hopewell Indian burial site.

77. Favretti, Rudy. *Landscapes and Gardens for Historic Buildings*; Second edition, rev.; 1991; fig. 44, p. 43.

78. Tuttle, op.cit., p. 2. Perhaps this structure was the original wood building sited in the earliest tax records, dating 1835.

79. This well served the household until 2009.

80. Hammond, M., op. cit., "The Land."

81. Howe, Jennifer., *Cincinnati Art-Carved Furniture and Interiors*, p. 54.

82. By the time Sadie arrived in the Queen City, Mr. Pittman was no longer teaching. Chewning and Burke think that his protégée, Elizabeth Martin Lupton (Miss Katherine's sister), may have been Sadie's tutor.

83. The exhibit was entitled "Chillicothe: 200 Years of Art," and displayed were Sadie's carved library table and a quilt stitched by Margarite.

84. Commencement program, Adelphi High School, 1892.

85. Delano's engagement announcement letter to stepbrother. Punctuation changed for clarification.

86. Letter from Martha to Margarite, dated January 20, 1904.

87. Letter from Martha to Margarite, dated February 2, 1904.

88. *The Bicentennial*, a special publication by *The Chillicothe Gazette*; April 27, 1996; p. 81.

89. Sadie's letter to her mother, dated Dec. 22, 1903.

90. From an interview with former teacher Helen Arrington, September, 2008.

91. According to Pat Medert, Ross County Historical Society, at this time there were no trains going near Bourneville from Chillicothe. Reference: the Ohio Rail Map for 1898.

92. In the later 19th century before electricity was widely used, some houses had their own private small-scale gas generators. (From an interview with house historian, Liz Miller Tuttle.)

93. This newspaper clipping was undated.

94. Obituary, undated, *Scioto Gazette*.

95. Again, letter from Aunt Asenath to Maggie (Margarite), "My darling niece," dated Nov. 24, 1911.

96. Surviving letters to Margarite from Robert Fleming, Architect.

97. Friedlander, Alfred, M.D., Carey P. McCord, M.D., Frank J. Sladen, M.D., and George M. Wheeler, M.D. "The Epidemic of Influenza at Camp Sherman, Ohio." *The Journal of the American Medical Association*, Chicago, 1918, p. 12.

98. Medert, Pat, *Chillicothe, Ohio and The Great War*, 1914-1918, p. 176.

99. Hammond, George. "A Brief and Sketchy History of the Farm; 1984." George was son-in-law of Delano and Sadie Butler.

100. Hammond, M., op. cit., "The Land."

101. Interview with Helen Arrington, September, 2008

102. Butler, Philemon, PDB Farm Ledger

103. One article was dated 1939, the other clipping was undated.

104. *Musical Progress*, Washinton, DC, Oct 1912, Vol. 1, Nos. 3 ; *"Songs and Peace"*, p. 11, 12.

105. Anderson, M. Margarite; *Cabinet of Blue and Purple and Gold*; Broadway Publishing Company, New York, 1904.

106. Hammond, M., op. cit., "The Land."

107. According to Marian's diary, the Bourneville Fish Fries were held from 1920-26, and resurrected again in 1939 and 1940.

108. From an interview with Ed Steele, Sept. 1, 1992.

109. Hammond, M., op. cit., "The Land." Editor's note: it was not in May that Wilgus drowned, but June 5.

110. Butler, Delano. In Memory of Wilgus Anderson Butler, June, 1922.

111. An interview with Helen Arrington, see above.

112. Marian's paper, dated 1921.

113. Marian's letter to her brother, 1923.

114. *The Lyceum*, 1826.

115. Interview with Ed Steele, see above.

116. Interview with Helen Arrington, see above.

117. Brochure from Farmers' Institute, 1929

118. Pat Medert corroborated this story by telling me that during the depression her step-father was one of eight DeLong children facing starvation when Mr. Butler gave his father work.

119. Marian's letter "Honey dear" to George, written shortly before their wedding and dated Wednesday, 9:15 p.m.; Note: dots in letter are Marian's.

120. Marian's letter to George, undated.

121. Mother's Day letter from Marian to Sadie, May 14, 1933.

122. Newspaper clipping, probably *The Scioto Gazette*.

123. Rogers, Wm. H., and Dively, Penn, G., *"Hell and High Water" Saga of the Second Johnstown Flood; A Pictorial Resume of the St. Patrick's Day Disaster, March 17, 1936*.

124. I would later learn that the tribe of Native Americans who had lived in our area used needles made of bone.

125. Marian. (Cannot relocate source of this quote.)

126. Interview with Helen Arrington, see above.

127. Hammond, M., op. cit., "The Land."

128. From the interview with Ed Steele.

129. Hammond, M., op. cit., "The Land."

130. Marian; Mother's Day letter.

131. Delano's letter to daughter Marian, undated.

132. Letter found inside Lynn's little green diary, "Travels Abroad."

133. From Lynn's little green diary, "Travels Abroad."

134. See Upper Arlington yearbooks, *The Norwester*; 1956-1959.

135. From Lynn's white diary, "My Trip," November 2, 1959.

136. Ibid, April 3, 1960.

137. My father, along with another ISA parent, confronted Mr. Jaeger. They threatened to go public with the accusation if he did not sit out the next year of ISA or meet with a counselor. He chose the former.

138. Information about Paint Valley High School's class of 1960 is courtesy of graduates Linda and Don Carroll.

139. Excerpt from Lynn's letter to Doug in New Haven, dated Apr. 25, 1964.

140. Doug would eventually edit and publish his mother-in-law's book in 1996. In his editor's notes, he commented that the book "…provides us an historical insight in-to Marian's life and the times in which she lived. Her goals were, I'm sure, to establish a mood for her readers so that they could appreciate the qualities of appearance, aroma, and taste that hand-wrought meals provide compared to the fast-food versions becoming available in grocery stores."

141. Hammond, M., op. cit., "The Land."

142. Watson, Fran. *Truth in Action*, City Beat Magazine, Cincinnati Ohio, Mar. 27, 1997.

143. Sullivan, Kimberly. *Eastern Hills Journal Press*, Oct. 16, 1991.

144. Zegeer, Jill. *Chillicothe Gazette*, Lifestyles, July 29, 1992.

145. Quotes from "It Began at the Lloyd: An Artist's Journey," a publicity poster for Lynn's retrospective show at Lloyd Library and Museum, February 2–April 30, 2008.

146. Watson, Fran. "Botany for the Brave," *City Beat Magazine*, June 25, 1998.

147. Note on loose scrap of paper, found in Lynn's grey journal. Date unknown.

148. Agnes Carden lived to be 100 and died in 2009; Wade Carden, age 96, died in 2006.

149. Notes from Lynn's grey journal, Nov. 1, 1994.

150. Carden, Jenny, *Telling Time*, (award-winning video): Northwestern University, 1994.

151. Hammond, G., op. cit., "Brief and Sketchy History of the Farm."

152. Carden, Lynn, and Doug, eds. School Stories, Recollections of School Days; 1889–2001; Bourneville Twin School, Ross County, Ohio; 2009.

153. The Diggs house was torn down in 2016.

154. Hammond, M. op. cit., "The Land."

Citations for Graphics

Drawings are by the author and depict artifacts discovered in Robertson Place. Both the artifacts and their drawings remain in its archives. Unless otherwise cited, the photographs, newspaper clippings, architectural drawings, art work, ledgers, maps, invitations and other memorabilia are from the archives of Robertson Place. Additional information and sources are listed below:

Map of Northwest Territory: https://www.ncpedia.org/media/map/colonial-north-america

Etching of General Massie from *Henry Howe's Historical Collections*, p. 513.

Etching of Shawnee man, ca. 1796, courtesy Ross County Historical Society

Etching of Tecumseh: https://www.lib.umich.edu/online-exhibits/exhibits/show/great-native-american-chiefs/group-of-native-american-chief/chief--tecumseh

Etching of Oakland Farm: Gould. *Atlas Ross County, Ohio, 1875*, reprint, p. 66.

Engraving of Salem Academy: Gould, p. 13.

Engraving of General Morgan: https://commons.wikimedia.org/wiki/File:John_Hunt_Morgan_portrait.jpg

Escape route from Libby Prison: https://library.blog.wku.edu/2013/06/a-daring-escape/

Bourneville plot map: Gould, p. 67.

Engraving of Hillsboro Female College, Williams Bros., *History of Ross and Highland Counties, 1880*, p. 380.

Engraving of Ross County Courthouse: Gould, p. 79.

Paintings by author:

Iris; 2005; Mixed media on raw canvas (wall hanging); 96x51.

Mandolin with Cherry Blossoms; 1995; acrylic on canvas; 30x24.

First Snow Storm; 1993; watercolor, ink; 22x30.

Helleborus; 2003; mixed media on canvas; 48x36; Coll. of Mr./Mrs. Richard Hildbold.

Selected Bibliography and Primary Sources

Arthur, T. S. *Women to the Rescue*, (one of 12 volumes in a set on temperance), Queen City Publishing Co., Cincinnati, Ohio, 1874.

Baum, Nancy. *History of Bainbridge*, 1994.

Bennett, Henry Holcomb, ed. *The County of Ross*, Selwyn A. Brant, Madison, Wisconsin, 1902.

Bolton, Sarah K. *Lives of Girls Who Became Famous*, Thomas Y. Crowell Company, New York, 1886.

Carden, Jenny. *Telling Time, 1850-1950, A Century of Stories*, (Video) C-THRU Productions, Evanston, Illinois, 1994.

Carden, Lynn and Doug, eds. *School Stories, Recollections of School Days, 1889-2001*, Bourneville Twin School, Ross County, Ohio, 2009.

"Chronological Guide to the History of Ross County," printed by Ross County Historical Society, date unknown. It only goes to 1940, but it appears to have been printed after 1975. (Pat. Medert)

Cooke, Maud C. *The Great 20th Century Cook Book*, L.W. Walter Company, Chicago, Illinois, 1902.

Eckert, Allan W. *The Frontiersmen*, Little, Brown and Co., Boston, Massachusetts, 1967.

Evans, Lyle S., ed. *A Standard History of Ross County*, Volumes I and II, Lewis Publishing Company, Chicago and New York, 1917.

Finley, Issac and Putnam, *Rufus. Pioneer Record and Reminiscences of the Early Settlers and Settlement of Ross County, Ohio*, R. Clark & Company, Cincinnati, 1871.

Gragg, Rodney. *The Story of Bourneville (Ohio), Paint Creek Valley Folk Research Project*, Chillicothe, Ohio, 1963.

Green, Harvey. *Light of the Home, An Intimate View of the Lives of Women in Victorian America, Pantheon Books*, New York, 1983.

Gould, Hueston T. *Illustrated Atlas of Ross County and Chillicothe, Ohio*, H.T. Gould & Co., Columbus, Ohio. 1875. (Reprint by The Bookmark, Knightstown, Indiana, 1975).

Hammond, Lynn (Carden). Diaries and Journals: first diary: 1954; little green diary, 1958: *Travels Abroad*; white diary, 1959: *My Trip*.

Hammond, Lynn (Carden). Letter addressed to Mr. Douglas Carden, in New Haven, Connecticut, dated April 25, 1964.

Hammond, Marian. "The Land," an unpublished essay, April, 1953.

Hammond, Marian. (Douglas Carden, ed.) *Shall We Cook?* Cincinnati, Ohio, 1996.

Hammond, George. "Brief and Sketchy History of the Farm," unpublished, 1984.

Harper, Robert S. *Ohio Handbook of the Civil War*, The Ohio Historical Society, Columbus, Ohio: 1961.

Heran, Margaret. "It Began at the Lloyd: An Artist's Journey, "Lloyd Library and Museum, Cincinnati, Ohio, 2008.

History of Ross and Highland Counties, Ohio, Williams Brothers, Cleveland, Ohio, 1880.

Howe, Henry, LL.D. *Historical Collections of Ohio*, Vol. I, Published by State of Ohio, C.K. Krehbiel & Company, Cincinnati, Ohio, 1888. (This was Ohio Centennial Edition; I believe there to have been an earlier edition).

Howe, Jennifer L. *Cincinnati Art-Carved Furniture and Interiors*, Ohio University Press, Athens, Ohio, 2003.

Kerns, Willam. *Civil War Diary* (South Salem's 89th Regiment).

Massie, David Meade. *Life of Nathaniel Massie*, Robert Clark Company, Cincinnati, Ohio, 1896.

Mathews, Nancy Mowll. *Mary Cassatt, A Life*, Villard Books, New York, 1994.

McDonald, John. *Biographical Sketches of General Duncan McArthur, Captain William Wells, and General Simon Kenton*, Osborn & Son, Dayton, Ohio, 1852.

Medert, Patricia F. *Stories from Chillicothe's Past*, 1998.

Medert, Patricia F., ed. *The Memoirs of a Pioneer Family*, Ross County Historical Society, Chillicothe, 2000.

Medert, Patricia F. *Chillicothe, Ohio and The Great War, 1914-1918*, published by the author, Chillicothe, Ohio, 2016.

Mendelson, Anne. *Stand Facing the Stove: The Story of the Women Who Gave America The Joy of Cooking*, Henry Holt and Co., New York. 1996.

Military History of Ohio Illustrated (Soldiers Edition), H. H. Hardesty, Publisher, N.Y., 1887.

Moore, Frank. *Women of the War: Their Heroism and Self-Sacrifice*, S. S. Scranton & Company, Hartford, Connecticut, 1867.

Nochlin, Linda. *Women Artists*, Thames & Hudson Inc., New York, 2015.

Perkins, George. *A Summer in Maryland and Virginia, or Campaigning with the 149th O.V.I.* Chillicothe, Ohio, publish date unknown.

Richter, Conrad. *The Trees*, Alfred A. Knopf, Inc., New York, 1940.

Richter, Conrad. *The Fields*, First published 1946. Published by arrangement with Al-fred A. Knopf, Inc., Ohio University Press, Athens, Ohio, 1991.

Richter, Conrad. *The Town*, First published 1950. Published by arrangement with Alfred A. Knopf, Inc., Ohio University Press, Athens, Ohio, 1991.

Rodgers, Wm. H., and Dively, Penn G."Hell and High Water" The Saga of the Second Johnstown Flood, Chas. M. Henry Printing Co., Greensburg, Pennsylvania, 1936.

Squier, Ephraim and Davis, Edwin. *Ancient Monuments of the Mississippi Valley, 1821-1888,* Smithsonian Institution Press, Washington and London, 1998, (originally published by Smithsonian Institution in 1848).

Sullivan, Kimberly. *Eastern Hills Journal Press,* October 16, 1991.

Tuttle, Elisabeth H. *Robertson Place, Twin Township,* Ross County, Ohio, Cincinnati, Ohio 1987.

Watson, Fran. "Truth in Action," *City Beat Magazine,* Cincinnati, Ohio, March 27, 1997.

Watson, Fran. "Botany for the Brave," *City Beat Magazine,* Cincinnati, Ohio, July 2, 1998.

Zegeer, Jill. *Chillicothe Gazette,* Lifestyles, July 29, 1992.

Index

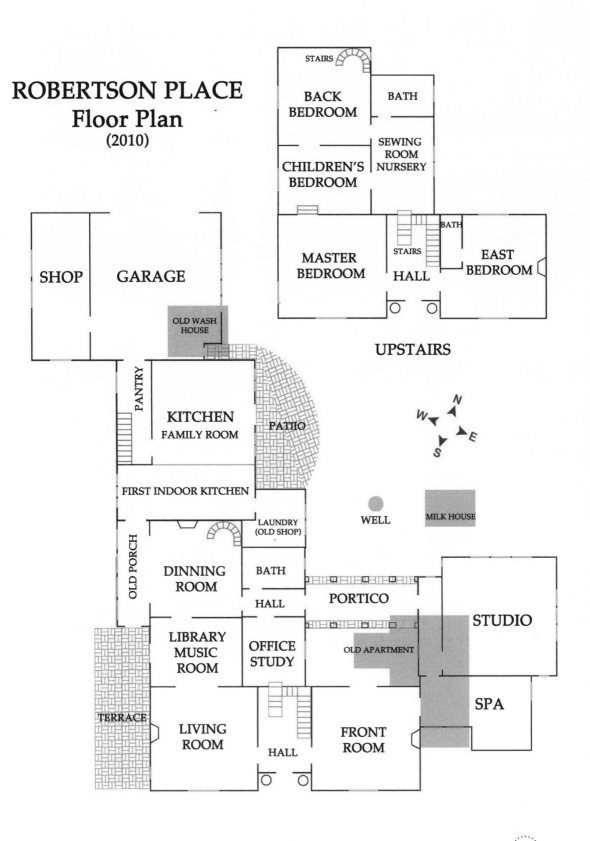

ROBERTSON PLACE
Floor Plan
(2010)

SHOP

GARAGE

STAIRS

BACK BEDROOM

BATH

SEWING ROOM NURSERY

CHILDREN'S BEDROOM

MASTER BEDROOM

STAIRS

HALL

BATH

EAST BEDROOM

UPSTAIRS

OLD WASH HOUSE

PANTRY

KITCHEN
FAMILY ROOM

PATIO

N
W E
S

FIRST INDOOR KITCHEN

WELL

MILK HOUSE

OLD PORCH

LAUNDRY (OLD SHOP)

DINNING ROOM

BATH

HALL

PORTICO

STUDIO

TERRACE

LIBRARY MUSIC ROOM

OFFICE STUDY

OLD APARTMENT

SPA

LIVING ROOM

HALL

FRONT ROOM